STRATEGIC ASIA 2010–11

D1444361

STRATEGIC ASIA 2010–11

ASIA'S
RISING POWER

and America's Continued Purpose

Edited by

Ashley J. Tellis, Andrew Marble, and Travis Tanner

With contributions from

Richard A. Bitzinger, Abraham M. Denmark, Nicholas Eberstadt,
Charles D. Ferguson, Aaron L. Friedberg, Sumit Ganguly, Mikkal E. Herberg,
Richard A. Matthew, Manjeet S. Pardesi, Peter A. Petri, and Ashley J. Tellis

THE NATIONAL BUREAU *of* ASIAN RESEARCH
Seattle and Washington, D.C.

THE NATIONAL BUREAU *of* ASIAN RESEARCH

Published in the United States of America by
The National Bureau of Asian Research, Seattle, WA, and Washington, D.C.
www.nbr.org

This material is based upon work supported in part by the Department of Energy (National Nuclear Security Administration).

This report was prepared as an account of work sponsored by an agency of the United States Government. Neither the United States Government nor any agency thereof, nor any of their employees, makes any warranty, express or implied, or assumes any legal liability or responsibility for the accuracy, completeness, or usefulness of any information, apparatus, product, or process disclosed, or represents that its use would not infringe privately owned rights. Reference herein to any specific commercial product, process, or service by trade name, trademark, manufacturer, or otherwise does not constitute or imply its endorsement, recommendation, or favoring by the United States Government or any agency thereof. The views and opinions of authors expressed herein do not necessarily state or reflect those of the United States Government or any agency thereof.

NBR makes no warranties or representations regarding the accuracy of any map in this volume. Depicted boundaries are meant as guidelines only and do not represent the views of NBR or NBR's funders.

Design and publishing services by The National Bureau of Asian Research

Cover design by Stefanie Choi

Front cover photo: "Airshow China 2006 - Day Two" © Guang Niu/Getty Images

Note: The fighter jets depicted on the cover are Russian Sukhoi Su-27s at an air show in Zhuhai, China in 2006. Variants of the Su-27 (including those designated as Su-30s) have been acquired by several Asian militaries including China, India, Indonesia, Malaysia, and Vietnam. India and China are licensed to produce these jets.

Publisher's Cataloging-In-Publication Data
(Prepared by The Donohue Group, Inc.)

Asia's rising power and America's continued purpose / edited by Ashley J. Tellis, Andrew Marble and Travis Tanner ; with contributions from Richard A. Bitzinger ... [et al.].

    p. : ill., maps ; cm. -- (Strategic Asia 1933-6462 ; 2010-11)

    Based upon work supported in part by the Department of Energy (National Nuclear Security Administration).
    Includes bibliographical references and index.
    ISBN: 978-0-9818904-1-8

    1. Asia--Foreign relations. 2. Asia--Politics and government--1945- 3. Asia--Foreign economic relations--United States. 4. United States--Foreign economic relations--Asia. 5. Globalization--Asia. 6. Asia--Strategic aspects. I. Tellis, Ashley J. II. Marble, Andrew. III. Tanner, Travis. IV. Bitzinger, Richard. V. National Bureau of Asian Research (U.S.) VI. Series: Strategic Asia ; 2010-11.

DS35.2 .A85 2010
327.5

Printed in Canada

The paper used in this publication meets the minimum requirement of the American National Standard for Information Sciences—Permanence of Paper for Printed Library Materials, ANSI Z39.48-1992.

Contents

Overview

> An overview of the themes and conclusions of the volume that both highlights how key international trends are affecting Asia and draws implications for U.S. policy.

Thematic Studies

> An examination of a range of possible geopolitical futures for Strategic Asia and an evaluation of the likelihood of each outcome based on the prospective performances of the U.S. and Chinese economies, potential political reform in China, and other factors.

> An analysis of Asia's likely economic expansion through 2030, including implications for U.S. policy.

Indicators

Preface

Richard J. Ellings

That the Strategic Asia Program has survived the vicissitudes of the past ten years—even prospered through them—is a remarkable testament not only to the need for the program but to the tremendous people who have led and otherwise contributed to it. With only myself to blame, it took all of the 1990s to figure out how to market the concept effectively. Even then, it took the tremendous help of people like General (ret.) John Shalikashvili, former chairman of the Joint Chiefs of Staff, and Brigitte Allen, NBR's director of institutional development. Through the dramatic events that marked the end of the Cold War and the twilight of the second millennium, almost no one was systematically tracking the historic changes unfolding. There certainly was a deluge of reports and books on what had and what was taking place (including those published by NBR), but there were no sustained studies that systematically tracked and analyzed the extraordinary data and developments of the times. And there were indeed extraordinary developments: the take-off of China, the fragmentation and problems plaguing the Asian and Islamic portions of the former Soviet empire, reforms in India, the integration of Asia into the global economy, and the utter transformation of the global balance of power.

In August 2000, on the outskirts of Seattle, NBR assembled a group of scholars to plan the program, and then in 2001 we secured the support necessary to launch it. Envisioned was a comprehensive assessment of the driving forces and important features of the dramatic economic and geopolitical changes taking shape in the region. Ultimately, our purpose was to understand the relevance of these changes to U.S. interests. With founding research director Aaron Friedberg's inspiration we named the program and published the first volume in the series, *Strategic Asia 2001–02: Power and Purpose*. We developed an executive summary and a companion database; we aimed the program at a diverse set of intellectual, policy, and business leaders; and we hoped that new generations of students and analysts would gain deeper knowledge from it. Ashley Tellis, an original contributor, assumed the helm from Aaron as research director when Aaron took a senior position in government in 2004.

Strategic Asia 2010–11: Asia's Rising Power and America's Continued Purpose is the tenth in the series, and is Ashley's seventh volume as research director. The title and content of the volume honor these milestones and address head-on both the challenges our nation faces today and the challenges we think our nation will face in Asia for many years to come. The volume assesses the region by providing an integrated perspective—an issue-based assessment to get at the "big picture." Aaron returns to the program with a thought-provoking, strategic assessment of alternative, geopolitical conceptions of the future. The volume throughout aims to provide a deeper examination of the core concerns of international relations today: power and influence, domestic political and ideological transformation in key countries, economic growth and trade, national security threats stemming from military competition and nuclear proliferation to energy and resource scarcity, demographic trends, international cooperation, and the politics of climate. This is a daunting mission that we thought had to be undertaken. As it turns out, the authors have been up to the task and have done a marvelous job by drawing invaluable comparisons and identifying the cumulative and interactive effects of the most important developments in Asia for a net assessment for the United States.

The Very Big Picture

Over the last 30 years the strategic landscape of the world has transformed, as the Asia-Pacific replaced the Atlantic as the locus of global power, challenges, and opportunities. The tectonic shift was caused by the collapse of the Soviet empire as well as by the rise of Japan, South Korea, then China, and now India. Current economic weakness in the United States and Europe is further accentuating China's rise. The political will to sustain international leadership, long an issue for Europe, is increasingly a question asked about the United States.

With such rapid change has come ambiguity in the distribution of power and decisiveness to use power. In this environment, some nations may seek opportunities that fulfill international ambitions. Others may lose capacity to fulfill existing international responsibilities or expectations. There is the resulting danger—indeed, likelihood—that nations will aggressively exploit real opportunities or at a minimum misperceive their competitors' capacities and purposes. Painful "lessons" of history will be trumpeted by nationalists. In fact, nationalisms of different sorts, some variations more threatening than others, will rise. Feeling increasingly insecure, nations will seek to spur their economic growth and will modernize and build up their militaries. They will reach out to strengthen their alliances and attract new strategic partners. Often they will deepen their engagement even with the competitors that present the greatest long-term threats. The latter behavior may have several motivations. Nations will want to learn from competitors— about their technology and capabilities, their plans, their top people, and their institutions. Through engagement, many nations will also hope to build mutual interests in peaceful cooperation. For similar reasons many will seek to add to the spirit and substance of international cooperation through multilateral mechanisms with the aim of adding stability to their fragile strategic environment. Rapid change and resulting ambiguities in nations' power and purposes explain so much of the character and pace of what we observe today in this region we have dubbed Strategic Asia.

The variables over which Americans have profound control are their own country's capabilities and international strategy. Americans find their country burdened with difficult and expensive wars in distant places and find themselves deeply divided over how to grapple with basic economic policy. Although the daily plight of Americans, albeit fragile, seems not so dire as in the 1930s, the ideological divisions seem as great indeed as in the Great Depression. At question are no less than the relationship between the federal government and private enterprise and property; more broadly, the roles and size of the federal government in society; very different approaches to macro-economic policy; and the choice between significant redistribution of wealth versus encouragement of entrepreneurs and individualism.

For good reasons much of the world roots for Americans to be successful in resolving these fundamental issues in ways that reinvigorate the U.S. economy and enable the United States to craft successful foreign and defense policy. Given the challenges ahead, the judgment of the Strategic Asia Program, like the judgment of so many governments around the world, is that for the foreseeable future—probably for decades—the world will depend on the United States for leadership for adapting the post– World War II international system to new developments. With America's leadership, that system has avoided great-power war and sustained crucial values and structures for promoting stable, regional balances of power, free trade, freedom of the seas, economic growth, international institutions, economic stabilization, democracy, rule of law, human rights, self-determination, international humanitarian and development assistance, and so on. What other major power or powers seem able and prone to take on such leadership?

Linked to the future of United States leadership are the core issues of how China will chart its path and toward what goal. Simply put, beyond China's capacity as an international actor, the principal source of uncertainty is China's strategic intentions. No matter the intentions, how will China and the United States interact? The role of other powers will also be crucial to the course of the future. How will China and the United States interact with key countries such as Japan, India, the Koreas, the members of ASEAN, the Central Asian states, and so forth? Ultimately, how will China affect the functioning and underlying values and salient features of the postwar system? At the bad end of the spectrum of imaginable outcomes is the bifurcation of the system into contending spheres of influence leading to major war. At the good end is the full and peaceful incorporation of China into an international system compatible with our interests, a system mostly like the one described above that we have been shepherding for over 65 years.

Ahead, all the major powers, and especially the United States and China, will need to display remarkably adept diplomacy and national security policies. Such are the requirements in a rapidly changing world in which relative power and the will to use power are ambiguous.

The Strategic Asia Program

NBR developed the Strategic Asia Program to fulfill three objectives, which comport with undertaking analysis of the major trends within Asia: (1) to provide the best possible understanding of the current strategic environment in Asia, (2) to look forward five years, and in some cases beyond, to contemplate the region's future, and (3) to establish a record of data and assessment for those interested in understanding the changes taking place in the Asian strategic landscape.[1]

In keeping with this tradition, *Strategic Asia 2010–11: Asia's Rising Power and America's Continued Purpose* is designed to complement the series' existing work, to broaden the current political and economic debates to include issues related to Asia, and to provide U.S. decisionmakers with the most authoritative information and analysis. Through a collection of

---

[1] The Strategic Asia Program considers as "Asia" the entire eastern half of the Eurasian landmass and the arc of offshore islands in the Western Pacific. This vast expanse can be pictured as an area centered on China and consisting of four distinct subregions arrayed clockwise around it: Northeast Asia (including the Russian Far East, the Korean Peninsula, and Japan), Southeast Asia (including both its mainland and maritime components), South Asia (including India and Pakistan, and bordered to the west by Afghanistan), and Central Asia (Kazakhstan, Kyrgyzstan, Tajikistan, Turkmenistan, Uzbekistan, and southern Russia). The Strategic Asia Program also tracks significant developments across the Asia-Pacific to the United States and Canada.

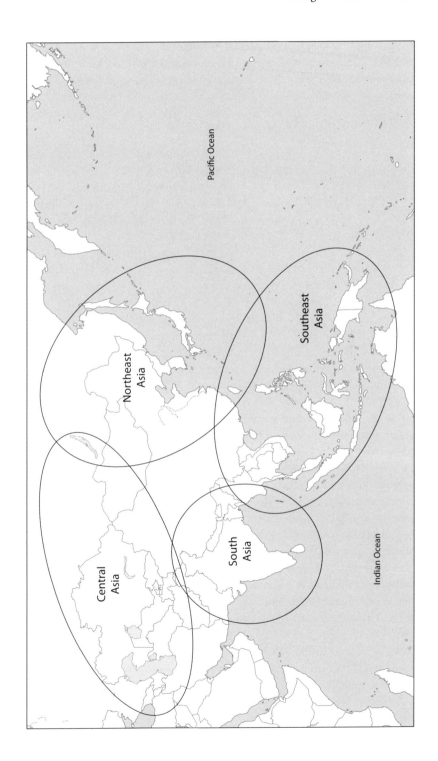

"across Asia" thematic studies, this volume also moves beyond analysis and identifies policy options for U.S. decisionmakers that we believe will facilitate and strengthen efforts to craft effective policy toward Asia.

Acknowledgments

The publication of this year's *Strategic Asia* volume comes at a pivotal time not only in international relations but also in NBR's history as an institution. The year 2010 has been a momentous time for us, marked by the launch of the National Asia Research Program (NARP) with the Woodrow Wilson International Center for Scholars. This is our most ambitious undertaking to date to bridge the gap between scholars and policymakers. The exciting new program selected 39 research associates and fellows to serve as the inaugural class of scholars receiving support to encourage and highlight policy-relevant Asia studies research. In June 2010, the NARP associates and fellows joined the nation's leading Asia studies scholars to present their findings to policymakers in Washington, D.C., at the inaugural Asia Policy Assembly. The NARP, as a logical extension of the Strategic Asia Program's mission, provides another platform for ensuring that U.S. policymakers are provided with the most current, relevant research available.

In late 2009 we were also thrilled—relieved may be a more accurate term—to settle into our permanent headquarters in Seattle's University District, in a building named for one of NBR's closest friends and long-time supporters, our chairman emeritus George F. Russell Jr. We are grateful to everyone who has made this move possible. We have also worked this year to build a living legacy to the extraordinary national and international contributions of Senator Slade Gorton by opening the Slade Gorton International Policy Center. The Gorton Center will incorporate and build on ongoing NBR initiatives to sponsor research in economics and trade, energy security, energy and the environment, and terrorism-related studies.

As always, producing this year's volume would not have been possible without the dedication and hard work of the staff and associates that carry out all of NBR's projects. The program's two senior advisors—General (ret.) John Shalikashvili and the founding research director Aaron Friedberg, professor of politics at Princeton University and former deputy national security advisor to the vice president—are important to this effort. Their guidance serves as the foundation for our work on the Strategic Asia program as well as for other research initiatives at NBR.

NBR is fortunate to have Ashley Tellis continue in his seventh year as the Strategic Asia Research Director. The substantive theme, framework, and structure of this year's volume are largely the product of his superb intellect and research direction. I would be remiss if I did not also acknowledge Ashley for his commitment to numerous other NBR projects. His contributions to several NBR initiatives make for a heavy workload amid his many other professional pursuits. Travis Tanner, director of the Pyle Center for Northeast Asian Studies, continues to direct the Strategic Asia Program as part of his extensive portfolio at NBR. As Strategic Asia program director, Travis contributed to every stage of the book and worked to build cohesiveness across the program's activities. Andrew Marble, NBR editor, has been a key contributor to the *Strategic Asia* series over the last six years, with his editorial skills contributing to a seamless volume. Together, Ashley, Travis, and Andrew provided outstanding leadership to the Strategic Asia research and program teams.

I also want to acknowledge the central role that NBR staff played behind the scenes. Melissa Colonno, Strategic Asia program manager, provided essential logistical and production support for this year's publication and book launch events in Washington, D.C. Members of NBR's editorial team—Jessica Keough, managing editor; Joshua Ziemkowski, NBR copy and style editor; and interns Jacquelyn Allen and Kelly Mallahan—were instrumental in the technical editing, layout, and proofreading processes. The publication of the volume would not have been possible without their efforts and careful management.

Much of the day-to-day work in the program has relied on NBR fellows and interns. Bridge Award fellow Daniel Alderman and Next Generation fellows Jared Bissinger, Ryan Zielonka, and Lyle Morris provided extensive research assistance for the scholars and made valuable contributions throughout the process. We hope their experience at NBR will serve them well as they embark on future endeavors in the field of Asian affairs.

I would also like to extend my gratitude to the other individuals who have helped make the Strategic Asia Program possible. Members of our Board of Directors, especially our chairman John Rindlaub and chairman emeritus George Russell, have been core supporters of and advisors to all of NBR's projects. Karolos Karnikis and Michael Wills have worked with persistence and innovation to sustain the program's institutional support.

The leadership team in NBR's Washington, D.C., office serves as the brain trust for our policy outreach activities. Roy Kamphausen, senior vice president for political and security affairs and director of the Washington, D.C., office, is at the forefront of these efforts. Under Roy's direction, NBR has become increasingly effective at integrating policy outreach into its projects, and his support is without a doubt a critical factor in the high-level impact NBR has with key leaders in Washington. Meredith Miller, vice president for trade, economic, and energy affairs and outreach, plays a pivotal role in fulfilling our mandate to inform multiple constituencies. NBR is extremely fortunate to have people of such high caliber working behind the scenes.

Our stellar group of authors did an excellent job assessing the strategic implications of the major issues currently facing Asia. This year's topic was highly challenging because of the breadth of issues and geography covered. Nevertheless, we are confident that their research findings not only are timely but also will be enduring. Special thanks to them for such diligent work in wrestling with the challenges implicit in the research design while meeting the volume's tight publication schedule. These authors join a community of nearly one hundred other leading specialists who have written for the series. The anonymous reviewers, both scholars and government experts, also deserve acknowledgement for their substantive evaluations of the draft chapters that were essential to developing the final product.

Finally, I would like to express my deep gratitude to the Strategic Asia Program's core sponsors—the National Nuclear Security Administration (NNSA) at the U.S. Department of Energy and the Lynde and Harry Bradley Foundation. NNSA was early to recognize and appreciate the vision of the Strategic Asia Program, supporting it since 2002 and becoming a partner and participant in our many activities and events. Likewise, the Bradley Foundation has generously supported the Strategic Asia Program since the beginning. It is indeed an honor to have counterparts at these organizations who share NBR's commitment to strengthening and informing policy in the Asia-Pacific.

Richard J. Ellings
President
The National Bureau of Asian Research
August 2010

STRATEGIC ASIA 2010–11

OVERVIEW

EXECUTIVE SUMMARY

This chapter overviews the themes and conclusions of the volume, both highlighting how key international trends are affecting Asia and drawing implications for U.S. policy.

MAIN ARGUMENT:
Power in the international system continues to shift to Asia from the West, spurred by the superior growth of Asia's major economies. This growth is not uniform, however, and is causing a new struggle for strategic alignments among Asian states and with the U.S. While Asia's rise has brought new opportunities, it has also created challenges, including increased energy demand and environmental damage. Economic growth has allowed Asian states to invest more in modern military capabilities, which could threaten U.S. hegemony and regional stability. Economic growth has not democratized Asia's authoritarian states, raising concerns about the long-term prospects for continental peace and stability. By virtue of its economic, military, and political ties to the region, the U.S. will remain indispensable to the balance of power in Asia in the years to come.

POLICY IMPLICATIONS:

- Despite the steady emergence of new centers of power in Asia, the U.S. will remain the only country with truly "comprehensive national power," implying the continuance of American hegemony.

- The U.S. will continue to be the predominant military power in Asia and an integral part of the region's economic success as a source of technology and innovation, as a market for exports, and as an investment destination, while remaining the provider of choice for key public goods.

- To maintain its position in the long term, the U.S. must renew the domestic foundations of its power, strengthen its partnerships with Asian friends and allies, and deepen its military superiority through greater investment and innovation.

Strategic Asia: Continuing Success with Continuing Risks

Ashley J. Tellis

The National Bureau of Asian Research initiated the Strategic Asia Program ten years ago. Begun at a time when Asia was exhibiting clear signs of dominance in the global economy, the Strategic Asia Program sought to generate the intellectual capital necessary to assist U.S. policy to cope with the new realities of growing Asian power. Other annual surveys of Asia at the time focused primarily on examining the political developments occurring in the previous year. In contrast, Strategic Asia sought to analyze the "deep structure" of the transformations occurring in the eastern half of the Eurasian landmass—a region centered on China and the four major sub-regions surrounding it: Northeast, Southeast, South, and Central Asia. The scope of this analysis included each country's external relations with both their immediate neighbors and key states lying further afield, especially the United States.

From the very beginning this research program accordingly fastened on the concept of "grand strategy," that is, on understanding how the key Asian states were developing, managing, and utilizing the totality of their national resources to secure certain political aims—and how these aims were shaped by their history, geography, resources, culture, institutions, and threats and opportunities. Through this unvarying gaze, over the last decade the Strategic Asia Program produced a series of volumes that form an integrated assessment of Asia's capability and performance, with each individual volume focusing on a specific dimension in great, comparative depth.

Ashley J. Tellis is Senior Associate at the Carnegie Endowment for International Peace and Research Director of the Strategic Asia Program at NBR. He can be reached at <atellis@carnegieendowment.org>.

The first volume, *Strategic Asia 2001–02: Power and Purpose*, provided a systematic analysis of the grand strategies of key Asian states with a view to creating a baseline assessment of the balance of power in Asia. The second volume, *Strategic Asia 2002–03: Asian Aftershocks*, examined the consequences of the September 11 attacks on the United States for Asian geopolitics, including the problem of radical Islam and the implications of expanding U.S. military operations in Asia connected with the war on terrorism. The third volume, *Strategic Asia 2003–04: Fragility and Crisis*, examined the sources of fragility in Asia with particular reference to structural weaknesses in the changing balance of power, in the political and economic systems of key states, and in regional security and economic institutions. The fourth volume, *Strategic Asia 2004–05: Confronting Terrorism in the Pursuit of Power*, analyzed the U.S.-led war on terrorism in Asia in the context of the power-political changes taking place across the continent from Northeast Asia to the Middle East. The fifth volume, *Strategic Asia 2005–06: Military Modernization in an Era of Uncertainty*, re-examined a theme that was first explored in the inaugural volume, namely the military capabilities and modernization programs of various Asian states in the context of their grand strategies. The sixth volume, *Strategic Asia 2006–07: Trade, Interdependence, and Security*, assessed the growing economic and trade linkages throughout Asia with a view to understanding how various Asian states perceived their growing connectivity with the global economy as advancing their grand strategies and how this increasing economic integration might affect critical issues of war and peace. The seventh volume, *Strategic Asia 2007–08: Domestic Political Change and Grand Strategy*, examined the various transformations taking place in the domestic politics of pivotal Asian states and how these changes are affecting, or could affect, their respective grand strategies. The eighth volume, *Strategic Asia 2008–09: Challenges and Choices*, focused on analyzing the challenges in Asia and the range of policy choices facing the new U.S. president after almost a decade of distinctive, if controversial, policies pursued by the Bush administration. The ninth volume, *Strategic Asia 2009–10: Economic Meltdown and Geopolitical Stability*, analyzed the impact of the global economic crisis on key Asian states and explored the strategic implications for the United States.

This tenth volume, the decennial anniversary edition, takes stock of where the "Strategic Asia" region stands today, ten years after the first book in the series was published. Although, like its predecessors, this volume remains concerned with illuminating the changing continental balance of power as manifested by the performance of key regional actors (and to the degree relevant, the United States), it adopts a different approach. Whereas all previous volumes were composed primarily of country and regional studies that tracked either overall national performance or achievements and limitations in certain specified areas, this volume examines how growing Asian performance is revealed in nine key functional areas that have a great impact on power and security:

1. Geopolitics, regional institutions, and political integration

2. Economic growth, trade, and integration

3. Military modernization and capability

4. Energy and resource security

5. Nuclear power and nuclear proliferation

6. Security and the global commons

7. Climate change and environmental impact

8. Population trends and national power

9. Domestic politics, ideology, and political change

Viewing the interests and the achievements of key Asian states through each of these lenses provides a rich and textured picture of what recent Asian economic growth has wrought in its complexity. This picture clarifies the causal drivers and their relative strengths in regard to the various outcomes produced, and thus illuminates the potential for change or surprises. It also explores the current and likely effects of these outcomes for internal stability, continued growth, and regional conflict and cooperation, as well as the impact of all these variables for the United States, its interests in Asia, and U.S. interests globally.

Taken together, the nine chapters in this year's volume paint a picture of continuing Asian success—but success that is accompanied by significant internal and external risks. Five basic propositions elaborate this perspective succinctly.

Economic Growth and the Global Distribution of Power

First, there is a continuing long-term shift in the global distribution of power from the West—understood as the United States and Europe—to the East—understood as encompassing Asia's twelve largest economies. This shift in global distribution, which began in the postwar period and has continued even after the ending of the Cold War, has proved to be no fluke. Although the rate of change has been affected by the vicissitudes of economics and politics both in Asia and globally, the fact and direction of change are manifested clearly in the growing concentration of economic capabilities in the East. In the earliest iteration, Asia's growing economic strength was illustrated by the rise of Japan; subsequently, by the dramatic improvement in economic performance in South Korea, Taiwan, and the "tigers" of Southeast Asia led by Singapore; and in the most recent incarnation, by the huge expansion of the Chinese economy, now joined by a rapidly transforming India. The economic growth occurring in these two huge continental-sized states shows no signs of tapering and most observers have by now concluded that growth in China and India is what is most likely to drive the expansion of the global economy for some time to come.

The continued expansion of Asian economic power is not a flash in the pan—and in fact presages a return to the pre-Columbian era when Asia was in fact the center of the global economic system. This view appears to be confirmed by the felicity with which the continent has survived two major economic crises—first, the Asian financial crisis in the late 1990s and, more recently, the global financial crisis of the last few years. Although Asian states were affected differently by these cataclysms, the most significant fact remains that they weathered these crises remarkably, and having survived them, bounced back to become the engines of growth spearheading the recovery.

Peter Petri's chapter in this volume puts this dramatic story into global perspective. Noting that the rise of Asia is unprecedented in speed and scale, improbably led by blistering growth in China and India, countries with half of the world's people, including some of its poorest, Petri flags the dramatic geopolitical consequences of this change when he declares that "between 1990 and 2030, a stylized East, consisting of major Asian economies, and West, consisting of the United States and the European Union, will have roughly traded places in [...] measures of economic mass."

But the rise of Asia that Petri documents is unique in other ways as well. Asian growth is increasingly being driven by large economies with huge numbers of relatively poor populations—a growth process that simultaneously involves the large-scale absorption of subsistence labor into new domestic markets even as it produces a gut-wrenching transformation of the overall economy more generally. Petri observes then that Asian states will become dominant in the international political economy long before their societies become as rich as the West is today. For the foreseeable future, therefore, the international order will be characterized by the apparently anomalous phenomenon of large and impressively growing states behaving as if they were still disadvantaged entities. While these states will seek many of the status gains that they believe ought to be associated with their growing national power—such as new places at the

status gains
U.S.
protection

high tables of global politics, economics, and governance—they will also simultaneously seek to preserve the protections offered by various global regimes to the weakest and most vulnerable developing states. Managing the tensions between these two ~~antinomous~~ impulses will likely dominate all discussions with the West about the reordering of the global system for some time to come.

Even as the Asian economies continue to expand their national product to impressive levels, one of the many pieces of good news in Petri's story is that the United States is integral to these nations' continued success. This is usually assumed to be the case because of the protective benefits that U.S. security guarantees provide directly to allies such as Japan, South Korea, and Australia and indirectly to Singapore and the ASEAN states, not to mention the externalities of such arrangements enjoyed even by non-aligned states such as India. Without discounting these contributions, however, Petri's analysis underscores the importance of the United States as an economic actor in Asian success. Because intra-Asian economic integration still lags behind connectivity to the West for both political and economic reasons, the role of the United States as a major market, as the fountainhead of innovation, and as the provider of international reserves looms large. Asian economic success, therefore, continues to benefit the United States at multiple levels. Moreover, many Asian states—both the economically mature, such as Japan, Korea, Singapore and Australia, and the developing entities, such as India, Indonesia, and even China—seek continued U.S. economic involvement in Asia because of the political benefits and the economic opportunities afforded to these states.

Yet, for the United States to gain maximally from its economic involvement in Asia, changing the current patterns of interaction will be necessary. This change is essential because, as Petri declares succinctly, "global imbalances [today] are largely trans-Pacific." Since "the United States retains the largest single stake in managing the global economy," cooperation with Asia will become central to the challenge of rebalancing. To be sure, this requires important economic decisions on the part of key Asian exporters, but it entails equally critical policy changes in Washington. Some of the policy tools that can be implemented predominantly through U.S. action at home include changes in fiscal policy that sustain increased domestic savings, increasing investments in education at all levels and in R&D, and expanding U.S. trading opportunities through new free trade agreements with various Asian states (admittedly an interim solution until a consensus can be forged on enlarging the open trading system universally). These tools, though, would have the consequence of integrating the U.S.

economy more deeply with a growing Asia to the United States' own economic advantage.

The Alignment of Power in Asia

Second, the sustained economic growth that has characterized Asia's superior economic performance for many decades now is by its very nature not uniform but variegated, thus creating new geopolitical winners and losers within the continent and without—and, as a consequence, a struggle for new strategic alignments. Although Asian economic performance has been superior to most other regions of the world during the postwar era, it is worth remembering that "Asia" is fundamentally an artifact of geographical imagination; it is not an inherently unified political entity. Hence, the gains of growth—which have materialized thus far mainly in littoral Asia and neither uniformly nor proportionately even there—have not only failed to produce any significant Asian unity but, more problematically, have created fissures owing to the differential distribution of success in continental geopolitics.

Clearly the great success story of Asian growth, at least in this most recent iteration, is China, followed at some distance by India. China's economic success has been both rapid and, to the surprise of many, sustained—and, even more improbably, shows no signs of losing steam any time soon. China's explosive economic growth, which the *Economist* has described as "the most dynamic burst of wealth creation in human history,"[1] has occurred despite being embedded in an authoritarian political system and a still highly controlled political economy. Nonetheless, China's economic successes have been significant and robust enough to transform the country from its previous status as a marginal economic actor barely three decades ago into one of the largest global economies today. China is the third-largest trader internationally and the possessor of the world's largest foreign exchange reserves, which have made it an important source of investment capital not simply for many in the developing world but equally importantly for the most powerful global power, the United States. India's more recent economic achievements, though dramatic in comparison to its own post-independence history, nevertheless pale in comparison to China's post-1978 growth record. It is possible that India may sustain high rates of economic growth for longer than China over time, owing to India's favorable demography, open society, capacity for innovation, and superior public and private financial system. However, for the moment at least,

---

[1] "China's Growing Pains," *Economist*, August 19, 2004.

China's achievements not only overshadow India's but have had the effect of disconcerting New Delhi politically as well.

Thus, even among the most conspicuous recent winners of the Asian growth sweepstakes, there are already signs of unease as the weaker performer, India, fears the prospect that China will—as it already has—reallocate increased resources to military instruments that could eventually be used to threaten New Delhi's security interests. India is not alone in this regard. All along the Asian littoral, from Russia in the far north, to Japan in the northeast, to Singapore in the southeast, to Australia in the far south, the question of China's strategic intentions has become the most important geopolitical uncertainty confronting Asia. Although China has always been a significant Asian power, its ambitions mattered little when it was economically otiose; now that the country is growing by leaps and bounds, its emerging capabilities are viewed widely throughout Asia with concern, if not distrust.

This is particularly true in those states that until recently were capable of balancing China independently—Russia and Japan—but that now appear to be sliding sideways, if not downward, each for different reasons. Russia's political system after the fall of Communism has produced a new authoritarian regime supported by new oligarchs whose prosperity appears to derive from rents expropriated from an increasingly weakening society. This strategy seems sustainable so long as global demand for Russia's natural resources continues. But even this source of income could dry up over the long term because of the continued failure of Russian elites to sustain the requisite investments in physical and industrial infrastructure, human capital (especially public health), and R&D (outside of a gradually weakening military-industrial complex). Japan's failures, which have become more prominent in recent years, flow from the inability of the country's paralyzed political system to stimulate an economy that, despite high levels of technological capacity, has remained moribund for the better part of two decades in the face of a rapidly graying population that offers few solutions to the necessities of labor force growth.

Faced with such limitations, Russia and Japan confront this newly confident and powerful China with conflicted strategies: both states seek to redeem their economic prospects by increasing trade with China wherever possible, but are also deeply concerned about contributing further to Beijing's growth in power, even as they wonder what deepened ties to China might mean for their own geopolitical autonomy. For Russia, the way out appears to be continuing to sell raw materials to China, while restraining the impetus to part with its best conventional military technologies (as occurred in the 1990s); depending even more strongly on nuclear weapons; and seeking, to the degree possible, improved ties with India, Japan, Europe, and the United States as a hedge against continued dependence on China. For Japan, safeguarding national interests against China's rise has involved reaffirming the security alliance with the United States, even as Tokyo seeks adjustment in the terms of that relationship, while simultaneously maintaining strong conventional military forces, accelerating a new strategic partnership with India, and attempting to promote a still inchoate vision of an enlarged East Asian community. Whether these strategic modifications will yield lasting dividends for Russia and Japan still remains to be seen. Yet despite being among the more prominent losers in the evolving Asian transformation, these two countries do share with one of the current winners, India, certain commonalities in strategic response: namely, a desire to engage China to the degree possible while simultaneously seeking to build with one another and with the United States the political assurance that could serve as objective constraints on future misbehavior by China.

As Aaron Friedberg pointedly argues in his chapter, the choices exercised by the United States will be crucial in this context for geopolitical stability. Washington could surrender its prevailing primacy either deliberately or inadvertently in favor of duopolistic management with China (a "group of two," or G-2), regional multipolarity dependent on the success of offshore balancing, or reliance on multilateral institutions bereft of supporting U.S. military power in Asia. To the extent that the United States settles for one of these three outcomes, the stage could well be set for key Asian security managers to make geopolitical decisions that redound to the disadvantage of the United States. As Friedberg concludes plainly, "if balancing [China] appears fruitless, and possibly dangerous, it should come as no surprise that many [Asian states] will opt for bandwagoning [with China] instead." "Without active U.S. participation," Friedberg observes, "the balance of power in Asia is unlikely to remain balanced." And this conclusion holds because, among other reasons, purely multipolar systems often succumb to the pathology of "passed bucks," where the rational logic of relying on others to contain rising powers, such as China, could produce failures of balancing that are just as serious as the inability to contain the damage that could be wrought by failing powers, such as Pakistan, given that both types of contingencies are likely to become manifest in the Asia of the future.

New Military Capabilities

Third, the sustained dynamism of the Asian economies in the face of continued uncertainties due to ongoing changes in the regional distribution of power has produced an abiding demand for new military capabilities—and with such capabilities has come greater lethality, extended strategic reach, and potentially serious threats to the hegemonic stability provided by the United States in Asia. It is almost a truism among practitioners of international relations that any durable expansion of national economic power inevitably leads to increases in defense expenditures. The standard explanation for this phenomenon among realists is that as nations become wealthier, their valuation of their assets also increases and, by extension, the resulting investments made in protecting such assets. Given the impressive growth in Asian economic power in recent years—not simply in China and India, but even among smaller states such as Indonesia, Vietnam, and Thailand—it is not surprising that arms acquisitions throughout the region have displayed healthy growth despite being depressed occasionally by economic crises.

When scrutinized closely, however, the reasons for such sustained military modernization differ depending on the country and circumstances. Yet certain critical drivers can be readily identified. The rise of China, and the doubts that accompany it, shape both conventional and nuclear acquisition decisions in Russia and India and conventional modernization, at least in Japan and Australia. The presence of other local threats, as well as the widespread prevalence of interstate disputes in Asia, drives military modernization in the Korean Peninsula, the maritime and continental states of Southeast Asia, and India and Pakistan in South Asia. In addition, the otherwise general need to preserve internal security, protect sovereignty, and defend economically important places both on land and at sea provides sufficient motivation for improving national military capabilities, even if specific threats are not at issue in any given case.

The Strategic Asia region, therefore, does not lack for motivation where modernizing military instruments is concerned. As Richard Bitzinger argues in his chapter, however, what is distinctive about the expanding military capabilities in Asia is not simply the fact that such an expansion is occurring but rather that it is manifested through "hardware [acquisitions] that, on the surface at least, imbue [Asian] militaries with new capacities for warfighting when it comes to mobility, speed, precision strike, firepower, battlespace intelligence, communications, and command and control." Beyond the fact that this demand for leading-edge technologies is sustained by the availability of resources, Bitzinger also calls attention to two other variables. The first is the seductive promise of the "revolution in military affairs," as epitomized by the network-centric warfare proficiencies displayed during the recent U.S. military campaigns in Bosnia and Iraq—campaigns that China's People's Liberation Army (PLA), for example, has attempted to both emulate and counter. The second is the availability of advanced arms in the international market due to the increased willingness of both traditionally major suppliers (such as the United States and Russia) and second-tier producers (such as Germany, the United Kingdom, France, and Israel) to make commercial sales. Owing to the proliferation of such capabilities, Bitzinger concludes that many Asian states now enjoy extended strategic reach at least in nominal terms. Although deficiencies in integration may reduce the effectiveness of the Asian militaries for a while longer, the long list of new military acquisitions suggests that future conflicts in and around the Asian continent will be more lethal in terms of their violence and more devastating in terms of their effects.

The problems posed by these military acquisitions for political stability within Asia are only compounded by the threats increasingly posed to the hegemonic stability provided by the United States. There is little doubt now that U.S. security guarantees to key Asian allies—underwritten by the promise of protective military power—were critical to engendering the "Asian miracle" in the postwar period. The ability of the United States to dominate the Asian littoral effectively mitigated local security competition and thereby sustained the conditions for the growth of economic interdependence, which has produced unprecedented prosperity. The hegemonic power of the United States was also the pivot that enabled the provision of various global public goods. In the economic realm, such public goods included the availability of the dollar as an international reserve currency and U.S.-backed international institutions that upheld the global trading regime; in the security realm, such goods included the protection of the global commons in the maritime, air, space, and, most recently, cyberspace domains. For most of the postwar period, the ability of the Asian powers to mount sustained challenges to the United States in these arenas was largely limited—the Soviet Union being the most conspicuous exception during the high tide of the Cold War—but as Abraham Denmark points out in his chapter, the Asian continent may once again be poised to witness a resurgence of this threat.

Partly as a result of local competitions, partly as a result of the ongoing revolutions in military technology, and partly as a result of the desire of some Asian nations to challenge the United States for various geopolitical reasons—all occurring against the backdrop of continued economic growth—Denmark notes that the "emergence of new Asian military powers" is creating an emerging class of "pivotal states," which he defines as "states with a significant degree of influence over the security of a commons." The emergence of such powers, which will "simultaneously drive two countervailing trends: cooperation and competition," portends important dangers to traditional U.S. hegemony and, by implication, to the customary benefits flowing from a secure global commons. Dealing with these challenges will remain among the most important strategic tasks for the United States specifically, as well as for Asia and the larger international community—since all three entities profit from the continued freedoms that make sustained economic growth possible. Mitigating these threats, Denmark argues, will require a twofold approach. The first is strong diplomatic leadership by the United States to forge an international consensus that codifies the preservation of freedoms in the global commons. The second is simultaneously investing in the necessary military capabilities to defang the emerging challenges so as to protect U.S. interests in those arenas that are critical to both continued U.S. global dominance and prosperity. The common ingredients underlying the success of both endeavors, however, remain American initiative and leadership, for without these resources neither strategic solution is assured of success. In this context, Secretary of State Hillary Clinton's remarks at the ASEAN Regional Forum in Hanoi, Vietnam—stating firmly America's national interest in maintaining freedom of navigation in the South China Sea and willingness to facilitate multilateral negotiations on territorial disputes in the area—are an important sign of U.S. willingness to maintain its leadership role in preserving the security of these commons.

The Demands and Repercussions of Success

Fourth, the continued demands associated with Asia's economic success are producing consequential direct repercussions as well as externalities of global impact, and in the process are suggesting that the sustainability of Asia's growth may be more challenging than is often imagined. The continued economic growth witnessed in Asia over the past several decades is not simply another evolutionary development in global economic history, a continuation of past trends with merely a change in pace. Rather, this growth is genuinely a discontinuity because it is unprecedented in scope and speed, encompasses numerous states and huge populations, and is being sustained at high rates in a fashion not witnessed before. Consequently, economic growth in Asia must be judged as an authentically systemic transformation whose culmination is not yet in sight. By all accounts, the growth of China and India at the core of the Asian system, followed by continuing expansion in the second-tier states of Southeast Asia and the steady, if slower, growth in the mature East Asian economies, will persist for a long time to come. This implies that the Strategic Asia region will continue to remain the locomotive for growth in the global economy writ large.

While this phenomenon is undoubtedly significant for geopolitical reasons, it is also intriguing for economic reasons alone. After all, there is simply no precedent for a country as large as China growing so fast for such a long period of time. And if India continues its slower, but still high, rates of economic growth for another two decades, that too would make the record of Asian economic growth all the more incredible. This unique phenomenon of high sustained growth can be partly explained by the fact that such growth begins from a relatively low base and, hence, is owed to the increasing returns to scale that are often witnessed in the early phases of economic expansion. To that degree, high sustained growth rates, at least for a while, may not be surprising. But something else may be afoot in a country such as China—and with serious consequences. As Prem Shankar Jha argues in his masterly comparison of Chinese and Indian political economy, *Crouching Dragon, Hidden Tiger*, China's explosive growth may owe as much to its political economy as to the laws of economics. Arguing that "the struggle for control over investable resources between the central and local levels of government" accounts for China's runaway expansion, Jha asserts that the "continued state monopoly of the banking system" is what has made China's economic expansion "fatally easy."[2] He argues that this is so because the state banking monopoly has permitted local authorities to sustain an enormous—and still continuing—expansion in investment through their control of bank credit provided by local banks, their ability to allocate land for new industrial ventures by fiat, and their control over local taxation and local markets.

Given this anatomy of success, Jha demonstrates that China's economic expansion has been sustained primarily because it remains a sterling example of "extensive" growth, that is, growth based on rapidly expanding the quantity of inputs committed in order to increase a given level of output. In the absence of a genuine internal market capable of effectively aligning prices with relative scarcity, China's reliance on extensive growth has had many consequential effects. First, it has produced an insatiable drive for raw materials and other natural resources because continually increasing levels of inputs are required to maintain the desired growth in output (that is, economic growth) if the social compact that keeps the Chinese Communist Party (CCP) in power is to be sustained indefinitely. Second, China's reliance on growth has led to dreadful levels of economic inefficiency, waste, pollution, and environmental abuse deriving from the rampant overexploitation of both national and international natural resources. Third, it has put a premium on increasing the size of the labor

---

[2] Prem Shankar Jha, *Crouching Dragon, Hidden Tiger: Can China and India Dominate the West?* (New York: Soft Skull Press, 2010), 64, 65.

force as one of the key elements necessary to sustain extensive growth over the long-term—at precisely the time when China's social policies are at cross purposes with this objective and in circumstances where Beijing does not appear to be doing too well in fostering technological change, thus putting at increasing risk over the long term its undeniable achievements in regard to capital accumulation.

Each of these three consequences is illustrated in this volume in different ways. Mikkal Herberg's chapter on energy and resource security challenges in Asia demonstrates that China's and, more broadly, Asia's economic growth is likely to make enormous demands on imported energy. Increased demand obviously remains at one level a direct function of the expansion in economic activities at home. But to the degree that this expansion is driven by the pathologies of political economy of the kind found in China or in the failures to create efficient domestic markets for energy, as is the case in India and in other developing countries, the growing demand for energy and rare earth minerals is necessarily higher than it ought to be ordinarily. Both kinds of weakness combine to increase the demand for natural resources beyond what is actually necessary, given current levels of technology. The upshot of such rising demand is steadily increasing prices globally. Whereas the developed world and the fast-growing developing countries can cope with the consequences of energy price increases either through technology substitution or simply through absorption, the poorer states in the global economy end up bearing significantly onerous burdens.

As Herberg emphasizes, however, the implications of increased energy demands from a rapidly growing Asia go beyond mere economic discomfort into the contested arenas of power politics. This is because many emerging Asian economies, most notably China's, are quite distrustful of market mechanisms as a matter of both ideology and practice. Given Jha's analysis, the latter may in fact be more important: the CCP's continued political survival depends on assured inputs in order to sustain continuous growth domestically. According to Herberg, this political need has resulted in China pursuing "an increasingly nationalistic and competitive approach to energy security" according to which its national oil companies with strong state support have sought to secure control of oil and gas supplies through "[technical] investments, financial largesse, and various trade and aid emoluments in key energy-exporting regions." This strategy has not only propelled Chinese investments in far-flung areas but also in countries run by some fairly odious regimes, such as Iran, Sudan, and Burma. Worse still, this strategy has provoked emulation by others, most notably India, though to a lesser degree. It has also opened the door to a mercantilist competition over energy and raw materials in Asia, where if the flag were to follow trade and investment, the stage could truly be set for malignant rivalries in the future.

The perils of depending on natural resources from abroad, especially energy resources, has provoked a renewed interest in nuclear energy in Asia. Charles Ferguson's chapter in this volume details how the demands of economic growth in Asia have produced an "astonishing upsurge" in nuclear power investments led by China, India, and South Korea. More interestingly, many smaller Asian states, including some that have experienced high growth levels recently (such as Indonesia, Bangladesh, Malaysia, the Philippines, Thailand, and Vietnam), have expressed a new interest in acquiring nuclear power plants. Because the availability of electricity is a fundamental requirement for sustaining economic growth, it is not surprising that many Asian states are now examining nuclear energy as a source for producing electricity, especially at a time when there are growing price and access pressures on fossil fuels and increased concerns about greenhouse gas emissions. Nuclear energy production, however, embodies a variety of risks; the possibility of catastrophic accidents, the management of waste, and the dangers of engendering further nuclear proliferation all combine to make expanding access to nuclear energy a delicate proposition where commercial and national interests intersect in complex ways.

Ferguson's conclusions are eminently realistic. Accepting that the expansion of nuclear power in Asia is inevitable and that this expansion will both have direct impact on possessors of nuclear technology and produce externalities for others, Ferguson argues that the United States ought to focus attention on maximizing the positive gains while minimizing the global risks. In a succinct summary, he notes that the United States can achieve these objectives clearly by "ensuring the highest international standards of nuclear safety and security, maintaining access to all components of the fuel cycle, upholding adequate controls on enrichment and reprocessing components of this cycle, shoring up security alliances, and working to bring pariah states into the international system." To do so, however, will require that Washington be just as attentive to sustaining U.S. nuclear capabilities at both a military and a civilian level as it is to preserving the extant global nuclear regime.

Richard Matthew's chapter in this volume details the real and potential impact of climate change in Asia. His conclusions are indeed sobering. He notes that "the overall picture is quite alarming for Asia, as climate change models predict significant climate effects throughout the region." Matthew concludes not merely that much of Asia will be physically and socially vulnerable to the ravages of climate change—as manifested through health challenges, increasing population displacements, diminishing state capacity, growing development challenges, sharper resource scarcity, and biodiversity loss—but also that these casualties are in many ways the consequence of human choices. Again, the example of China is illustrative: the use, or more accurately misuse, of energy remains a crucial driver of environmental degradation and climate change, and China's political economy fosters wasteful investment that exacerbates rather than attenuates China's climate change burdens.

As Wang Qingyi has pointed out in his study of energy intensive industry in China using 2004 data, China operates 28,000 coal mines with an average annual output of 70,000 tons. This contrasts with Germany, which runs 9 mines with an average annual output of 5.56 million tons. China operates 56 refineries with an annual processing capacity of 4.19 million tons in contrast to South Korea's 6 refineries with an annual processing capacity of 21.47 million tons. Likewise, China operates 263 blast furnaces with an average annual steel production of 750,000 tons in contrast to the 29 in Japan that produce 2.83 million tons of steel annually. Finally, China operates 5,027 cement factories with an average annual output of 190,000 tons in contrast to Japan, which has 65 factories producing an average annual output of 1.14 million tons.[3]

While Chinese economic inefficiency may be egregious compared to Asia's other states, the problems of the misuse of energy and other natural resources are widespread and remain ultimately the products of institutional failures that either directly or indirectly contribute to resource depletion, environmental degradation, and climate change. In many countries, such as India, for example, these problems are exacerbated by state and regulatory weaknesses that further undermine the ability of the market to price various human decisions effectively, thus contributing to the creation of those societal hazards that exacerbate climate change. Matthew concludes correctly that in such circumstances "the potential for violent conflict ranging from riots to war is real, although there are also considerable opportunities for cooperation."

If the deleterious effects of climate change caused by state and societal decisions cast a shadow on the ability of the Asian states to sustain their remarkable growth over the long term, Nicholas Eberstadt's comprehensive overview of demographic trends in Asia provides further reason for concern. All models of growth in modern economic theory acknowledge that the supply of labor directly or indirectly remains one of the building blocks of economic growth. The size, rate of growth, and the quality of population, then, become fundamentally important

---

[3] Wang Qingyi, "Energy Conservation as Security," *China Security*, no. 3 (Summer 2006): 89–105, http://www.wsichina.org/curr05.html.

components in determining whether a country's growth can be sustained over the long term. In an extensive growth model, the steady availability of growing quantities of manpower becomes even more crucial because it can compensate for sluggish technological change while simultaneously contributing to capital accumulation.

Unfortunately for China, which appears critically dependent on extensive growth, Eberstadt's findings do not represent good news: given current fertility patterns, China appears poised to confront a severe "replacement deficit" involving a steep and continuing shrinkage in China's working-age population over the foreseeable future. Eberstadt notes that the size of the critical 15–24 year old cohort is fundamental from the perspective of economic growth, because it represents individuals with the best health, the highest levels of educational attainment, and the most up-to-date technical and scientific skills. Eberstadt concludes that this group has been shrinking in relative terms for a generation—and it stands to shrink still further, in both relative and absolute terms, in the decades just ahead. For those who assume that China's economic rise is inevitable or that its strategy of extensive growth can be sustained indefinitely, Eberstadt's prognostication puts a damper on all such expectations and raises an even more disconcerting question: can the Asian expansion, which relies deeply on integration with the Chinese economy, be sustained if the motor of that growth were to seriously slow down in the decades ahead?

It does not appear as if any of the other Asian great powers can seamlessly step in to replace China either. India's fertility rate is slowing as well, and although the country possesses a favorable demographic profile, the Indian economy is not as well integrated into the Asian trading system as China's is today—and may never be, as a deliberate matter of national strategy. Japan and Russia, confronted by serious problems of aging and depopulation, respectively, do not promise to be effective substitutes for China either. Where labor force growth is concerned, therefore, the Asian miracle is handicapped by vulnerabilities. Even a country such as India, which is better positioned in regard to population size and profile, still faces significant problems because of past failures to invest in human capital.

On balance, therefore, Asia's economic success, though likely to be sustained in the policy-relevant future, faces serious challenges in the years ahead. Even today, however, economic growth has come at a price: though essential for defeating poverty and raising the standards of living of the millions who live in the most populous areas of the continent, the processes of growth have not always been as efficient or equitable as they could be. This implies that the direct and social costs of growth have been higher than is desirable even as such growth has produced externalities of different kinds that affect indigenous populations, states lying further away, and the international system as a whole. For these reasons, sustaining Asia's economic success over the long term will remain a challenging endeavor.

Governance and the Prospects for Peace and Stability

Fifth, and finally, the economic transformations across Asia are occurring faster than the march of democratization throughout the continent, raising questions not only about the responsiveness of governments to their populations in the face of painful social change but also about the prospects for continental peace and stability. The issue of the spread and viability of democracy in Asia is not simply a matter of ideological preference, a manifestation of "superstructure" in the Marxian sense, but rather is organically connected to the deepest issues of internal stability and external peace. At a time when rapid economic growth has forced gut-wrenching transformations in domestic politics throughout Asia, the presence or absence of rule-bound and responsive governments could make a major difference to managing the challenges of social change. The desirability of democratic regimes in this context does not hinge on a preference for any particular type of democracy; rather, any political system that is constrained by a set of rules grounded in a fundamental respect for persons and that allocates power on the basis of respect for popular will ought to suffice for both normative and practical reasons.

The stark differences between China and India are illustrative in this regard. Both China and India have been exemplars of rapid Asian growth. Although China has been far more successful economically than India has been, the future of China's success appears to be more contingent because of the fundamental tension inherent in a social system that combines command politics with a partially free economy. The ability of such a system to absorb the stresses that are generated by inequity and losses in the marketplace is suspect, as the evidence of unrest throughout China increasingly demonstrates. Although social order in the short term can—and will—be maintained by force, the brittleness of the authoritarian regime remains an ever-present concern, in different ways, for the Chinese leadership and for outsiders. For the politburo, the chief danger is the decisive loss of control stemming from popular dissatisfaction that results in widespread violence, chaos, and, ultimately, forcible regime change. For the international community, China's authoritarian dispensation poses the danger of "diversionary" conflict abroad in the face of frayed legitimacy at home. In fact, it would not be an exaggeration to say that although China's size and growing economic and military power would give pause to all of the country's neighbors simply as a matter of course, these fears have certainly been reinforced throughout Asia and globally because Beijing's growing national power is wielded by a non-democratic regime.

India's democracy, in contrast, breeds fewer suspicions. Almost every Asian power, including the United States, welcomes India's rise—with the exception of Pakistan and China, which are special cases both because of their authoritarian internal structures and because of their long-standing rivalries with New Delhi—and seeks to integrate India ever more tightly into the evolving Asian strategic system as a counterbalance to China. This preference for a partnership with India, whether on the part of the United States, Russia, Japan, or the smaller powers of Southeast Asia, is undoubtedly shaped by perceptions of growing Indian power in the first instance, but it is certainly reinforced by the judgment that Indian democracy makes the country's national trajectory both stable and predictable. India's democracy provides irreplaceable benefits for its own polity as well. As the country has moved further along the trajectory of market society, liberal democracy has become the fundamental defense of the weak against the potential abuse of power by the strong—whether those be political or economic elites—and will increasingly become the instrument by which losers in the marketplace can protect their interests from being decisively effaced.

The comparison between India and China thus illustrates the basic point that the spread of democracy is desirable not merely as an ideological preference but because it is a vital instrument for preserving social stability in countries undergoing rapid economic transformation even as it simultaneously offers the hope of engendering more peaceful interstate relations. Sumit Ganguly and Manjeet Pardesi's chapter on democratization in Asia offers, however, only qualified optimism that the continent will enjoy these benefits in the years ahead. Although noting that democracy is well entrenched in two key states, Japan and India, they argue persuasively that "the global wave of democracy has seemingly stalled in most other states in Asia." More dangerously, China's success appears to have given a fillip to the "authoritarian state-market economy model," which despite its inherent contradictions could become a serious competitor to free market democracy in Asia. Although such a model has not yet demonstrated that it can satisfactorily manage the problems of inequity that arise in market societies—because, among other things, authoritarian state actions often tend to exacerbate inequality rather than mitigate it—China's recent successes will likely embolden some current power holders in Asia to attempt to emulate the Chinese model in order to maximize their own gains vis-à-vis their larger societies. That such regimes also offer poor hope for enlarging the democratic peace turns out to be an equally consequential problem, given the number of interstate disputes over territory and resources that are present in Asia.

As Ganguly and Pardesi attest, authoritarian capitalism remains only one of two challengers to democracy in Asia; the other is increasingly political Islam, which although requiring a specific milieu for expansion, most importantly a preexisting history of Muslim presence nationally, is nonetheless advantaged today by the interaction of technology and politics. The availability of new mass communications technologies has permitted transnational mobilization around certain specific Muslim grievances, transforming them into universal complaints that are embedded into a larger protest against Westernization, secularism, modernity, and, in its most empirical manifestation, the United States. The presence of a few wealthy states, most notably Saudi Arabia, that have subsidized the propagation of specific forms of political Islam, and the realities of state decay in other parts of Asia, most notably Pakistan, have produced a religiously radicalized population that is willing to challenge democratic societies worldwide through the use of violent force. Dealing with this threat, Ganguly and Pardesi conclude, will require the United States to develop "a global strategy that is sensitive to local conditions," where the selective targeting of al Qaeda cannot come at the cost of "ignoring other radical Islamist organizations in different parts of the world."

Where does all this leave the United States? One of the key objectives of the Strategic Asia Program from the very beginning has been not simply to understand Asian transformations but to analyze their impact on U.S. interests and particularly on the future of U.S. power. The volumes in the *Strategic Asia* series over the past decade, when read synoptically, permit a reasonably optimistic answer to this fundamental question: as the chapters in this decennial volume subtly corroborate, the Asian economic transformation that began in the early years of the postwar period will continue successfully well into the first quarter of this new century, but because of the many challenges affecting the nations implicated in this process, the rise of Asia will not translate into the demise of U.S. hegemony in Asia or globally for a long time to come. Despite the steady emergence of new centers of power in Asia during the period, the United States will still remain the only country in the world with truly comprehensive national power, which even by the most minimalist definition implies the continuance of U.S. hegemony.

This persistence of hegemony owes to the fact that even as Asia rises, the United States will continue to remain a vital component of Asia's economic success—a source of technology and innovation, a large and expanding market, and an unparalleled destination for investment by others. The

United States will also remain the provider of choice for the most important public goods necessary for the success of the region and the predominant military power in Asia despite the emergence of new challengers. These realities, however, cannot be an invitation for the United States to rest on its laurels. Rather, the country must focus resolutely on the three tasks that are essential for bolstering its hegemony if that is to survive over the secular future: renewing the domestic foundations of U.S. power, strengthening partnerships with key Asian friends and allies, and deepening military superiority through greater investments in technological and organizational innovation. Above all else, the United States should not—as it works through these demands—cede its geopolitical primacy to others as a matter of either diplomatic niceties or national policy, because it emphatically does not need to. Instead, Washington's attention ought to be focused on exercising effective international leadership even as it concentrates on renewing the foundations that will make that leadership last as long as possible.

STRATEGIC ASIA 2010–11

THEMATIC STUDIES

The shifting structure of power shapes the parameters within which states must act, setting limits on what they can achieve and creating imperatives that they ignore at their peril. How quickly and in precisely what ways states react to changing material conditions will depend on their goals and strategies. These, in turn, are the product of a variety of tangible and intangible factors, including the perceptions of key individuals, the power of various societal groups, the domestic political regimes within which they operate, and the content of prevailing ideologies. Structure is important, but so too is strategy. To paraphrase Marx, "nations make their own histories, but they do not make them just as they please."

These basic insights and beliefs have informed the Strategic Asia Program since its inception. Successive volumes in this series have sought to look forward as well as backward, speculating in a disciplined way about where the confluence of underlying trends and evolving policies seemed to be taking the region. Contributors have presented what the late Samuel Huntington used to call "policy-relevant basic research": probing, rigorous treatments of fundamental questions intended ultimately to inform the thinking of those charged with making and executing national strategy.

The purpose of this chapter is to analyze the evolving balance of power across "Strategic Asia," an area encompassing the entire eastern half of the Eurasian landmass and the arc of islands in the Western Pacific. As this is the tenth anniversary of the Strategic Asia Program, it seems appropriate to begin by looking back briefly over the events of the past decade, before considering the decade that has just begun. Because the future of the region is so contingent and uncertain, instead of making a single prediction about where Asia is headed, this chapter will offer a range of alternative futures. In each case, the chapter will identify both the factors that could make a particular configuration of power more likely and the possible implications for the countries of the region and for the United States.

A Geopolitical Retrospective: Strategic Asia, 2000–2010

The past ten years have been punctuated by geopolitical and economic shocks of exceptional, once-in-a-century magnitude. For an event similar in impact to the September 11 attacks on New York and Washington, one would have to go back 60 years to December 7, 1941. The closest equivalent to the global financial meltdown and deep recession that began in 2008–09 would be the October 1929 stock market crash that marked the start of the Great Depression. In terms of the diplomatic and domestic political furor unleashed, the invasion and occupation of Iraq most closely resembled the Vietnam War of the mid-1960s to mid-1970s.

Despite all this unanticipated turmoil, at least insofar as Asia is concerned, the basic economic trends visible at the beginning of the century have thus far played themselves out more or less as expected. The region as a whole has continued to grow faster than the rest of the world, with the result that its share of global GDP has increased from 33% in 2000 to nearly 40% in 2010. Within Asia itself, China and India remained the growth leaders, with their GDPs advancing at an average annual rate of 9.9% and 7.3%, respectively, between 2000 and 2009, and increasing from a combined total of 34% of the region's total output in 2000 to 48% in 2010. Thanks largely to an increase in oil prices, Russia managed to hold onto its share of world GDP (growing slightly over the course of the decade from 2.7% to 3.0%), while Japan's position continued to weaken (its GDP share falling from 7.6% to just under 6%). Both Russia and Japan also entered into what is likely to be an irreversible absolute drop in population, with unfavorable portents for their future prosperity, dynamism, and strength.[2]

The essential continuity of the region's economic trend lines, in spite of political upheaval, suggests that they are being driven by deeply rooted demographic and technological forces. Nonetheless, over the past ten years all the major regional powers (and some smaller ones, too) have provided illustrations of the ability of leaders and governments to influence, for good or ill, both the perception and the reality of national power and prestige, at least at the margins. During this period, Russia moved from the drunken buffoonery of erstwhile democrat Boris Yeltsin to the seemingly tough-minded pragmatism of the decidedly authoritarian Vladimir Putin. The fundamentals of Russia's position did not change perceptibly. The country made little progress toward modernizing its economy or armed forces, with the result that its increasingly questionable claim to great-power status continued to rest on little more than exports of non-renewable resources and an aging stockpile of nuclear weapons. But Putin's obvious determination to reassert Russian influence in its "near abroad," as well as in Europe and the Middle East, made his country look more like a force to be reckoned with at the end of the decade than it had appeared at the beginning.

Japan, meanwhile, went through a reverse cycle. The country started out in 2001 under the leadership of Junchiro Koizumi—an iconoclastic, popular reformer determined to smash long-established political and bureaucratic cartels, rouse his country from years of economic stagnation,

---

[2] International Monetary Fund, World Economic Outlook Database, April 2010, http://www. imf.org/external/pubs/ft/weo/2010/01/weodata/index.aspx; World Bank, World Development Indicators and Global Development Finance Database, http://databank.worldbank.org/; World Bank, *South Asia Economic Update 2010: Moving Up, Looking East*, advance edition (Washington, D.C.: World Bank, April 2010), 67; and "China Quarterly Update," World Bank, Beijing Office, March 2010, 10.

flex and strengthen its military muscles, and assert its right finally to play the role of a "normal nation" on the international stage. Yet by the decade's close, notwithstanding the fact that the Liberal Democratic Party (LDP) had finally lost its monopoly on power, the nation seemed to have lapsed back into an all-too-familiar pattern of weakness, deadlock, indecision, and underperformance.

Both China and India gave further proof of the importance of policy in shaping national destiny, albeit in very different ways. In the first instance, despite changes in top leadership, the ruling Chinese Communist Party (CCP) regime in Beijing maintained its single-minded focus on sustaining market-driven economic growth as the means to preserving social stability and fueling the acquisition of all other forms of "comprehensive national power." For all its messy inconsistencies, democratic India held firm to a similar commitment. In this case pro-growth policies were rooted not only in the convictions of a small ruling elite but also in a broad societal consensus, sustained across changes in elected governments.

In the introduction to the inaugural volume of the *Strategic Asia* series, I made a number of observations about the policies of the major Asian powers and about the patterns of interaction that seemed to be emerging among them and with the United States. As of 2001, all were pursuing "mixed, hedged" national strategies aimed at "fending-off short-term challenges, while at the same time preserving options for the future and attempting to build (or re-build) long-term power and influence." All were eager to enjoy the benefits of economic exchange, and none sought confrontation. Nevertheless, to varying degrees, and with differing impact on their policies, Russia, India, and Japan were all worried about the rapid growth of China's power, while Chinese strategists, for their part, feared that Japan, India, the United States, and perhaps someday Russia would "join together in an encircling alliance directed against them." These considerations produced a layered pattern of interstate relations in which day-to-day dealings were "dominated by trade and talk of peace" and in which all parties declared "a willingness to negotiate differences… participate in multilateral institutions and, in general, to abjure the threat or use of force," while, at the same time, harboring deep concerns about the capabilities and ultimate intentions of their counterparts. Despite the evident fluidity of the situation, I noted finally that there were signs of "an unmistakable movement toward polarization in Strategic Asia, with China and a handful of friends on one side, and an assortment of allies and quasi-allies on the other."[3]

---

[3] Aaron L. Friedberg, "Introduction," in *Strategic Asia 2001–02: Power and Purpose*, ed. Richard J. Ellings and Aaron L. Friedberg (Seattle: National Bureau of Asian Research, 2001), 18, 21, 22.

In the ten years that have passed since these words were written, the rise of China and the responses of other states to it have emerged even more clearly as the defining features of the Asian, and indeed the global, strategic landscape. To date, Beijing has been able to sustain annual growth at or near the average levels achieved since the start of "reform and opening up" in the late 1970s. What is more, at least as of this writing, China has managed to navigate a major crisis of precisely the sort that some analysts had long predicted would derail the nation's economy and destabilize its political system. The resulting compounding of China's GDP and the country's movement up the ranks of the world's largest economies were entirely predictable, but the reality nevertheless inspired awe and anxiety in other Asian capitals, as well as in Washington.

China's continuing growth has enabled the country to conduct a wide-ranging and rapid modernization of its armed forces and defense industrial base that, in terms of the burden imposed on the national economy, has been all but painless. Whereas at the turn of the century it was still commonplace to observe that China's jets, tanks, ships, and submarines lagged several generations behind those of the United States, the gap in many areas has clearly begun to close. More worrisome is the recognition that China has also been pursuing asymmetric approaches to deterring and defeating potential enemies by developing anti-satellite weapons, large numbers of precision-guided conventional ballistic missiles, and cyber warfare techniques that could prove disproportionately costly and difficult for the United States and its allies to counter.

Economic growth has also given Beijing a variety of tools that it previously lacked, including the ability to promise (or threaten to withhold) aid, investment capital, access to China's massive market for energy and raw materials, and its seemingly limitless supply of inexpensive labor. In recent years Beijing has become more subtle and sophisticated in using all these instruments of soft power to enhance its influence and shape its strategic environment. In addition, the mere fact of China's obvious economic success has boosted its prestige around the world, and its ability to combine growth with authoritarianism has encouraged the perception in some quarters that China provides a workable alternative to Western models of liberal democratic capitalism.

This last point deserves emphasis. Throughout the 1990s and into the start of the new century, concern over the possible strategic implications of China's rapidly growing wealth and power was offset to a degree by the widely held belief that the country was also on a fast track to political reform. Increasing wealth, it was thought, would lead to the emergence of a middle class, which would demand expanded political rights. Like several of its East Asian counterparts, including South Korea and Taiwan, China would eventually make the transition from authoritarian rule to liberal democracy. Once that happened, China would presumably enter the democratic "zone of peace," and the likelihood that Beijing would use China's newfound power to confront the United States, or its democratic allies, would decline dramatically.

Over the course of the past decade the prospects for change seem to have receded. Even as Beijing has kept the economy moving forward, the current regime has proven to be remarkably inventive, ruthless, and determined in crushing dissent, developing techniques for controlling information, and finding new ways to co-opt and intimidate potential opponents. As in the economic domain, sudden reversals are always possible. For now, however, it seems likely that China will continue to be ruled for some time by an authoritarian regime with growing resources at its disposal, whose wider ambitions and intentions are opaque, but whose determination to keep a tight grip on domestic political power, while exerting a growing influence across Asia, is unmistakable.

The questions going forward are: Will China continue to rise? And, assuming that it does, how will others respond? Due to the multiple uncertainties that necessarily surround these issues, this chapter will take a frankly speculative approach, looking in turn at six alternative geopolitical futures for Strategic Asia. For reasons that will be explained, the first four possibilities (a restoration of American hegemony, an East Asian community, Sino-American "bi-gemony," and a U.S.-India-China triangle) appear to be relatively less likely than the final two (either Chinese hegemony or a balance between a grouping of authoritarian, continental states centered on China and a coalition of maritime democracies led by the United States).

Strategic Asia, 2010–20: American Hegemony Restored?

In the immediate aftermath of the Cold War, the United States enjoyed a huge advantage in both economic and military capabilities over any nation in Asia, or in any other part of the world for that matter. Today, in relation to China and, to a lesser extent, India, the margins are somewhat smaller, though still substantial. While the narrowing of the "GDP gap" between the United States and China has received the most attention, the latter's ongoing military build-up is beginning to reach the point where it could produce a noticeable shift in the regional balance of power. Whereas twenty years ago U.S. air and naval forces could operate with impunity right up to the edge of China's coastal waters and airspace, the acquisition by the People's Republic of China (PRC) of layered anti-access capabilities will soon make this a more complex and risky task. China's deployment of larger, more secure intercontinental-range nuclear forces will also begin to raise questions about the ability of the United States to extend deterrence to some of its friends and allies in the region. In this respect, as in the economic and diplomatic domains, China is beginning to have the capabilities necessary to match or offset U.S. power in Asia, if not yet on a global scale.[4]

As noted above, at the time of writing China seems to have passed through the recent economic turmoil comparatively unscathed. After rising to a peak of 13% in 2007, its annual growth was cut almost in half (to around 7% on a year-on-year basis) during the initial stages of the global crisis.[5] Thanks to a very aggressive response by the central authorities, growth climbed back to just under 9% in 2009, and some estimates show it hovering between 9% and 10% for at least the next few years.[6] While Beijing chose to slow the rate of growth in defense spending in the wake of the crisis, there appears to be little reason why China cannot sustain a continued build-up at or near previous rates.[7]

For its part, the United States is entering the new decade tightly constrained fiscally and politically. The recession that began at the end of 2007 and extended into 2010 caused tax revenues to fall and the deficit to grow, and the federal government's efforts to contain the banking crisis and stimulate the economy produced even bigger imbalances. In the span of only a year, the deficit quadrupled in size from $459 billion (3.2% of GDP) to $1.85 trillion (13.1% of GDP), the most rapid deterioration on record and the largest deficit in relation to the economy as a whole since the end of World War II.[8] To cover the gap between revenues and expenditures the federal government had to borrow at unprecedented rates, causing the federal debt to balloon from 41% of GDP to 60%.[9]

---

[4] These shifts and their possible implications are discussed in Aaron L. Friedberg, "Here Be Dragons: Is China a Military Threat?" *National Interest*, no. 103 (September/October 2009): 19–25, 31–32.

[5] Pieter Bottelier, "China and the International Financial Crisis," in *Strategic Asia 2009–10: Economic Meltdown and Geopolitical Stability*, ed. Ashley J. Tellis, Andrew Marble, and Travis Tanner (Seattle: National Bureau of Asian Research, 2009), 72–76.

[6] See "OECD Sees Strong Growth, Low Inflation in China," Reuters, November 19, 2009, http://www.reuters.com/article/idUSSGR00205520091119. Based on surprisingly strong growth in exports, Morgan Stanley predicted that China would grow at around 11% in 2010. See Qing Wang and Steven Zhang, "China: Upgrading 2010 Forecasts on Improved External Outlook," Morgan Stanley, February 5, 2010, http://www.morganstanley.com/views/gef/archive/2010/20100205-Fri.html.

[7] "China's Defense Budget to Grow 7.5% in 2010: Spokesman," *China Daily*, March 4, 2010, http://www.chinadaily.com.cn/china/2010-03/04/content_9537753.htm.

[8] "Seeing Red," *Economist*, June 13, 2009, 33; Paul Swartz, "Quarterly Update: The Recession in Historical Context," Council on Foreign Relations, Center for Geoeconomic Studies, June 5, 2009; and "The Long-Term Budget Outlook," Congressional Budget Office (CBO), CBO Summary, June 2009, 2. http://www.cbo.gov/ftpdocs/102xx/doc10297/SummaryforWeb_LTBO.pdf.

[9] "The Long-Term Budget Outlook."

Unusually low interest rates have helped to hold down the cost of servicing this massive increase in debt. As rates rise, however, so too will the size of the federal government's payments to its creditors. Within the next decade, for the first time on record, annual payments on the federal debt could exceed outlays for national defense.[10]

The deflection of resources from productive investment to debt repayment, coupled with the tax increases and spending cuts that are likely to be imposed in order to shrink the deficit, will put a damper on growth rates. While there are some optimistic outliers, the emerging consensus among forecasters is that the United States will not bounce back immediately to its pre-crisis performance. Instead of averaging 3.0%–3.5% per year, growth is expected to remain at about 2.0%–2.5% for much of this decade and perhaps beyond.[11]

The combination of rising interest costs, slower growth, and the long-awaited explosion in entitlement programs due to population aging will tend to squeeze all forms of "discretionary spending."[12] Of these, the defense budget is the biggest and may turn out to be the most politically vulnerable. As the United States disentangles itself from Iraq and Afghanistan, there will be calls to pocket the resulting "peace dividend" and to direct more resources to urgent domestic needs. Instead of being freed to spend more on systems relevant to a possible long-term competition with China, the Defense Department is likely to face the necessity of making cuts in R&D and procurement over the coming decade.[13]

If present trends continue, then, over the next ten years China will begin to pose an increasing challenge to American preponderance in Asia. But, of course, these trends may not continue. Despite its recent success, China may not manage to keep growing at anything resembling the rates attained over the past three decades. The enormous sums that both the central and local authorities have pumped into the economy since the start

---

[10] "U.S. Interest vs. Defense Spending," Council on Foreign Relations, Center for Geoeconomic Studies, October 26, 2009.

[11] The historical average for the period since 1875 is 3.4%. See David J. Lynch, "U.S. May Face Years of Sluggish Economic Growth," USA Today, May 7, 2009, http://www.usatoday.com/money/economy/2009-05-07-slow-us-economic-growth_N.htm. For a relatively optimistic prediction of 2.6% for the period 2010–20, see Martin S. Feldstein, "U.S. Growth in the Decade Ahead," National Bureau of Economic Research, Working Paper, no. 15685, January 2010.

[12] The intensity of this pressure will depend in part on the outcome and fiscal impact of the ongoing debate over health care reform. If reform winds up slowing the growth of health care costs, as promised, the pressures will obviously be less. Unfortunately, the opposite scenario is at least equally plausible. For one pessimistic assessment, see Robert Samuelson, "A Parody of Leadership," Washington Post, December 21, 2009.

[13] See Dov S. Zakheim, "Security Challenges Arising from the Global Economic Crisis," remarks to the House Committee on Armed Services, Washington, D.C., March 11, 2009, available at http://www.fpri.org/enotes/200903.zakheim.securityeconomiccrisis.html.

of the recent crisis may soon produce asset price bubbles and contribute to massive overcapacity in certain key sectors. In the process of staving off immediate danger the Chinese government may have set the stage for an even bigger crisis in the years just ahead.[14]

Even if China manages to stay on track for the next few years, and even for the next decade, the burdens imposed by environmental, demographic, and natural resource constraints; official corruption; increasingly dysfunctional development policies; foreign protectionism; energy price shocks; and social unrest could combine to knock China off its current steep trajectory.[15] By contrast, despite recent difficulties, the United States' economic fundamentals still look extremely strong. In addition to the entrepreneurial culture, stable political and legal institutions, deep capital markets, natural resource endowments, well-funded corporate research establishments, and great universities, if it remains open to immigration, the United States—unlike China and virtually all of the advanced industrial democracies—will be able to sustain a favorable ratio of workers to retirees. In the mid to long term, the prospects for restoring growth to historic levels thus appear good. What is more, projected constraints on defense budgets are the result of politics rather than of any absolute scarcity of resources. Should the country and its leaders perceive a sufficient threat, then even in hard times the United States can ramp up spending very quickly, much as it did in the late 1970s and early 1980s, to say nothing of the late 1930s and early 1940s.

Present trends point to a further erosion in U.S. hegemony rather than to its restoration. Should China stumble, however, and if, at the same time, the United States were able to rejuvenate its own economy, then the era of American preponderance in Asia could be extended well into the future. Even if this were the case, however, the United States would be unlikely to regain its previous position of overwhelming advantage over all comers. Unless China experiences a truly catastrophic systemic crisis, the country's wealth and power will probably continue to grow, albeit perhaps less steadily and at a slower pace. India, too, will become stronger and more influential, certainly in South and Southeast Asia and perhaps beyond. One way or another, the United States' unipolar moment in Asia is drawing to a close.

---

[14] For a debunking of many of the more pessimistic appraisals of China's performance and prospects, see Bobo Lo, "China and the Global Financial Crisis," Centre for European Reform, April 2010. http://www.cer.org.uk/pdf/essay_974.pdf.

[15] For useful surveys of these problems, see Charles Wolf Jr. et al., *Fault Lines in China's Economic Terrain* (Santa Monica: RAND Corporation, 2003); and C. Fred Bergsten, Bates Gill, Nicholas R. Lardy, and Derek Mitchell, *China: The Balance Sheet* (New York: Public Affairs, 2006), 18–72.

An East Asian Community?

Throughout the Cold War, Asia, like Europe, was divided along ideological lines. For a mix of historical and geographical reasons, the United States' non-Communist friends and allies in Asia were also largely separated from, and suspicious of, one another. Furthermore, from the 1960s onward, the Communist camp was itself split between China and the Soviet Union. Since the early 1990s, there has been a steady stream of proposals for new multilateral structures intended to remedy this fragmentation and knit the region together into a more coherent institutional whole. The most ambitious of these have called for the creation of an East Asian community loosely modeled on the European Union. While there are many variants under discussion, such an entity would presumably include both an economic component (perhaps a free trade zone or a tariff union of some kind) and a deliberative body to deal with a variety of issues, including security.

Adherents of "realist" theories of international politics believe that institutions reflect the power and preferences of the nations that make them up rather than any shared commitment to lofty abstract principles. The process of institutional design generally involves political struggle among the potential participants, with each pushing for the plan that best serves its own interests. Such struggle is clearly visible just beneath the surface of recent discussions of a possible East Asian community, with China, Japan, and the United States all trying to shape whatever may ultimately emerge. Not surprisingly, Beijing has tended to favor mechanisms such as ASEAN +3 (the ten smaller nations of Southeast Asia plus Japan, China, and South Korea), in which China would be the biggest and most powerful member. Japan, meanwhile, has advanced proposals in which China's strength would be offset by the addition of other major players (including, at a minimum, India, Australia, and New Zealand).[16] The United States has made clear its preference for open, pan-Pacific organizations as opposed to pan-Asian ones, but Washington has been careful not to appear too eager or to put itself in a position where it might seem to be actively opposing the wishes of a substantial group of Asian nations.

Is it conceivable that ten years from now most or all of Strategic Asia could be organized around a set of institutions that not only would seek to promote trade but also would address serious regional and global issues,

---

[16] For a useful overview of the "conceptual rivalry, if not geopolitical conflict," between China and Japan on this issue, see Yoshihide Soeya, "An East Asian Community and Japan-China Relations," East Asia Forum, May 17, 2010, http://www.eastasiaforum.org/2010/05/17/an-east-asian-community-and-japan-china-relations. See also Aurelia George Mulgan, "Hatoyama's East Asia Community and Regional Leadership Rivalries," East Asia Forum, October 13, 2009, http://www.eastasiaforum.org/2009/10/13/hatoyamas-east-asia-community/.

resolve disputes, and keep the peace? Given the present distribution of power and interests, the probability of such an outcome appears remote at best. As a rising power with expanding ambitions, China has little to gain by locking itself into arrangements that will restrict its future freedom of action or give the United States a perpetual voice in the affairs of the region. Conversely, the weaker powers (especially Japan, but also South Korea and Australia, among others) will be wary of joining organizations that a powerful, opaque China can easily dominate.

A comparison to the circumstances that gave rise to the EU is instructive. In that case the process took several decades to unfold, and by the time it began to reach fruition, all the participants were stable, open, liberal democracies (indeed, this became a precondition for membership in the new European institutions). Furthermore, the societies and economies of the major players were increasingly interwoven, and they were also members of a strategic alliance led by the United States. At the same time, as they converged ideologically and developed habits of cooperation, nations that had only recently been deadly enemies were thus able to reconcile and reach a mutually acceptable understanding regarding their tragic shared past. Here, again, the ability of a friendly outside power to act as go-between and referee was vitally important, as was the menacing, unifying presence of the Warsaw Pact on Europe's eastern frontiers.

Compared to Europe at the close of the Cold War, Asia today remains divided by ideology, history, the lack of any prior experience of regional integration, and the absence of a trusted arbiter and guarantor. Despite claims about the existence of an "Asian way," and the search for "universal values" that somehow transcend differences in political ideology, the fact that China is authoritarian as well as strong still matters. The regime's lack of transparency, the absence of any internal checks on its power, and the degree to which the CCP is closed to outside influences make China far more difficult for others to trust than it would be if it were a democracy. In contrast to Germany, Japan's failure to come to terms adequately with its past, coupled with the CCP's deliberate efforts to keep Tokyo off balance and alienated from Japan's other neighbors, has helped to keep the history issue very much alive. Even though several East Asian states maintain strong strategic connections to the United States as part of the latter's hub-and-spokes system, they have never been integrated into anything resembling a true multilateral alliance, and, of course, throughout the Cold War China, Russia, and India remained in orbits of their own. The fact that the United States would not even be a full member of some proposed organizations means that there would be no one to play honest broker, a role that, in any event, China would be exceedingly unlikely to grant.

promise of alignment to both. (The Soviet Union attempted to do this with Nazi Germany and the Anglo-French alliance before the outbreak of World War II, and the United States tried a similar gambit for a brief period in the late 1960s and early 1970s with the Soviet Union and China.) But this is a game that cannot be played indefinitely. Triangles have a tendency to collapse into simpler, two-sided structures.

In the situation now emerging in Strategic Asia, India might be tempted to pursue a policy of equidistance, avoiding overly close alignment with either the United States or China. While there seems little prospect at present of a true Sino-Indian entente, New Delhi could hold out the prospect of maintaining its traditional posture of non-alignment in order to win concessions from Beijing, while at the same time dangling the promise of closer strategic cooperation with Washington. Beijing, meanwhile, might respond by intimating that it is willing to consider an eventual spheres-of-influence arrangement in which it would no longer seek to challenge New Delhi in South Asia in return for an understanding that India would not meddle in East Asia.

There are several reasons to be skeptical that this kind of flirtation would ever amount to much. Based on current trends, Beijing is unlikely to regard India as an equal in ten or even twenty years time. Especially if China has by then managed to head off or contain potential threats from its eastern shores, it will have more resources to devote to the south, making the distribution of effective power with India even more lopsided than it would otherwise be. Beijing may therefore feel little pressure to give New Delhi what it wants. Following a more accommodating course would also involve a major reversal in long-standing Chinese strategy and the abandonment of some substantial commitments and investments. Leaving South Asia to India would require easing back on support to Pakistan and Myanmar and accepting a settlement of outstanding border disputes that many in Beijing would see as leaving China dangerously exposed to Indian meddling in Tibet. Moreover, it is not at all clear what China would gain in return for such concessions. Commitments from New Delhi to limit involvement in East Asia and to forgo actions that might threaten China's use of vital sea lanes across the Indian Ocean could easily be reversed at some point in the future. By contrast, if it were to abandon the positions that presently give China leverage against India in South Asia, Beijing would have a very difficult time in recreating them. China's growing reliance on energy imports from the Persian Gulf and Africa makes an expansion of its activities in the Indian Ocean seem far more plausible than a willing contraction. For its part, an ever more powerful India will probably be less inclined to tolerate what it regards as Chinese intrusions into "its" region and more willing, and better able, to oppose such actions in various ways.

The problem for India is that drawing closer to China is unlikely to win the kind of concessions New Delhi wants but could very well limit the kinds of cooperation (on technology, trade, and intelligence-sharing) that it needs from the United States. On the other hand, in addition to Indian concern over the continuing growth of Chinese power, other, more positive factors are already inclining India to lean toward the United States (or, rather, are causing the two to lean toward one another). Among these factors are growing economic, educational, and familial links between the two societies; common concern over Islamist terrorism; and the somewhat belated recognition of the depth of the two nations' shared commitment to democratic values.

After eight years of priority treatment from the United States, some in India now worry that the Obama administration is less committed than its predecessor to cultivating a new "special relationship."[19] There are also a number of important issues on which the two countries differ and could collide, including Iran's nuclear program, strategy for Afghanistan, and climate change. Such differences could impose limits on how far and how fast cooperation can progress, but they are unlikely to throw relations into reverse. The underlying forces of attraction between the two countries now appear strong enough to hold them together, regardless of the ebb and flow of policy. In the years ahead it is more likely that the United States and India will become closer to one another than that either will draw close to China.

Chinese Hegemony?

The extension of American preponderance in Asia would come as a surprise to many people. The emergence of China as the dominant power in East Asia, if not the entire region, would not. A recent Chicago Council on Global Affairs poll of public opinion in Japan, South Korea, Indonesia, and Vietnam found, for example, that large majorities of those questioned expect Beijing to become "the leader in Asia," though what this means and when it is anticipated are not clear from the survey data.[20] The fact

---

[19] See, for example, G. Parthasarathy, "The Axis of Grudging Cooperation," *Wall Street Journal*, May 4, 2010, http://online.wsj.com/article/SB10001424052748704608104575221303790430846. html?mod=wsj_india_main; and Sumit Ganguly, "America's Wounded Ally," *Newsweek*, April 2, 2010, http://www.newsweek.com/2010/04/01/america-s-wounded-ally.html.

[20] "Soft Power in Asia: Results of a 2008 Multinational Survey of Public Opinion," Chicago Council on Global Affairs and East Asia Institute, 2008, 5, http://www.thechicagocouncil.org/UserFiles/File/POS_Topline%20Reports/Asia%20Soft%20Power%202008/Chicago%20Council%20Soft%20Power%20Report-%20Final%206-11-08.pdf.

arrangement, this time with China at the center and the other regional players (including Japan, South Korea, India, Australia, and Russia) maintaining amicable, but strategically detached, relationships with one another. In such circumstances, China might not be able to exert positive control over its neighbors, but it would have considerable influence over all of them and perhaps an effective veto over the policy choices of some. In addition to deterring attacks, threats, or other actions deemed contrary to its interests, Beijing would be in a strong position to persuade or coerce others to accede to its wishes on issues ranging from trade and investment, to alliance and third-party basing arrangements, to the treatment of ethnic Chinese populations, and, at least in the case of some of its closest neighbors, to the character and composition of their governments.

A Continental-Maritime Divide?

Without active U.S. participation, the balance of power in Asia is unlikely to remain balanced. Instead of stable multipolarity, or a post-polar regional system bound together by strong multilateral institutions, what is likely to emerge in the wake of U.S. disengagement is some form of Chinese hegemony. Conversely, if China's wealth and power continue to grow, the United States will find it increasingly difficult to provide an adequate counterweight without the vigorous support of friends and allies.

If China continues to rise but its regime does not change, and if the United States remains engaged in Asia, relations between the two powers are likely to become increasingly competitive and contentious rather than more cooperative. As China's power increases, so too will the sphere of its interests. Like other rising powers of the past, China will seek to reshape the regional and global orders in ways that better reflect its preferences and serve its needs. The United States, for its part, is likely to push back and to encourage others to do the same rather than give way before a power that it sees as hostile to its own liberal democratic vision for Asia and the world.

Instead of being dominated by Beijing or overseen by a Sino-American condominium, Asia could thus be divided into two camps. On the one hand would be a grouping of continental nations physically contiguous to, and strategically centered on, China. Most of these countries would be economically dependent on and comparatively weak in relation to the PRC, and each would have its own form of authoritarian government. Included in this coalition would be North Korea, Russia, Kazakhstan, Kyrgyzstan, Tajikistan, Pakistan, Myanmar, Laos, and possibly Vietnam. On the other side would be a group consisting primarily of liberal democracies; aligned with the United States; physically separated from China by oceans, mountains, or intervening territory; and with a largely maritime orientation. Among these countries would be Japan, South Korea, the Philippines, Indonesia, Australia, Singapore, Thailand, India, and possibly Mongolia.

As noted in the first volume of the *Strategic Asia* series, the outlines of such a structure were already visible at the turn of the century. This final scenario would thus involve the playing out of current trends. Depending on how events unfold (and depending, in particular, on the course of Sino-American relations), the degree of polarization between the continental and maritime groupings—and the extent to which their members coalesce—could vary considerably. At one extreme would be something resembling a new Cold War, with the United States and China sharply at odds with one another, and each trying to bind its friends into a more tightly integrated coalition. At the other extreme, relations within and between the two coalitions could remain highly fluid, even to the point that the distinction between them might begin to disappear. A general mellowing in U.S.-China relations, resulting from a liberalization of the latter's domestic politics, would likely be accompanied by the dissolution of any continental-maritime divide.

Assuming a continuing, and perhaps mounting, measure of tension and rivalry between them, Washington and Beijing may both try to weaken each others' nascent coalition, by neutralizing or peeling away one or more coalition members. China seems already to be attempting this in its relations with South Korea, Thailand, Australia, India, and now Japan. The United States may eventually respond by wooing Vietnam and, if Moscow's anxieties about Chinese expansionism continue to grow, Russia as well. While in all but the most dire circumstances these states would continue to trade and talk with one another, the members of the two coalitions would also engage in intelligence-sharing, joint weapons development programs, and military exercises meant to enhance their collective ability to threaten or use force. The resulting patterns of interaction within and between the two groups of nations could come eventually to resemble those among the great powers of Europe in the nineteenth and early twentieth centuries—not an entirely comforting thought for those who know their history.

Conclusion

No student of geopolitics should be surprised by the conclusion that the future shape of Strategic Asia will be determined in large part by the power and preferences of its two biggest players. If China fails to fulfill its potential, the United States will remain dominant in at least the eastern portion of this vast domain. If the United States stumbles, on the other hand, the chances of Chinese hegemony will grow. If both powers remain strong and engaged, Strategic Asia will likely be split along geographic and ideological lines.

The probability of other scenarios will depend on factors that lie outside the realm of normal geopolitical calculation. It is much easier to imagine the United States and China (or the United States, China, Japan, and India) collaborating to keep order in Asia if all share the same democratic values and institutions. Similarly, an East Asian community modeled on the EU is more likely if China liberalizes than if it does not. With all that has transpired in the interim, this prospect appears no closer today than it did ten years ago.

EXECUTIVE SUMMARY

The chapter examines Asia's likely economic expansion through 2030 and explores the consequences for U.S. policy.

MAIN ARGUMENT:
Between 1990 and 2030, Asia and the West (defined as the U.S. and Europe) will have roughly traded places in terms of output and other measures of economic mass. Asia's rise will require adjustments around the world but should have a conservative influence on the world system. Given the region's stake in global interdependence and pragmatic focus on development, Asia should help to sustain existing institutions, while also resisting new, more restrictive agreements. Commercial, institutional, and people-to-people contacts will expand and mitigate tensions.

POLICY IMPLICATIONS:
- The U.S. can prepare for this transition by investing in technology, education, and exports, and by putting its finances on a sound footing. With complementary reforms in Asia, these initiatives should help to reorient U.S. production and employment toward rapidly growing Asian markets.

- Deepening trans-Pacific linkages should become Washington's highest international economic policy priority. Asian regional integration is a natural by-product of Asia's rise, and trans-Pacific partnerships can help to keep Asian cooperation outward-looking rather than turning discriminatory.

- As the established power that will benefit most from Asia's integration into the global economy, the U.S. is well positioned to lead the search for global institutions that deliver effective cooperation and reflect Asia's rise.

- Asia-U.S. relations will face major opportunities in 2011 as a legislative window opens in the U.S. for passing the Korea-U.S. Free Trade Agreement and making progress on the Trans-Pacific Partnership. As the host of APEC in 2011, the U.S. also has an excellent platform for promoting the benefits of trans-Pacific ties to both sides.

Economic Performance

Asia and the World Economy in 2030: Growth, Integration, and Governance

Peter A. Petri

Between 1990 and 2030, in the span of one generation, a stylized East, consisting of the major Asian economies, and West, consisting of the United States and the European Union (EU), will have roughly traded places in purchasing power GDP and other measures of economic mass. The world is already adjusting, as reflected by the group of twenty (G-20) replacing the group of eight (G-8), the proliferation of Asian cooperative mechanisms, and the focus of attention on bilateral meetings between the United States and China and other Asian countries. How will world economic institutions change as they acquire Asian characteristics?

The world's emerging economic leadership is far more heterogeneous than in past transitions of economic power: put simply, Asia will become dominant before it becomes rich. The functional implications of these shifts are unclear. Large changes in regional weights might bring radical changes in the institutions and mechanisms of world trade and finance. Or they might not: if the rising and declining powers generally benefit from the existing economic framework, or at least cannot agree on alternatives, the transition could proceed with modest adjustments within the system, in variables such as the direction of trade and investment and voting shares in global institutions. This chapter assesses the scope of likely changes and, in that context, considers options for U.S. policy.

The preeminent example of revolutionary change in global institutions is the reinvention of the international economic system at the end of World War II. In three consequential weeks in July 1944, the United States and its

Peter A. Petri is the Carl J. Shapiro Professor of International Finance at the International Business School at Brandeis University and a Senior Fellow at the East-West Center. He can be reached at <ppetri@brandeis.edu>.

allies created a dazzling array of new institutions, including the International Monetary Fund (IMF), the World Bank, and mechanisms for liberalizing trade (which eventually became the World Trade Organization, or WTO).

Evolutionary change, however, is more common. In the Bretton Woods era, the rise of Europe, Japan, and the "Asian tigers," also representing a substantial redistribution of economic mass, did not lead to systemic change. Adjustments occurred—notably in the exchange rate system—without altering basic institutions. If anything, the success of the "miracle" economies enhanced U.S. efforts to build a market-based, liberal economic order. The Bretton Woods institutions prospered, and the United States shared leadership of them comfortably with rising powers. Eight rounds of trade negotiations were successfully concluded. Despite disagreements, major stakeholders sustained the system even as their roles changed within it.

Will Asia's rise, the salient trend of the new century, lead to revolutionary or evolutionary change? At least three outcomes can be envisioned:

- Rules and institutions will be strengthened, facilitating deeper integration, and Asia's rising economies will continue to converge toward liberal norms. This scenario would sustain trade and investment, stimulate innovation and specialization, and provide opportunities for the United States to participate in Asian growth.

- Norms for international behavior will be relaxed or ignored, leading to more disparate national practices. For example, Asia might discriminate against non-regional partners, relax intellectual property enforcement, pursue pollution-intensive growth, and manage currencies. This path would disadvantage smaller countries and rules-oriented countries such as the United States.

- Protectionist rhetoric and initiatives will rise and the world economy will segment into blocs separated by trade and financial barriers. Some regions could prosper initially, but general uncertainty would dampen investment and growth. This scenario, though unlikely, would undermine global prosperity and peace.

Globalization is the "elephant in the room." In contrast to previous transitions of economic power, today's shifts are taking place alongside—and as a result of—deepening economic interdependence. In the liberal Bretton Woods era, Asian and Western economies converged on strategies that are predicated on interdependence. The largest emerging economies—China, India, and Indonesia—are early in their "catch-up" and need economic integration to continue to grow. The advanced economies, especially the United States, are deeply engaged in and benefit from integration, although governments face urgent pressures to divide the gains more fairly. This is a positive-sum game: Asia is rising relative to the West, not at the expense of the West.

For these reasons, Asia is likely to become a conservative force in the global economy. Assuming that Asian policymakers remain motivated by rational economic interests, they will criticize the system they inherit but will be cautious about changing it. For decades to come, Asian policymakers will face huge challenges at home—giant, poor, diverse, and aging populations, not to mention internal political tensions—and will need a stable global environment to manage these challenges. Policymakers will shade policies to national advantage—as all countries do—but will participate in and support global institutions. They will act when the global system needs to be saved (as in the frightening fall of 2008) and resist efforts to make rules more complex or restrictive. They will not rock the boat. Moreover, it is in the United States' interest to reinforce this trend, guiding the future to somewhere between the first and second scenarios.

The chapter begins by reviewing Asia's economic rise and the region's stake in the global system. It then considers how recent crises shaped Asia's prospects and explores the strategic interests of the United States. Political and security environments willing, Asia and the United States should be able to cooperate with benefits to both. These bets would be off in a hostile climate in which countries seek to impede each other's progress—for example, for fear that a rival's success will lead to military confrontation.

Asia Rises

Using Angus Maddison's well-known estimates,[1] after dominating the world economy until the early 1800s, Asia fell into more than a century of relative economic decline.[2] Since World War II, however, Asia has grown more than twice as fast as the rest of the world, even allowing for stretches of poor performance in countries such as Maoist China and pre-reform India. Asian development is again setting global records. Seven of the ten

---

[1] Angus Maddison, *The World Economy: A Millennial Perspective* (Paris: Organisation for Economic Co-operation and Development [OECD], 2001).

[2] A narrow, pragmatic definition of Asia is used here—essentially East Asia and India—to facilitate data collection and analysis, based on Asian Development Bank, *Emerging Asian Regionalism: A Partnership for Shared Prosperity* (Manila: Asian Development Bank, 2008). The study's "integrating Asia" concept defines Asia as including the ten ASEAN countries plus China, Hong Kong, Japan, South Korea, Taiwan, and India. These economies have strong linkages, significant systemic influence, and better data. In some data references, an even narrower twelve-economy definition is used, omitting the four smaller ASEAN economies (Brunei, Cambodia, Laos, and Myanmar). These definitions account for 90%–95% of the economic activity of fully inclusive definitions of Asia.

most rapidly growing economies in the world since 1955 have been Asian.[3] Although other countries have also experienced rapid growth over several years,[4] the recent Asian cluster of sustained, consistent performance has no parallel. This section examines the background of Asia's rise and how this ascent has shaped Asian attitudes toward the global economy.

The Asian Economic Model

Asia's development strategy, often described as the "East Asian economic model," has consisted of varied, loosely similar approaches to penetrating international markets, absorbing and developing technology, and raising productivity.[5] Variants of this strategy are now practiced throughout Asia and elsewhere. At the risk of oversimplification, the model provides a starting point for analyzing how Asia has benefited from the world economic system and how the region might shape this system in a decisionmaking role.

Competitive export industries, eclectically built, helped to spearhead Asian growth starting with Japan in the late 1950s. Exporting was anything but an obvious choice at the time. But unlike richer and more diversified economies, Japan and other Asian countries could not afford a big push of investments into import substitution, as favored by the policy consensus. Densely populated, inadequately endowed with resources, and lagging in technology, Asia turned outward—to exports—in order to survive. For example, in the mid-1950s South Korea (simply called Korea hereafter), having only a few years to replace the dollar inflows associated with the Korean War with other sources of foreign exchange, developed a large-scale export industry based on wigs made of human hair.

From simple, labor-intensive manufactures, Asian economies graduated to more sophisticated products, leaving markets behind to the next development cohort. The liberal global order managed by the United States—featuring trade liberalization under the General Agreement on Tariffs and Trade (GATT) and good access to U.S. markets—supported this

---

[3] Asian Development Bank, *Emerging Asian Regionalism*. For deeper analysis of the roles of China and India, see Wendy Dobson, *Gravity Shift: How Asia's Powerhouses Will Shape the 21st Century* (Toronto: University of Toronto Press, 2009).

[4] Ricardo Hausmann, Lant Pritchett, and Dani Rodrik, "Growth Accelerations," *Journal of Economic Growth* 10, no. 4 (2009): 303–29.

[5] Generalizations about Asia defy the region's extraordinary diversity. Asia encompasses essentially the full variation observed in the world in country size and income; endowments of natural, human, and capital resources; and political organization, language, culture, and history. Asia is also intensely competitive and a battleground of historic rivalries. Yet there are important similarities among Asian economies in development strategies and linkages with the world economy, and one goal of this chapter is to tease out their shared interests. The chapter's conclusions will be accordingly limited and need to be complemented with more nuanced analysis for specific country cases.

strategy. The tactics varied from market-oriented approaches in Hong Kong and Singapore to purposeful industrial policies in Japan, Korea, and Taiwan. Foreign investment played a role in some cases, notably in late developers China and Southeast Asia, but Korea and Japan relied on indigenous firms and licensed technologies. The common denominator was exposing firms to international competition. *What doesn't kill you make you stronger*

This process has been famously compared to geese flying in formation.[6] As **Figure 1** shows, Japan's real per capita output growth rate hovered toward 8% through the early 1970s and remained reasonably high for another decade. This growth spurt was replicated about a decade later by the newly industrializing economies (Hong Kong, Korea, Singapore, and Taiwan), and still later by Southeast Asia. China's acceleration began in the late 1970s and has been steadier and appears to be lasting longer than those of previous champions. India's takeoff, following China's by about fifteen years, is similarly solid but is more recent than the takeoff of the other Asian "miracles." Given this remarkable record, Asian policymakers have become generally committed to integration. If this strategy remains viable—with whatever adjustment may be required to achieve greater balance—countries are unlikely to switch to alternatives such as isolationism or narrow regionalism.

On the financial and macroeconomic side, the Asian model relied on fiscal and monetary discipline coupled with incentives for production, especially of exports.[7] Initially incentives included subsidies now disallowed by the WTO. The policy mix also repressed markets for basic factors of production, such as labor and capital, to keep production costs low. For example, some countries restricted the outflow of domestic savings and imposed interest ceilings to reduce capital costs. Some also restricted labor unions and adopted measures to keep wages low.

The legacy of factor-market repression continues to haunt Asian development. Producers still have greater influence on policy than consumers and investors do, and this may account for Asia's chronic saving surpluses. Also, while firms compete aggressively in product markets, governments have helped to ensure their access to factors of production, especially capital. Thus, successful firms are often connected to the government, and such relationships remain important relative to markets and rules. While financial market development is also underway in Asia, progress has been

---

[6] Kaname Akamatsu, "Historical Pattern of Economic Growth in Developing Countries," *Developing Economies* 1, no. 1 (1962): 3–25.

[7] World Bank, *East Asian Miracle: Economic Growth and Public Policy* (Washington, D.C.: World Bank, 1993).

FIGURE 1 Waves of Asian growth: Japan, NIEs, ASEAN, China, and India measured in 5-year moving averages of growth rates of per capita real GDP

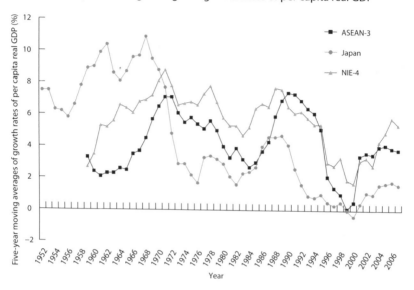

SOURCE: Calculations based on the Penn World Table, version 6.3, http://pwt.econ.upenn. edu/php_site/pwt_index.php.

NOTE: The NIE-4 (newly industrialized economies) consists of Hong Kong, South Korea, Singapore, and Taiwan. ASEAN-3 consists of Indonesia, Malaysia, and Thailand.

more gradual and ambivalent than in real markets. All this will slow Asian efforts to rebalance economies toward domestic demand.

The Asian Financial Crisis: Lessons and Legacies

Efforts to end financial repression set the stage for the Asian financial crisis. Given that the financial sector often served as a conduit for policy, Asian capital markets generally lagged behind markets elsewhere.[8] To catch up, Japan, Korea, and other countries began to liberalize their financial systems in the 1980s and 1990s by deregulating interest rates, allowing greater competition among financial institutions, permitting foreign institutions to enter, and easing restrictions on international capital flows.[9] In some countries, deregulation and "hot money" inflows raised the complexity of macroeconomic management and provided opportunities for risky activities by financial and non-financial firms.

In this volatile context, the currencies of Thailand, Indonesia, Malaysia, the Philippines, and Korea came under speculative attacks and collapsed in late 1997 following several years of high growth and investment. The financial system in these countries froze and their economies declined sharply. The crisis was exacerbated by deflationary policies adopted under IMF programs or advice, including monetary and fiscal tightening, and the rushed closing or reorganization of failing firms.[10] A few months later, macroeconomic policies were loosened, credit began to recover, and output rebounded. Except for Indonesia, where the calamity brought prolonged political turmoil, the crisis-affected economies were growing again by 1999.

While much of Asia experienced a wrenching recession during this period, China was barely affected. With its capital account closed, China faced no capital flight and could sustain aggregate demand by replacing exports with investment. Growth scarcely dipped. To create similar room to maneuver, Malaysia also restricted capital movements in September 1998. The impact of this decision is difficult to assess because by then currency markets were beginning to stabilize; however, at a minimum, the controls did not prevent Malaysia from attracting direct investment and returning

---

[8] See Ronald I. MacKinnon, *The Order of Economic Liberalization: Financial Control in the Transition to a Market Economy* (Baltimore: Johns Hopkins University Press, 1993); and P. Arestis and P. Demetriades, "Financial Development and Economic Growth: Assessing the Evidence," *Economic Journal* 107, no. 442 (May 1997): 783–99.

[9] See, for example, Yung Chul Park and Kee-Hong Bae, "Financial Liberalization and Economic Integration in East Asia" (report of PECC Financial Forum Conference, Hawaii, 2002).

[10] Andrew Berg, "The Asia Crisis: Causes, Policy Responses, and Outcomes," International Monetary Fund (IMF), Working Paper, no. 138, October 1999.

TABLE 1   Asia's rising economic importance as shares of world totals

Country/region	% of world total			% of change
	1990	2010*	2030*	2010–30
Population				
Asia-12	53%	50%	49%	40%
United States and EU	13%	12%	10%	0%
East/West ratio	4.1	4.3	4.9	211.1
GDP (PPP)				
Asia-12	21%	32%	43%	49%
United States and EU	50%	41%	31%	25%
East/West ratio	0.4	0.8	1.4	1.9
Trade				
Asia-12	14%	24%	35%	37%
United States and EU	55%	43%	28%	25%
East/West ratio	0.3	0.6	1.2	1.5
Market capitalization				
Asia-12	35%	24%	38%	41%
United States and EU	55%	54%	31%	26%
East/West ratio	0.6	0.4	1.2	1.6
Energy consumption				
Asia-12	23%	32%	41%	64%
United States and EU	38%	33%	28%	15%
East/West ratio	0.6	1.0	1.4	4.2
CO2 emissions				
Asia-12	22%	35%	46%	78%
United States and EU	36%	30%	25%	10%
East/West ratio	0.6	1.2	1.9	8.1

SOURCE: Author's projections (see Appendix).

NOTE: Asia-12 includes China, Hong Kong, India, Indonesia, Japan, Malaysia, Philippines, Singapore, South Korea, Taiwan, Thailand, and Vietnam. Asterisk indicates values for the given year are projected.

2010 and 2030. As is well known, China and other Asian economies are actively accumulating energy assets abroad through direct purchases and long-term contracts. The military and strategic implications of such acquisitions are outside the scope of this paper, but the economics deserve precise analysis because they are often misunderstood. Asia would certainly benefit from such acquisitions if energy prices and associated asset values were to rise, but this would not give the region the broad advantages that many presume.

A useful point of departure is to assume that markets will remain important mechanisms for distributing supply in the future even if the role of officially owned energy supplies increases. Markets are likely to remain substantial because of the wide dispersion of production and utilization of energy worldwide and, over any significant stretch of time, will balance demand and supply by changing prices. Indeed, expectations about future market prices are built into current prices, given that owners of energy assets can limit supply if they expect prices to rise. Of course, these current expectations about future market conditions could be wrong and prices could rise substantially more than is now expected. If prices were to rise sharply, China and other countries would realize significant windfalls from having accumulated foreign energy assets.[29] But they would still have strong economic reasons to price energy for their own use at rates that are similar to world market prices. In effect, the ownership of energy assets will affect the global distribution of wealth but not necessarily global patterns of energy use or production of energy-intensive goods and services. As Asia accumulates wealth, prudence dictates that a significant portion of it be invested in energy resources, including those abroad. Yet the main economic benefit of these investments is financial and is available to investors worldwide.

Regionalism

A final and powerful implication of Asian growth is deepening regional integration. So far, this has been a largely market-led process, the result of rapidly expanding Asian supply and demand. Asia had been closely integrated before World War II, but after the war the region's economic connections turned toward the United States and the global economy. Intra-Asian trade began to expand rapidly only a half-century later, with the region's accelerating growth and intraregional investments.[30] In the wake of the Asian financial crisis, intraregional linkages further intensified. **Figure 4** compares pre- and post-crisis indicators of economic integration in trade

---

[29] Reserve purchases might also help to insure Asia against short-term disruptions in supply, much as strategic reserves provide insurance within countries. Of course, this assumes that reserves are not the subject of disruption and can be accessed in a crisis.

[30] Peter A. Petri, "The East Asian Trading Bloc: An Analytical History," in *Regionalism and Rivalry: Japan and the U.S. in Pacific Asia*, ed., Jeffrey Frankel and Miles Kahler (Chicago: University of Chicago Press, 1993), 21–52. The analysis is updated in Peter A. Petri, "Is East Asia Becoming More Interdependent?" *Journal of Asian Economics* 17, no. 3 (June 2006): 381–94.

rate policy will continue to induce inflation at home and remain a source of tension with trade partners, including the United States.

Integrating the Asia-Pacific

In the longer term, the central priority of the United States' trade policy should be to build stronger linkages with Asia's rapidly growing economies. Much U.S. trade is already with Asia, and, as discussed above, an even larger share of world trade growth is projected to come from the region. Trade with Asia represents a potentially powerful engine for the U.S. economy. Although U.S. firms are well positioned in Asian markets, their market shares have declined in the context of large U.S. deficits. Reversing these trends will require an active, Asia-focused trade policy.

A general context for U.S. engagement with Asia is provided by the APEC forum. Established in 1989, APEC was upgraded into a meeting of the region's leaders in 1993 by President Clinton. Two decades later, the United States again hosts the APEC summit in 2011. This event, which will occur under a president who frequently notes the importance of Asian linkages, could provide a fitting backdrop for reinvigorating the United States' trans-Pacific relationships.

APEC's mission is to promote trade and investment, and specifically the Bogor Goals adopted in 1994 to create free trade and investment by 2010 in developed Asia-Pacific countries and by 2020 in developing countries. The Bogor Goals have not been met in a literal sense, but APEC has made significant contributions to denser networks and to policy cooperation in the Pacific. After unsuccessfully negotiating trade agreements in its initial years, APEC shifted to non-binding approaches. In that format, the forum has sponsored initiatives in trade facilitation, policy reviews, the alignment of standards, and sharing best practices.[40] APEC has also created a sense of community among Pacific leaders, on the one hand, and mid-level policymakers, on the other. Even if APEC is given credit for only a small part of the region's success, the forum's achievements provide ample return on investments.

Still, few would argue that APEC has lived up to its potential. APEC's agenda has not been sufficiently coherent or productive. As already noted, there are now many competing forums for regional and global economic dialogue. The U.S. year will provide an opportunity to sharpen APEC's focus and ratchet up the forum's accomplishments. A plan to generate deliverables by the 2011 summit in Honolulu would help to sell Asia-U.S.

---

[40] Matthias Helble, Ben Shepherd, and John S. Wilson, "Transparency and Trade Facilitation in the Asia Pacific: Estimating the Gains from Reform," World Bank, Working Paper, 2007.

cooperation to skeptical public opinion on both sides. The plan could rely on the "pathfinder" approach of initiating regional agreements with like-minded countries. For example, the 2011 agenda could feature major pathfinders for an open regional investment zone and for eliminating all barriers to trade in environmental goods and services. In addition, APEC could spotlight critical, shared socio-economic issues, such as the economic impact of population aging and best practices in engaging women in economic activity. Ideally, this agenda would be supported by an ambitious public diplomacy effort.

Because APEC is not an effective negotiating body, the United States also must counter the trend of Asia-only trade agreements with parallel formal trans-Pacific agreements and negotiations. An overdue step is to pass the Korea-U.S. Free Trade Agreement. Also important is the decision (under President Bush and confirmed by President Obama) to join the TPP Agreement. Launched in 2002 by Chile, New Zealand, Singapore, and eventually Brunei, this agreement represents a high quality economic partnership that could attract many new members, eventually paving the way to an APEC-wide free trade area of the Asia Pacific (FTAAP). The first stage negotiations now also include Australia, Peru, and Vietnam (although at this writing Vietnam's full participation is uncertain), and Malaysia and Japan may join as well.

The TPP enables the United States, first, to promote global economic integration despite the stalemate of the Doha round of the WTO and the contentious politics of trade in Congress.[41] Second, the partnership explores a range of new issues that reflect social and technological change. Positioned as a template for 21st century agreements, the TPP could go well beyond the topics that stalled the WTO and engage issues such as services, investment, environmental protection, innovation, job creation, trade facilitation, and capacity-building. Third, the agreement can bring a stream of new partners into an open, dynamic group. Thus, the TPP could offer Asian and Latin American countries a fresh start in shaping trade policy and might lead to progress on both the FTAAP and the Doha round.

The TPP has been criticized for addressing small, open countries (several already have FTAs with each other and the United States). But what matters is not which countries participate initially, but whether a

---

[41] See, for example, C. Fred Bergsten and Jeffrey J. Schott, "Submission to the USTR in Support of a Trans-Pacific Partnership Agreement," Peterson Institute for International Economics, January 25, 2010; and Claude Barfield and Philip Levy, "Tales of the South Pacific: President Obama, the Trans-Pacific Partnership and US Leadership in Asia," VoxEU.org, January 28, 2010. For a more detailed analysis of the structure of the TPP, see Deborah Elms, "From the P4 to the TPP: Explaining Expansion Interests in the Asia-Pacific" (paper prepared for the Asia-Pacific Trade Economists' Conference, Bangkok, November 2–3, 2009).

dynamic group results. The alternative is not a large, wide negotiation, but no negotiation at all, or an unsuccessful one. In the crowded global policy agenda after the global financial crisis, trade policy lacks urgency. Charting a path forward is valuable.

Managing the Global System

The United States retains the largest single stake in managing the global economy, but cooperation with Asia is now central to this effort. Global imbalances are largely trans-Pacific. Although there are also significant imbalances within Europe, those are closely associated with features of the EU and will need to be managed regionally rather than globally. Appropriately, the United States has led efforts to bring Asian and other large emerging economies into global decisionmaking. The G-20 already responds to Asian voices—Asian countries, for example, helped make the case for fiscal stimulus instead of financial regulation in early responses to the crisis. Given Europe's preoccupation with internal matters, the success of the G-20 will continue to depend on Asia-U.S. cooperation. Even though bilateral dialogue, especially between the United States and China on imbalances, is essential for preparing the groundwork for the G-20, few would want a G-2 (group of two) of the United States and China making decisions by itself.

Given the transitions underway, the institutions of global cooperation will be in flux for some time. Eventually, a new, multi-layered framework is likely to emerge. Contemporary global economic governance faces three inconsistent requirements: it is expected to be simultaneously universal (include all influential members), democratic (accept input from all members), and effective (make timely decisions).[42] To mitigate this "trilemma," multiple institutions are needed in different functions and regions, much as multiple layers of government operate in national jurisdictions. For some time, new institutions and coalitions will form and disband as they compete for decisionmaking roles. This fluidity is evident in Asia, where several ASEAN + groupings, APEC, two "communities," and a host of bi- and mini-lateral meetings compete for attention. Unexpected events and unusual leaders will eventually tip this competition toward one or another institution; there is every reason for the United States to stay engaged.

---

[42] "Asia in Global Governance: A Case for Decentralized Institutions," Asian Development Bank Institute, Working Paper, no. 157, October 2009, reprinted in *Asian Regionalism in the World Economy: Engine for Dynamism and Stability*, ed. Masahiro Kawai, Peter A. Petri, and Elif Sisli Ciamarra (Cheltenham: Edward Elgar, forthcoming, 2010).

Conclusions

The realignment of global economic power, which has been accelerated by the global financial crisis, presents new challenges to the global system requiring strategic responses. Asia and the United States have much adjusting to do, but their interests are deeply connected.

Between 1990 and 2030, Asia and the West (the United States and Europe) will have roughly traded places in broad measures of economic activity. Asia will become more important than the United States and Europe in producing, trading, investing, using resources, and causing environmental harm. Asia will have a larger voice in managing the global economy, and its regional institutions will become more prominent. Asia will still be relatively poor, however, and its progress will depend on cooperation with the United States and other advanced countries. Barring adverse political scenarios, interdependence should remain vigorous.

These shifts have far-reaching policy consequences. In the medium term, the world faces daunting challenges in repairing the damage from the financial crisis; generating demand is especially urgent. Emerging Asia needs to diversify its economy, liberalize factor markets, and reorient output toward Asian demand. In turn, the United States must strengthen its competitiveness and put its finances in order.

In the longer term, given their long-established economic structures, Asia and the United States have a common stake in sustaining an open and stable system of trade and investment. Of course, their management styles and specific interests differ. Emerging Asia will be less willing, for example, to pay to avert climate change. Competition may intensify for energy and other resources in limited supply. Mostly, Asia will seek time and space to develop before contributing to global public goods. Impending political transitions, large populations, low incomes, and demographic change all complicate the region's policy agenda. These differences will create tensions but are manageable in the context of Asia's likely economic progress. Hopefully, Asia will also remain pragmatic and free of the triumphalism that sometimes accompanies periods of strong economic performance.

Thus, probabilities favor evolutionary adjustments. Asia's rise does not foreshadow drama comparable to Bretton Woods, because today's world system serves Asian interests and is resistant to change. Asian governments—the newcomers to the leadership elite—are conservative and pragmatic, and are likely to support preserving existing agreements until clearly better alternatives are found. To be sure, they will also be reluctant to take on new, stricter obligations. Global economic management may become more contentious but perhaps also more stable. In the meantime, the bridges linking Asia and the West will continue to multiply, engaging a wide range of commercial, institutional, and people-to-people contacts. These will be crucial for managing tensions and minimizing the danger of conflict.

Given a graceful transition, the United States should benefit from Asia's rise. There will be periods of tension, as is the case now over rebalancing the global economy. But as a flexible, technologically advanced, and internationally connected economy, the United States can profit from the opportunities created by this unprecedented expansion of world markets. To be sure, the adjustments will require new efforts to maintain U.S. competitiveness and to engage Asia through forward-looking initiatives.

In this complex but favorable context, Asia-U.S. relations face major milestones in 2011. That year offers a narrow legislative window for passing the Korea-U.S. FTA and for making significant progress in the TPP negotiations. International economic policy is traditionally an area of bipartisan cooperation in the United States, and 2011 will be an important test of American vision. 2011 is also the United States' year to host APEC, culminating in the visit of Asian heads of state. Volatile political and financial markets willing, 2011 could be the year to confirm Secretary of State Clinton's claim that the United States is "back in Asia."[43]

---

[43] Hillary Rodham Clinton, "Remarks on Regional Architecture in Asia: Principles and Priorities" (remarks at the East-West Center, Honolulu, January 12, 2010), http://www.state.gov/secretary/rm/2010/01/135090.htm.

Appendix: Projections of Asian Population and Output

Projections of Asian and world growth are based on several available studies. Projections up through 2015 are taken from the IMF's World Economic Outlook Database. The 2015 IMF values are then projected forward using expected 2015–30 growth rates for population, real GDP in PPP terms, and real GDP in international dollars. Growth rates were set by the author with reference to the results of three recent studies:

- Sandra Poncet, "The Long Term Growth Prospects of the World Economy: Horizon 2050," Centre d'Etudes Prospectives et d'Informations Internationales (CEPII), CEPII Working Paper, no. 2006-16, 2006.

- Goldman Sachs Economics Group, "BRICS and Beyond," Goldman Sachs, 2007.

- OECD, *Environmental Outlook to 2030* (Paris: OECD, 2008).

Growth rates of purchasing power GDP from these studies and ones used in this study are summarized in **Table A1**.

Projections of real market price GDP (in international dollars) require additional assumptions about the so-called Balassa-Samuelson effect. This effect predicts a gradual appreciation in the real exchange rates of low-income countries as they catch up with high-income countries (eventually eliminating differences between the PPP and market price

TABLE A1   Comparison of projections of real GDP growth rates, 2015–30 (%)

Country/ region	CEPII	Goldman Sachs	OECD	This study	Balassa- Samuelson
United States	2.8	2.3	2.4	2.3	-0.2
EU	1.6	1.1	2.0	1.5	0.2
Japan	1.4	1.2	–	1.0	0.2
China	4.2	4.7	4.5	5.0	3.0
India	4.1	6.0	4.9	5.5	3.0
ASEAN-5	3.8	5.0	4.0	4.5	2.0
NIE-4	3.3	2.6	–	3.0	1.0
Other	–	–	–	3.0	1.0
World	–	–	–	3.2	0.5

SOURCE: Projection sources explained in the text. Some sources provide only partial coverage of the ASEAN-5 and NIE-4 groups.

and the political-military factors driving this process. The second section discusses three key dynamics affecting this modernization process: defense spending, arms imports, and the "revolution in military affairs." The third section then evaluates recent trends in regional military modernization, particularly the types of new military equipment and weapons systems being procured and the new warfighting capabilities they might bring to local militaries. The fourth section makes a net assessment of these acquisition efforts, examining whether and how much overall military modernization activities in the Asia-Pacific have actually added to regional military capabilities as well as where critical shortcomings may still lie. Finally, a conclusion sums up this analysis of militaries capabilities in the region.

Why Military Modernization?
The Regional Political-Military Context

Countries in the Asia-Pacific have many reasons for acquiring new defense hardware and improving national military capabilities. The region is clearly one of constantly shifting security dynamics, with rising great powers (China and India), new threats and security challenges (missile attacks, terrorism, proliferation of WMDs, international crime, and the like), ongoing territorial disputes (for example, the Senkaku/Diaoyutai Islands and the Spratlys), and new military commitments (such as contingency and stabilization operations) that require new capabilities for surveillance, force projection, mobility, firepower, and joint operations. All of these factors, in one way or another, are affecting regional military modernization activities.

At the same, changes within the U.S. military are also having a considerable impact on the security calculus of states in the Asia-Pacific and therefore on military modernization activities in the region. Increasingly, the U.S. armed forces must be prepared to manage both global and regional contingency operations. As these forces become more mobile and expeditionary, they will significantly alter the size, character, and scope of the U.S. military in the Asia-Pacific. The U.S. military's "center of gravity" will shift farther south and east as troops are removed from South Korea and especially as 8,000 marines of the III Marine Expeditionary Force are relocated from Okinawa to Guam. In particular, the U.S. territory of Guam will grow in importance as a forward-basing area and become the home for B-2 and B-52 bombers and attack submarines deployed to the Pacific area of operations. Moreover, as U.S. forces transition to fighting mobile high-tech wars—which will require that they become more expeditionary, operationally flexible and agile, and capable of dealing with global as well as regional contingencies—so too will the military increasingly require the support and assistance of allies and other partners. Interoperability, therefore, particularly in regional or even out-of-area operations, will become a much higher priority for the U.S. military. Overall, U.S. forces are being drawn down in the Asia-Pacific and reoriented for global as opposed to static operations, and this shift is influencing the military modernization decisions made by countries in the region.

China and India, of course, possess great-power aspirations that drive their requirements for modern militaries that are capable of projecting and sustaining power, delivering firepower and precision strikes, and dominating the information battlespace. Beijing, for example, seeks to gain "hard" power commensurate with growing "soft" power (i.e., economic, diplomatic, and cultural). Naturally, China still seeks sufficient military capabilities to deal with any "Taiwan contingency"—that is, the ability to isolate the island, invade and occupy it if necessary, and engage in anti-access/area denial operations to interdict U.S. forces seeking to come to the island's defense. Additionally, China wants to be able to press its territorial and exclusive economic zone (EEZ) claims in the East and South China seas. Finally, Beijing increasingly seeks the military means to police and protect sea lines of communication (SLOC) in order to safeguard Chinese shipping and trade as well as to secure energy supplies, given China's reliance on oil and gas imports.

Consequently, China is keen to build expeditionary forces capable of projecting power out to the "second island chain," which is delineated by Guam, Indonesia, and Australia. Eventually, it hopes to be able to project sustainable force throughout the whole of the Western Pacific and into the Indian Ocean. In particular, this goal has led Beijing to deemphasize ground forces in favor of building up the naval, air, and missile forces of the People's Liberation Army (PLA). China's 2006 defense white paper states that the PLA Navy "aims at gradual extension of the strategic depth for offshore defensive operations and enhancing its capabilities in integrated maritime operations." The PLA Air Force, for its part, "aims at speeding up its transition from territorial air defense to both offensive and defensive operations, and increasing its capabilities in the areas of air strike, air and missile defense, early warning and reconnaissance, and strategic projection."[1]

Additionally, the PLA increasingly sees considerable force multipliers in network-centric warfare—the stuff of the current revolution in military affairs (RMA) led by advances in information technologies (IT). Consequently, the PLA is putting considerable effort and resources into

---

[1] Information Office of the State Council of the People's Republic of China, *China's National Defense in 2006* (December 29, 2006), http://www.chinadaily.com.cn/china/2006–12/29/content_771191.htm.

building its capabilities for "informationalized" warfare by expanding its infrastructure in command, control, communications, computers, intelligence, surveillance, and reconnaissance (C4ISR); by pursuing integrated joint operations via networking; and by adopting information warfare (IW) as a key offensive tool.[2] *inspection (exploration of an area*

India also aspires to become a regional great power, particularly in terms of asserting military strength throughout the Indian Ocean area. In particular, this entails the protection of local SLOCs (90% of the country's trade, and most notably oil and gas supplies, transits through the Indian Ocean), sovereignty enforcement, and sea area denial to adversaries.[3] India is increasingly keen to build national capacities for power projection, long-range surveillance and intelligence, and expeditionary warfare.[4] These taskings particularly favor the Indian Navy, which in turn is increasingly becoming the high-tech focus of the military.[5] Additionally, these great-power aspirations are manifested in the country's efforts to develop its nascent nuclear forces (including land- and sea-based missile delivery systems) and in continuing interest in how the country might harness its growing expertise in IT in order to pursue an IT-led RMA.[6]

Japan's current military modernization efforts are driven by three factors: the need to deal with new emerging regional threats, the requirement for increased interoperability with an expeditionary U.S. military, and the desire for the "normalization" of Japanese foreign and defense policy. As the threat of a Soviet attack on the Japanese mainland has disappeared, other security concerns have arisen, particularly missile threats from North Korea, international terrorism, and instability in regions far from Japan that could nevertheless affect Japanese economic, political, and military security. At the same time, within Northeast Asia, China has become a growing security concern, as evidenced by large Chinese military exercises that took place in April 2010 near Japanese territorial waters[7] as well as by the ongoing dispute over the Senkaku/Diaoyutai Islands.

Additionally, Japan is a critical U.S. ally in Asia and, as such, serves as a forward-operating area for U.S. forces in the region. The Japan

---

[2] You Ji, "Learning and Catching Up: China's Revolution in Military Affairs Initiative," in *The Information Revolution in Military Affairs in Asia*, ed. Emily O. Goldman and Thomas G. Mahnken (New York: Palgrave MacMillan, 2004), 97–123.

[3] Rahul Bedi, "Getting in Step: India Country Briefing," *Jane's Defence Weekly*, February 6, 2008.

[4] Ibid.

[5] Rahul Bedi, "Indian Navy Strives for Regional Dominance," *Jane's Defence Weekly*, December 21, 2005.

[6] Thomas G. Mahnken and Timothy D. Hoyt, "Indian View of the Emerging Revolution in Military Affairs," *National Security Studies Quarterly* 6, no. 3 (Summer 2000): 55–80.

[7] Greg Torode, "Exercises Off Japan and Taiwan Show PLA Navy's New Strength," *South China Morning Post*, April 18, 2010.

Self-Defense Forces (SDF) are also increasingly partners with U.S. forces (and by extension, with NATO and Australian forces) in contingency operations, such as security-building in the Indian Ocean; patrolling the Straits of Malacca; and stabilization operations in Iraq and Afghanistan. Consequently, Japan's security interests have expanded far beyond Northeast Asia, and the SDF have accordingly greatly increased their mobility and expeditionary capabilities, firepower, and C4ISR.

Finally, Japan is keen to pursue a foreign and defense policy more befitting a "normal" nation, and Tokyo has permitted the country's military to play a larger and more active role in regional security missions. Japan's Liberal Democratic Party (LDP), in particular, has sought to upgrade the status of the SDF and legitimize their role as a military force. In addition, many politicians have called for the revision of Japan's so-called Peace Constitution in order to explicitly permit the maintenance of self-defense forces and to allow these forces to be used in international peacekeeping and security operations.

Australian defense planning is increasingly driven by growing concerns over a militarily rising China, as well as by emerging requirements to interoperate with U.S. forces in a variety of contingency and stabilization operations. Over the past decade Canberra has shifted its defense posture away from simply a defense of the Australian homeland to expeditionary operations both in the country's immediate neighborhood (e.g., East Timor and the Solomon Islands) and further afield (e.g., Afghanistan and Iraq).

Overall, the Australian Defence Force (ADF) wants to be capable of making a significant contribution to coalition and allied operations with the United States, while at the same time maintaining an independent deployment capability that can contribute to peace and stability within the country's geographic area of responsibility, either alone or as the head of coalition operations. These conditions, in turn, have translated into new requirements for greater mobility (in particular, the ability to move and sustain a 3,000-man brigade), versatility, firepower ("robustness"), sustainability, and jointness. The ADF must be more deployable, more sustainable over long periods and across long distances, and capable of engaging in both low-level and high-intensity high-tech wars.[8] As a practical result, the ADF is currently seeking to improve its capabilities in a number of key areas: amphibious and expeditionary capacity; enhanced survivability

---

[8] Australian Department of Defence, *Australia's National Security: Defence Update 2005* (Canberra: Commonwealth of Australia, 2005).

and firepower; intelligence-gathering, surveillance, and reconnaissance; logistics; and networking and communications.[9]

Military modernization activities within the smaller countries of the Asia-Pacific have enjoyed their own particular momentum. The Republic of Korea (ROK, or South Korea), in addition to being confronted by a possibly growing threat from North Korea, also has growing pretensions of becoming a regional power. As such, Seoul is pursuing military acquisition programs intended to increase the capacities of the ROK Armed Forces in order to permit them to act more independently of the U.S. military and in support of a more nationalistic, self-reliant, and self-assertive foreign and defense policy.[10] This is apparent in South Korea's efforts to acquire a blue water navy (complete with a large fleet of ocean-going submarines) that will rival Japan's and China's maritime forces.

In Southeast Asia, there are renewed concerns over China's "creeping assertiveness" in the South China Sea and growing military strength.[11] China has been building up its military forces in the area (particularly on Hainan Island, which is becoming a major base for nuclear-powered submarines), and Beijing has become more adamant in pressing territorial claims over the Paracel and Spratly islands.[12] Additionally, Southeast Asian countries face new unconventional threats, particularly piracy, terrorism, international crime, and human trafficking. At the same time, many Southeast Asian states are just as often suspicious of each other as they are of external powers such as China, with historical animosities still existing between Malaysia and Singapore, Malaysia and Indonesia, and Thailand and Burma, to name but a few. Moreover, competing claims over EEZs in the South China Sea and over the Spratly Islands are just as strong between the various Southeast Asian nations as they are between these nations and Beijing. Consequently, these tensions have also been powerful motivators behind recent national military build-ups in the region, especially when it comes to acquiring

---

[9] Australian Department of Defence, *Australia's National Security: Defence Update 2005*; and Australian Department of Defence, "The Hardened and Networked Army," 2005.

[10] Hoon Noh, "South Korea's 'Cooperative Self-Reliant Defense': Goals and Directions," Korea Institute for Defense Analyses, KIDA Paper, no. 10, April 2005, 5; and the Republic of Korea, Ministry of National Defense, *2004 Defense White Paper* (Seoul: Ministry of National Defense, 2004), 92–98.

[11] See Ian Storey, "China's 'Charm Offensive' Loses Momentum in Southeast Asia [Part I]," Jamestown Foundation, China Brief, April 29, 2010; and Ian Storey, "China's 'Charm Offensive' Loses Momentum in Southeast Asia [Part II]," Jamestown Foundation, China Brief, May 13, 2010.

[12] See Richard A. Bitzinger, "The China Syndrome: Chinese Military Modernization and the Rearming of Southeast Asia," S. Rajaratnam School of International Studies (RSIS), Working Paper, no. 126, May 2, 2007.

capabilities—particularly long-range naval and air forces—for patrolling and protecting EEZs and promoting sovereignty rights.[13]

Three Key Dynamics Affecting Military Modernization in the Asia-Pacific: Defense Spending, Arms Imports, and the Revolution in Military Affairs

Defense Spending

Certainly, rising military budgets have underwritten a significant regional arms build-up. Defense expenditures have increased significantly over the past decade or more; even the Asian financial crisis of the late 1990s appears to have had no permanent effect on military spending. China, for example, has experienced real (i.e., after inflation) double-digit increases in defense expenditures nearly every year since 1997. Between 1997 and 2005, Chinese military expenditures grew 13.7% per annum, according to the country's own statistics. China's official 2010 defense budget of $78 billion constituted "only" a 7.5% rise over the previous year—compared with a 15% increase in 2009—but this was more than enough to vault the country into second place among the world's top military spenders. China now outspends Japan, France, Russia, and the United Kingdom on national defense. Overall, Chinese military expenditures have more than quintupled in real terms since the late 1990s, permitting Beijing to put considerable resources into the hardware and software of military modernization.

Other Asia-Pacific nations have also greatly increased defense expenditures over the past decade. Indian defense spending has grown by two-thirds between 1998 and 2008, according to data provided by the Stockholm International Peace Research Institute (SIPRI);[14] in 2010, Indian military expenditures have totaled approximately $32 billion. Australia's defense spending has increased by 46% over the same period, while South Korea's has increased by 48%.[15] Of all the larger countries in the Asia-Pacific, only Japan and Taiwan have needed to contend with relatively static military budgets. Even so, Taipei recently secured additional funding for arms acquisitions and in 2008 finally closed a $6.5 billion deal with the United States for the purchase of several types of weapons systems, including

---

[13] Andrew Tan, "Force Modernization Trends in Southeast Asia," Institute of Defence and Strategic Studies, Working Paper, 2004, 30–31.

[14] Stockholm International Peace Research Institute (SIPRI), SIPRI Military Expenditure Database, 2010, http://milexdata.sipri.org.

[15] Ibid.

Patriot PAC-3 missiles, AH-64 attack helicopters, Harpoon antiship cruise missiles (ASCM), and Javelin antitank precision-guided munitions (PGM).

Defense spending in Southeast Asia has in particular recovered from the Asian financial crisis, thus permitting a new round of arms acquisitions. According to SIPRI, Malaysia's military budget more than doubled between 2000 and 2008 from $1.7 billion to $3.5 billion (as measured in constant 2005 dollars). Indonesian defense spending over the same period grew from $2.2 billion to $3.8 billion (a 72% rise), while Thailand increased military expenditures by 43% from $2.1 billion to $3 billion. Singaporean defense expenditures rose 26% from $4.6 billion in 2000 to $5.8 billion in 2008 (again, in constant 2005 dollars); in 2010, Singapore's military budget totaled $8.4 billion. Altogether, military spending in Southeast Asia rose by at least 50% in real terms between 2000 and 2008.[16]

The remarkable economic growth experienced by most Asia-Pacific nations over the past twenty years or so has enabled this expansion in military spending and procurement. According to the International Monetary Fund (IMF), China's GDP grew five-fold from 1990 to 2008. India's GDP nearly tripled over the same timeframe. China and India, in fact, have been the fastest and second-fastest growing economies in the world, respectively. Other countries in the Asia-Pacific have experienced similar economic expansion: from 1990 to 2008, South Korea's GDP grew 160%; Taiwan's, 140%; Malaysia's, 200%; and Singapore's, 200%.[17]

This near-continuous long-term growth in local economies has meant that the burden of defense spending has remained manageable even as military expenditures have increased. China's defense budget for the past decade has never exceeded 2% of the country's GDP, for example. From 1998 to 2008, defense spending in India was nearly constant at around 2.8% of GDP, while South Korea's military expenditures averaged around 2.6% of GDP and Malaysia's approximately 2.1%. Japan's budget is unofficially pegged at about 1% of GDP. Only Singapore (and probably North Korea, as well) has devoted a relatively high percentage of GDP to defense (an average of 4.7% during 1998–2008), and even then that figure has dropped from a high of 5.4% in 1998 to 4.1% in 2008.[18]

---

[16] SIPRI, SIPRI Military Expenditure Database.

[17] International Monetary Fund, World Economic Outlook Database, April 2005, http://www.imf.org/external/pubs/ft/weo/2009/02/weodata/weoselgr.aspx.

[18] SIPRI, SIPRI Military Expenditure Database.

Arms Imports

Along with rising regional defense spending, the highly competitive nature of the current global arms market has also meant that there are a lot of motivated sellers on the supply side. Asia accounted for 42% of all arms deliveries—and 41% of all arms sales agreements—between 2001 and 2008, according to the Congressional Research Service.[19] The region is second only to the Middle East in terms of arms imports. Some of the world's largest arms buyers are located in Asia. India, for example, bought nearly $31 billion worth of weaponry during the 2001–08 period, while China signed arms agreements worth $12.5 billion over the same timeframe. Singapore and Malaysia are some of the largest arms buyers in Southeast Asia. Singapore took delivery of some $3.8 billion worth of arms from 2005 to 2009, placing it seventh among all arms importers, according to SIPRI.[20] Meanwhile, Kuala Lumpur has purchased over $5 billion worth of arms since the late 1990s.[21] India is a large buyer of weapons systems from Russia (e.g., Su-30 MKI fighter jets, Kilo-class submarines, and T-72 tanks), while Australia, Japan, and South Korea have historically made major purchases from the United States of combat aircraft (e.g., F-15, F-16, and F/A-18) and naval systems (e.g., the Aegis air-defense system and the Standard surface-to-missile system), to name but a few.

Because military procurement budgets have fallen significantly since the end of the Cold War, arms producers have increasingly sought out new markets abroad to compensate for the shrinking ones at home. In particular, the leading European, Russian, and Israeli defense firms now typically export the vast majority of their industrial output. BAE Systems, for example, does less than 25% of its business inside the UK, while Thales derives roughly three-quarters of the firm's revenues from outside France. For Saab, only around 30% of its business is with the Swedish military. The Israeli defense industry typically exports more than 75% of its products, and the Russian arms industry is believed to rely on overseas sales for up to 90% of its income.[22] In other words, for some of the major players in the arms industry the overseas arms business has become larger—much larger, in fact—than domestic markets.

For their part, U.S. defense companies traditionally have not needed to rely on arms exports, given the huge domestic market. Even so, some

---

[19] Richard F. Grimmett, "Conventional Arms Transfers to Developing Nations, 2001–2008," Congressional Research Service, CRS Report, R40795, September 4, 2009, 34, 37, 48, 51.

[20] SIPRI, SIPRI Arms Transfers Database, http://www.sipri.org/databases/armstransfers.

[21] Grimmett, "Conventional Arms Transfers," 45, 59–60.

[22] Richard A. Bitzinger, "Introduction," in The Modern Defense Industry: Political, Economic, and Technological Issues, ed. Richard A. Bitzinger (Santa Barbara: ABC-CLIO, 2009), 5.

weapons systems, such as the F-15 and F-16 fighter jets, are now exclusively produced for foreign markets, and overseas sales are therefore essential to keeping these assembly lines open.

Unsurprisingly, many leading arms-producing nations have come to see the Asia-Pacific arms market—which is both large and increasingly bent on acquiring the most sophisticated weapons systems available—as a particularly lucrative one, and competition to sell to this market has become fierce. Between 2001 and 2008, for example, more than 70% of all Russian arms deliveries, worth approximately $26.5 billion, went to this region.[23] Whereas in the past the bulk of Russian arms exports to the Asia-Pacific were delivered mainly to China and India, as of late Moscow has been able to expand its customer base within the region, especially within Southeast Asia, by selling fighter jets to Malaysia and Indonesia, submarines to Vietnam, helicopters to Thailand, and tanks to Myanmar, to name but a few recent deals.

The leading Western European arms producers—the UK, France, Germany, and Italy—also depend heavily on the Asia-Pacific market. Together, these four countries exported nearly $10 billion worth of arms to the Asia-Pacific over the period 2001–08. Although this figure is down significantly from the more than $19 billion worth of deliveries during the period 1994–2001, the region nevertheless remains an essential market for many European arms manufacturers.[24] Nearly 45% of France's arms exports went to Asia during the 2005–08 period; for Germany, 56% of exports were delivered to Asia, and for Italy, 33%. Only the UK had a relatively low level of dependency on arms deliveries to the region (17%), due to a handful of sizable sales to the Middle East (e.g., a 5-billion pound deal with Saudi Arabia for 72 Eurofighter Typhoon combat aircraft).[25]

The United States also exports considerable numbers of weapons systems to the Asia-Pacific. Between 2001 and 2008, it delivered $18.4 billion worth of arms to the region, accounting for approximately one-third of all U.S. arms exports during this period. Only the Middle East, at $35.6 billion, was a larger arms market for the United States.[26]

As competition has heated up, supplier restraint has been replaced by a readiness on the part of the major arms producers to sell just about any type of conventional weapon system available. In addition, supplier states are increasingly prepared to offer technology transfers, licensed production,

---

[23] Grimmett, "Conventional Arms Transfers," 51, 53.

[24] Ibid.

[25] David Roberson, "BAE Confirms £5bn Eurofighter Sale to Saudi Arabia," *Times* (London), August 19, 2006.

[26] Grimmett, "Conventional Arms Transfers," 48, 51.

and other kinds of offsets as inducements to make a sale. Germany, for example, has transferred submarine technology to South Korea, and Russia has licensed the production of Su-27s to China and Su-30s to India.[27]

The Revolution in Military Affairs

Finally, certain aspects of the current IT-led revolution in military affairs must be factored into modernization activities taking place within Asia-Pacific militaries. The RMA is often described as a process of discontinuous and disruptive change in the nature of warfare. Andrew Krepinevich, for example, argues that an RMA occurs when

> the application of new technologies into a significant number of military systems combines with innovative operational concepts and organizational adaptation in a way that fundamentally alters the character and conduct of a conflict. It does so by producing a dramatic increase…in the combat potential and military effectiveness of armed forces.[28]

History is replete with numerous examples of RMAs, and, in general, these revolutions have entailed the linking of one or more technological breakthroughs (such as gunpowder, the internal combustion engine, radio, or nuclear weapons) with one or more organizational, institutional, or operational concept (for example, the *levée en masse* or *blitzkrieg*). The current IT-led RMA is generally seen as derived from the emerging notions of network-centric warfare made possible by the information revolution. IT advances have facilitated significant innovation and improvement in the fields of sensors, seekers, data management, computing and communications, automation, range, and precision. Network-centric warfare permits the "linking of people, platforms, weapons, sensors, and decision aids into a single network" that "creates a whole that is clearly greater than the sum of its parts," resulting in "networked forces that operate with increased speed and synchronization and are capable of achieving massed effects."[29] Consequently, network-centric warfare "generates increased combat power by networking sensors, decision makers, and shooters to achieve shared

---

[27] Richard A. Bitzinger, "Arms Exports to Asia-Pacific Region Increase," RSIS, November 13, 2006, available at http://www.isn.ethz.ch/isn/Current-Affairs/Security-Watch/Detail/?ots591=0c54e3b3-1e9c-be1e-2c24-a6a8c7060233&lng=en&id=52719.

[28] Andrew Krepinevich, "From Cavalry to Computer: The Pattern of Military Revolutions," *National Interest* (Fall 1994): 30.

[29] "Elements of Defense Transformation," Office of Force Transformation, U.S. Department of Defense, October 2004, 8.

awareness, increased speed of command, high tempo of operations, greater lethality, increased survivability, and a degree of self-synchronization."[30]

To be sure, the RMA as an operational concept has come under a good deal of criticism lately.[31] Nevertheless, many of the precepts of the current network-centric RMA—particularly the basic idea of more "expeditionary, agile, and lethal forces," capable of employing "operational maneuver and precision effects,"[32] informed by improved and shared situational battlespace awareness, and enabled by sophisticated C4 (command, control, communications, and computers), which is the very essence of network-centric warfare—still have significant appeal to currently modernizing militaries. Mobility, joint operations, power projection, precision-strike capability, and, above all, the potential of information warfare, the digitization of the battlefield, and networked systems to act as powerful force multipliers in combat also all continue to be important to countries in the Asia-Pacific as they grapple with military modernization in the 21st century.

Quantifying Military Modernization in Asia

Over the past decade or so, many countries throughout the Asia-Pacific have initiated ambitious military modernization programs. As a result of both indigenous production and arms imports, these militaries have gained or are currently gaining capabilities that they did not possess earlier, such as new means for power projection, precision strike, long-range attack, lethality and firepower, and, in particular, battlespace intelligence, communications, and command and control. These new capabilities are especially due to recent acquisitions by Asian countries of modern surface combatants, amphibious assault vessels, aircraft carriers, submarines, advanced fighter aircraft armed with long-range air-to-air missiles, missile defenses, and a host of new precision-guided munitions, including antiship and land-attack cruise missiles, stand-off weapons, and smart bombs (see **Table 1**). Additionally, these weapons acquisitions are being complemented by greatly improved C4ISR systems, including unmanned aerial vehicles and drones, airborne early warning aircraft, and state-of-the-art communications networks.

command, control, communications, computers, intelligence, surveillance, reconnaissance

---

[30] "Network-Centric Warfare: Creating a Decisive Warfighting Advantage," Office of Force Transformation, U.S. Department of Defense, 2003, 2.

[31] See Richard A. Bitzinger, "Is the RMA Dead?" in *Strategic Currents: Marking the Transition to the S. Rajaratnam School of International Studies*, ed. Yang Razali Kassim (Singapore: RSIS, 2006).

[32] "Elements of Defense Transformation," 8.

TABLE 1   Major Asia-Pacific arms acquisition programs

	Surface combatants	Amphibious ships and aircraft carriers	Submarines	Combat aircraft	Missiles and other systems
Australia	• Building 3 Hobart-class air warfare destroyers, equipped with Aegis combat system and SM-2 air-defense missile; could be upgraded to MD capability	• Building 2 Canberra-class LHDs; could be upgraded to STOVL-type aircraft carrier	• 6 Collins-class diesel-electric submarines, acquired in the 1990s and scheduled for upgrading; to be replaced after 2025	• Acquiring 24 F/A-18F • Partner in the Joint Strike Fighter (F-35) program and may acquire up to 100 F-35s	• AAM: AMRAAM • ASCM: Harpoon • AGM: JSOW, Popeye
China	• 6 Type-051C/-052B/-052C destroyers, acquired in the 2000s • 4 Russian-built Sovremenny-class destroyers, acquired in the 1990s–2000s • Building 8+ Type-054/-054A frigates	• 1 Type-071 LPD, more in this class may be forthcoming • May acquire aircraft carriers (ex-*Varyag* by 2011, plus additional indigenous carriers) • May build LHD-class vessel	• 20+ Song-/Yuan-class submarines • Acquired 12 Russian-built Kilo-class submarines • 2+ Shang-class nuclear-powered attack submarines • 2+ Type-094 ballistic missile submarines	• Approximately 300 Su-27/-30 fighters (some Su-27s locally produced) • Building 300+ J-10 fighters	• AAM: R-77, PL-12 • ASCM: 3M-54E/E1 Sunburn, 3M-80E Moskit, YJ-83 • LACM: DH-10 • SSM: DF-11/-15
India	• Building 3 (possibly more) Type-15A Kolkata-class destroyers	• Acquiring ex-Russian Kiev-class STOVL aircraft carrier, to be modified to fly MiG-29 fighters • Building indigenous aircraft carrier, INS *Vikrant*, to fly MiG-29 or Tejas fighters	• Acquiring 6 to 12 Scorpène-class submarines; later submarines could be AIP • Launched first nuclear-powered submarine in 2009	• Acquiring 240+ Su-30MKI fighters (some locally produced) • Plans to acquire up to 260 locally produced Tejas fighters • Plans to acquire 126 foreign-built fighters	• AAM: R-77 • ASCM: Exocet, Brahmos • SSM: Prithvi, Agni

Large Surface Combatants

Asia-Pacific navies have expanded considerably over the past ten to fifteen years, both in terms of quantity and in terms of capabilities. Many navies in the region that were once oriented mainly toward coastal defense—the so-called brown waters—are being upgraded to green water or even blue water (open ocean) capacities. Many countries in the region have consequently added larger surface combatants to their fleets, which greatly extends their range of operations as well as their sustainability and firepower.

Between 2000 and 2008, for example, China constructed six destroyers of three different types—including one class (the Type-052C Luyang II) outfitted with an Aegis-type air-defense radar and fire-control system. In addition, China has built twelve new frigates—including one class that features a stealth design—as well as a new-generation catamaran-hull missile fast attack craft (of which several dozens may be built). The People's Liberation Army Navy (PLAN) also acquired four Sovremenny-class destroyers from Russia in the late 1990s and early 2000s. Chinese-built warships are equipped with indigenous antiship cruise missiles (either the YJ-83 or YJ-62) and Russian or Chinese surface-to-air missiles, housed in vertical launch systems (VLS). The Russian Sovremenny destroyers are outfitted with the 3M-80E Moskit (also known as SS-N-22 Sunburn) ramjet-powered, supersonic ASCM, which has a range of 120 kilometers. Newer missiles have a 200-kilometer range.

Australia is planning to acquire and construct three air warfare destroyers (AWD), which will be based on the U.S. Aegis combat system and the SM-2 Standard surface-to-air missile. These AWDs, known as the Hobart-class, are especially important to the ADF's new expeditionary strategy, as they will provide necessary protection to new amphibious, sealift, and support ships from air-breathing attacks (aircraft and antiship cruise missiles).[33]

The Republic of Korea Navy (ROKN) has contracted for three 7700-ton KDX-III destroyers (also known as the King Sejong the Great–class) and has optioned for three more. The KDX-III is a vast improvement over other destroyers in the ROKN, being equipped with the U.S.-supplied Aegis air-defense radar and fire-control system as well as the Standard SM-2 Block IIIB air-defense missile. As with the Australian AWD, the KDX-III could be upgraded to the SM-3 missile for antitactical ballistic missile operations, although this is currently not being planned. In addition, the KDX-III is armed with the Hyunmoo-IIIC land-attack cruise missile (LACM) and

---

[33] Ian Bostock, "Country Briefing: Australia—Reaching Out," *Jane's Defence Weekly*, November 3, 2004.

either the Harpoon or the indigenous Haesung (Sea Star) ASCM. All these missiles are housed in 128 vertical launch cells.

The move from brown water to open ocean navies has been particularly pronounced in Southeast Asia. The Republic of Singapore Navy (RSN) recently acquired six Formidable-class frigates (based on the French Lafayette-class stealth vessel), armed with Harpoon ASCMs and the French Aster-15 air-defense missile; these frigates are a significant increase in the RSN's power-projection capabilities. Indonesia is currently acquiring four new Sigma-class corvettes from the Netherlands, equipped with Chinese C-802 (YJ-83) ASCMs, while Malaysia is presently building six German-designed MEKO A100 offshore patrol vessels as well as buying two British-built Lekiu-class frigates.

Force Projection, Expeditionary Warfare, and Aircraft Carriers

Many local navies either have expanded or are in the process of expanding their capacities for force projection and expeditionary warfare, in particular via the acquisition of platforms capable of operating rotary-wing and, increasingly, fixed-wing aircraft. China has recently launched the Type-071 LPD (landing platform dock), a 20,000-ton amphibious warfare ship equipped with two helicopters and two air-cushioned landing craft (LCAC) and capable of carrying up to eight hundred troops. The PLAN reportedly could acquire up to eight Type-071s, and these vessels could be complemented by a new larger LHD-type (helicopter-based) amphibious assault ship.[34]

Meanwhile, rumors continue to circulate that China plans to deploy one or more—and perhaps up to six—full-deck aircraft carriers. There is considerable speculation that the Chinese military is restoring the Russian-built *Varyag*—sold to China in 2001, ostensibly for the purposes of being turned into a casino in Macau—and will turn the carrier into a training carrier, commissioning it by 2011. More importantly, many believe that China will soon start building a fleet of indigenously designed carriers, and outfit these with either a Russian fighter (MiG-29 or Su-33) or Chinese fighter (a naval version of the J-10).

The Japan Maritime Self-Defense Force (MSDF) has also been expanding its capacities for power projection through the acquisition of high-speed sealift ships (for logistics and transport) and three large amphibious Osumi-class ships. Ostensibly designated as an LST (landing

---

[34] Ronald O'Rourke, "PLAN Force Structure: Submarines, Ships, and Aircraft" (paper presented at the conference "The Chinese Navy: Expanding Capabilities, Evolving Roles?" Taipei, November 29–December 1, 2007), 19; and "Type 071 Landing Platform Dock," Sinodefence.com, June 5, 2008, http://www.sinodefence.com/navy/amphibious/type071.asp.

ship tank), the Osumi-class vessel is of a size and design more resembling a LPD (including a large open deck for helicopters). The 13,000-ton Osumi can carry 330 troops and up to ten tanks, and is outfitted with four helicopters and two LCAC hovercraft transports. Additionally, the MSDF is currently acquiring four Hyuga-class "helicopter destroyers" (DDH). At 13,500 tons and with a through-deck design and below-deck hangars, the Hyuga DDH more resembles a small aircraft carrier, similar to the Spanish Navy's *Principe de Asturias* or the British Royal Navy's Invincible-class carriers. The Hyuga DDH, however, is intended only for use with helicopters for antisubmarine warfare.

Perhaps in order not to be outdone by Japan, South Korea is in the process of accepting into service the Dokdo-class amphibious assault vessel. The Dokdo-class LPX (landing platform experimental) displaces 14,000 tons and is capable of carrying seven hundred troops, ten tanks, fifteen helicopters, and two LCAC.[35] The Dokdo is intended to serve as a multifunctional vessel, in particular, serving as a fleet command ship for a "rapid response fleet" that would include one Dokdo-class ship and several destroyers, frigates, and submarines.[36] At least two Dokdo-class vessels have been ordered—designed and built by Korean shipyards—and the first was commissioned into the ROKN in 2007; the ROKN may eventually deploy up to four ships in this class.

Australia's growing requirement for amphibious and expeditionary warfare includes the ability to move and sustain a force of three thousand soldiers. Consequently, the Royal Australian Navy (RAN) plans to acquire two new 28,000-ton Canberra-class amphibious power projection (helicopter-based, LHD-type) ships, each capable of transporting one thousand troops and 150 vehicles (including the Australian Army's new M1A1 Abrams tanks) and carrying both landing craft and a mix of transport and battlefield support helicopters. These ships, based on a Spanish design, will provide air support, amphibious assault, transport, and command center roles. This program will cost 3 billion Australian dollars, and the first Canberra-class LHD is due to enter service around 2013.[37]

Though Japan, South Korea, and Australia have no plans at the moment to acquire fixed-wing aircraft carriers, their current classes of open flight-deck helicopter ships—the Hyuga, the Dokdo, and the Canberra—could

---

[35] "LP-X Dokdo (Landing Platform Experimental) Amphibious Ship," GlobalSecurity.org, http://www.globalsecurity.org/military/world/rok/lp-x.htm.

[36] Ibid.

[37] Brendan Nelson, "$3 Billion Amphibious Ship Will Strengthen ADF, Boost Australian Industry," Office of the Minster of Defence, Australian Department of Defence, June 20, 2007, http://www.minister.defence.gov.au/NelsonMintpl.cfm?CurrentId=6780.

conceivably be modified (for example, by adding a "ski-jump" deck) to serve as pocket carriers capable of operating short take-off/vertical landing (STOVL) combat jets, such as the F-35B Joint Strike Fighter (JSF). It is worth noting that the Canberra-class LHD retains the ski-lift for fixed-wing aircraft that was part of the original Spanish design.

For its part, India is already putting considerable resources into building a carrier-centered navy and is currently in the process of replacing its two aging British-built carriers. In the first place, the navy is acquiring the Soviet-built *Admiral Gorshkov*, a 45,000-ton Kiev-class carrier, decommissioned by the Russian Navy in 1996. After several years of strenuous negotiations, Moscow and New Delhi agreed to a deal whereby Russia would provide the carrier *gratis*, while India would pay Russia approximately $1 billion to refit and upgrade the vessel to be capable of flying navy MiG-29 fighters off its deck in a STOBAR (short take-off but assisted recovery) configuration.[38] This entailed stripping off the weaponry from the ship's foredeck and adding a 14.3 degree ski-jump on the bow and three arrestor wires on the angled landing deck. In addition, India will pay another $700 million toward the aircraft and weapons systems, which include twelve single-seat MiG-29K Fulcrum-D fighter jets, four dual-seat MiG-29KUB trainer aircraft, and six Kamov Ka-27 and Ka-31 helicopters, along with training, simulators, spare parts, and maintenance facilities.[39]

The carrier, which will be renamed the INS *Vikramaditya*, was supposed to have been delivered to the Indian Navy in mid-2008, but refitting the vessel has turned out to be much more challenging than originally envisioned, resulting in considerable cost overruns—Moscow has asked for an additional $1.2 billion to finish the upgrade—and delays. Consequently, the *Vikramaditya* is unlikely to enter service until 2013 at the earliest.[40]

The Indian Navy is experiencing similar problems with its indigenous aircraft carrier (IAC), formerly known as the air defense ship (ADS). The IAC, designated the INS *Vikrant*, is a 37,500-ton vessel and will utilize a STOBAR arrangement of ski-jump and arrestor wires and operate either the MiG-29K or India's indigenous Tejas light combat aircraft (LCA), currently in development. Construction began in 2005 at the Cochin shipyards, but production problems have delayed the IAC's in-service date by at least three

---

[38] Bedi, "Getting in Step."

[39] "The Vikramaditya [ex-Gorshkov] Aircraft Carrier," GlobalSecurity.org, http://www.globalsecurity.org/military/world/india/r-vikramaditya.htm.

[40] Edward Hooten, "Modernizing Asia's Navies," *Asian Military Review* 18, no. 1(January 2008): 18; and Bedi, "Getting in Step."

years, or until 2015 at the earliest.[41] Consequently, the Indian Navy will have to keep its 50-year-old INS *Viraat* (formerly the HMS *Hermes*, operating the Harrier) in service for at least another four or five years. Ultimately, however, the navy wants to operate a two-carrier battle group force—one on each coast—with the *Viraat* in reserve.[42]

Several Southeast Asian nations have also been acquiring ships for expeditionary, amphibious warfare. The Republic of Singapore Navy, for example, operates two indigenously designed and constructed Endurance-class landing ships, each capable of carrying 350 troops, eighteen tanks, four helicopters, and four landing craft. Meanwhile, both Indonesia and Malaysia are acquiring or considering buying foreign-built LPDs. Finally, it is worth noting that the Royal Thai Navy is the only other navy in Asia besides India to operate a fixed-wing aircraft carrier, the 10,000-ton, Spanish-built *Chakri Nareubet*. This vessel is outfitted with nine used AV-8A Harrier STOVL jets and six S-70B Seahawk helicopters. The *Chakri Nareubet* is rarely put to sea, however, due to its high operating costs, and the operational ability of the ship's Harriers is highly questionable.[43]

Submarines

The procurement of submarines is another area where Asia-Pacific nations have invested considerable time and effort. In some cases, nations that never before had submarine forces are now acquiring their first boats. China has acquired 12 Kilo-class submarines from Russia since the late 1990s; during the same period it has also constructed sixteen Song-class and four Yuan-class diesel-electric submarines, and at least two Type-093 Shang-class nuclear-powered attack submarines. In addition, China is building a new class of nuclear-powered ballistic missile submarines (SSBN), the Type-094 Jin-class SSBN, of which two so far have been delivered to the PLAN.[44]

Japan is currently building a new class of diesel-electric submarines (the Soryu) equipped with the Stirling engine for air-independent propulsion (AIP). At least four boats in this class are under construction and five more are planned, to be built at a rate of approximately one submarine a year.

---

[41] Hooten, "Modernizing Asia's Navies," 8; and "The Vikrant-class Air Defense Ship," GlobalSecurity. org, http://www.globalsecurity.org/military/world/india/ads.htm.

[42] Bedi, "Getting in Step."

[43] Richard A. Bitzinger, "A New Arms Race? Explaining Recent Southeast Asian Military Acquisitions," *Contemporary Southeast Asia* 32, no. 1 (April 2010): 50–69.

[44] O'Rourke, "PLAN Force Structure," 4–9, 13–18.

Australia took delivery of six Collins-class submarines between 1990 and 2003. In its 2009 defense white paper, Canberra announced that it would eventually replace the Collins-class with a fleet of twelve new boats by 2030.

South Korea is also increasing its submarine fleet. During the 1990s, the ROKN acquired nine German-designed Type-209 diesel-electric submarines, designated the KSS-I Changbogo-class, which were subsequently built in South Korea under license. These are now being replaced by the German Type-214 Chungji-class (KSS-II). The Type-214 is notable for being outfitted with fuel-cells for air-independent propulsion, permitting the boat to remain submerged much longer (up to three weeks) than conventional diesel-electric submarines. South Korea is building three Type-214 submarines under license—the first of which was commissioned by the ROKN in 2008—and holds options on six more.[45] However, South Korea may instead attempt to design and build its own class of submarine, the KSS-III (perhaps up to nine boats).[46] Depending on how many KSS-IIs and KSS-IIIs are ordered, the ROKN could be operating a fleet of up to eighteen submarines by 2020–25.

After protracted negotiations, India has finally signed an agreement to acquire six Franco-Spanish Scorpène-class submarines, which will be constructed under license at India's Mazagon Docks shipyard; six additional submarines may subsequently be ordered, which could be outfitted with the French MESMA (*module d'energie sous-marine autonome*) system for air-independent propulsion.[47] In addition, the country is keen to develop a nuclear submarine fleet, and it is currently leasing two Akula-class submarines from Russia. India also wants to build its own nuclear-powered submarines—both hunter-attack (SSN) and ballistic missile-carrying (SSBN)—and has consequently been working on its Advanced Technology Vessel (ATV) program for over 35 years. The Indian Navy launched its first ATV in 2009 and ultimately by 2015 would like to deploy a fleet of three SSBNs that are armed with the indigenously developed Sagarika submarine-launched ballistic missile (SLBM).[48]

Turning to Southeast Asia, Singapore possessed no submarine fleet at all until the late 1990s, when it acquired four used 1960s-era submarines from Sweden. In 2009, Singapore took delivery of two more former Swedish Navy submarines; significantly, these boats, renamed the Archer-class, have been

---

[45] Tim Fish, "Seoul Commissions Type 214 Sub," *Jane's Defence Weekly*, January 23, 2008.

[46] Robert Karnoil, "Team Prepares for 2007 Start on KSS-III Design," *Jane's Defence Weekly*, December 20, 2006.

[47] Rajat Pandit, "India Plans to Buy 6 New Subs, Says Navy Chief," *Times of India*, December 2, 2007.

[48] Sandeep Unnithan, "The Secret Undersea Weapon," *India Today*, January 17, 2008.

retrofitted with the Stirling AIP engine.[49] For its part, Kuala Lumpur has recently taken delivery of two Franco-Spanish Scorpène-class submarines for the Royal Malaysian Navy (RMN), both of which were commissioned in 2009, while the Vietnamese navy recently announced its intention to buy six Kilo-class diesel-electric submarines from Russia at a cost of $2 billion.[50] In the mid-2000s, rumors were floating around that Indonesia would acquire four Kilo-class and two Lada-class submarines from Russia to replace the navy's two aging German-built Type-209 boats. This deal apparently fell through, however, after Moscow refused to allow Jakarta to use Russian credits to construct a submarine base. Nevertheless, Jakarta still has an outstanding requirement for up to six submarines that will likely be bought from Germany, France, or Russia, or acquired used from South Korea.[51] Thailand also has a requirement for two or more submarines.

Advanced Combat Aircraft

Nearly every Asia-Pacific country currently possesses or is in the process of acquiring at least some fourth-generation or "fourth-generation-plus" fighter aircraft, capable of firing stand-off active radar-guided medium-range air-to-air missiles or delivering precision-guided air-to-surface munitions. China, for instance, has acquired approximately 300 Su-27 and Su-30 combat aircraft, including licensed production of the Su-27 at the Shenyang Aircraft Company in Manchuria. Moreover, the military is supplementing these purchases with the manufacture of its first indigenous fourth-generation-plus fighter, the J-10. The J-10 is an agile fighter jet in roughly the same class as the F-16C and features fly-by-wire flight controls and a glass cockpit.

Japan has completed acquisition of approximately 100 indigenous F-2 fighters (a heavily modified version of the F-16), to complement its force of over 200 F-15s. Tokyo intends to acquire, either through import or indigenous development, a fifth-generation fighter (F-22 or F-35 type) sometime over the next two decades. In South Korea, the ROK Air Force (ROKAF) is acquiring 61 F-15Ks, and plans to acquire up to 60 fifth-generation fighters. The Royal Australian Air Force (RAAF) is in the process of replacing its aging F-111 and F/A-18A/B fighters with the F-35

[49] Tim Fish and Richard Scott, "Archer Launch Marks Next Step for Singapore's Submarine Force," *Jane's Defence Weekly*, June 18, 2009.

[50] Nga Pham, "Vietnam to Buy Russian Submarines," *BBC News*, December 16, 2009.

[51] "Russia, Korea to Fight for RI Submarine Contract," *Jakarta Post*, August 11, 2009; and "Defense Ministry Postpones Purchase of Submarines," Antara News Agency, July 29, 2009.

Joint Strike Fighter (JSF). In the meantime, the RAAF has acquired 24 F/A-18F fighters to fill the gap.

India has obtained, either through import or licensed production, 240 Su-30MKI fighter jets, and could buy up to 50 more eventually.[52] India also plans to acquire up to 220 indigenous Tejas LCAs, although it should be noted that this program is heavily delayed. In the meantime, the Indian Air Force has opened a competition to buy 126 fighters from a foreign supplier; candidates include the F-16, the Swedish Gripen, and the MiG-29.

The Republic of Singapore Air Force (RSAF) is the most advanced of all Southeast Asian air forces. The RSAF, for example, possesses 74 F-16s of the latest Block 52/52+ type. In addition, in 2005 the RSAF placed its first order of F-15SG fighters for a total of 24 aircraft, the first 12 of which have been delivered and are stationed in the United States for RSAF training. Singapore, incidentally, is a partner in the international JSF program and could buy upwards of 100 F-35 fighters.[53] Other recent Southeast Asian fighter jet purchases include 18 Su-30MKM Flankers by Malaysia, with plans to buy another 18 fighter aircraft (either the Swedish Gripen or additional Su-30s); 6 to 12 Gripens by Thailand; and 10 Sukhois (two Su-27s and eight Su-30s) by Indonesia, with hopes to eventually purchase up to 40 Su-27/-30 aircraft.[54]

Missile Defenses

Japan, Australia, China, India, and Taiwan are all in the midst of acquiring missile defenses. Japan, for example, has recently completed upgrading its fleet of six Aegis-class destroyers to the U.S. Navy's Sea-based Midcourse Defense (SMD) missile defense mode. The SMD upgrade entails improvements to the current SPY-1 multifunction phased-array radar and fire-control system that increase the range and altitude of its search, detection, track, engagement, and control functions in order to handle exo-atmospheric anti-missile engagements. This program also entails the deployment of a new interceptor missile, the Standard SM-3 Block IA missile, which includes a third-stage for extended range and a Lightweight Exo-Atmospheric Projectile (LEAP) kinetic warhead for terminal homing and intercept. Japan's SMD system should be fully deployed by 2011. SMD is

---

[52] Rajat Pandit, "IAF Wants 50 More Sukhois to Counter China, Pakistan," *Times of India*, October 2, 2009.

[53] Jermyn Chow, "F-15 Training Cements Ties with US," *Straits Times*, November 21, 2009.

[54] Trefor Moss, "Painful Progress: Indonesia Country Briefing," *Jane's Defence Weekly*, October 16, 2009; and Tan, "Force Modernization Trends in Southeast Asia," 17.

complemented by the land-based Patriot PAC-3 system that provides endo-atmospheric protection against missile threats to the Japanese homeland.

Other Asia-Pacific nations are following suit with missile defense plans. India has purchased the Israeli Green Pine ballistic missile early-warning radar, and New Delhi is currently working to create a national missile defense system that uses both the Russian S-300 surface-to-air missile and a variety of indigenously developed exo-atmospheric and point-defense missile systems. China conducted a missile defense test in early 2010, and Taiwan is attempting to modify its indigenous Tien Kung II SAM into a working missile interceptor.[55]

Australia's and South Korea's planned acquisition of several Aegis-equipped warships could conceivably provide the basis for their national missile defenses, based on the SMD concept. In particular, Australia is attempting to integrate the indigenously developed Jindalee Over-the-Horizon Radar Network (JORN) into the U.S. missile defense configuration, thereby upgrading the JORN system—currently used to detect aircraft at long range—to give it the capability to detect incoming missiles during their early boost phase.[56] South Korea recently announced plans to inaugurate an indigenous missile defense system by 2012 in order to defend against North Korean ballistic missile threats. This program will likely include both land- and sea-based inceptors and will cost at least 300 billion won ($214 million).[57]

Long-range, Precision-strike Weapons

At least as important as the acquisition of modern military platforms throughout the Asia-Pacific is the steady proliferation of precision-guided weapons for stand-off strike. As mentioned already, many new surface combatants and submarines being deployed in the region are equipped with advanced antiship cruise missiles, such as the Harpoon on Australia's Hobart-class destroyer, Singapore's Formidable-class frigate, and Japan's Soryu-class submarine; the Exocet on Malaysian and Indian Scorpène-class submarines; and the Russian 3M-80E Moskit on Chinese Sovremenny-class destroyers. India has developed the Brahmos supersonic antiship cruise missile in cooperation with Russia, which will be deployed in a variety of

---

[55] "China: Missile Defense System Test Successful," *USA Today*, January 11, 2010; and "Taiwan to Upgrade to Tien Kung-2 SAM," Missilethreat.com, July 31, 2006, http://www.missilethreat.com/archives/id.419/detail.asp.

[56] Richard A. Bitzinger, "Asia-Pacific Missile Defense Cooperation and the United States 2004–2005: A Mixed Bag," Asia-Pacific Center for Security Studies, Special Assessment, February 2005, 4, http://www.apcss.org/Publications/SAS/APandtheUS/BitzingerMissile1.pdf.

[57] "South Korea to Complete Missile Defense by 2012," *Defense News*, February 15, 2010.

sea-, land-, and air-based modes, and Taiwan is currently developing the Hsiung Feng III (HF-3) supersonic ASCM.

Additionally, many countries are acquiring active radar-guided, medium-range air-to-air missiles for their fighter aircraft. These include the U.S. AMRAAM (advanced medium-range air-to-air missile) by Australia, Japan, South Korea, Singapore, and Thailand; the Russian R-77/AA-12 by China, Indonesia, and Malaysia; and the PL-12 by China. In the case of AMRAAM, this missile was embargoed for sale to many states in the region until recently.

At the same time, Asian-Pacific militaries are being increasingly equipped with stand-off land-attack munitions. Japan, South Korea, and Singapore are buying the GPS-guided Joint Direct Attack Munition (JDAM), while Australia and Singapore are also acquiring the Joint Stand-Off Weapon (JSOW), a precision-guided glide bomb with a range of up to 130 kilometers. More importantly, perhaps, several countries in the region have developed their own land-attack cruise missiles (LACM), many of them adapted from existing ASCMs. Taiwan, for example, is deploying the Hsiung Feng IIE (HF-2E) LACM, based on its HF-2 antiship missile, China has developed the Dong-Hai 10 (DH-10) LACM, and South Korea, the Hyunmoo-IIIC LACM.

Finally, it is important to not discount the strike value of ballistic missiles armed with non-nuclear warheads. China, of course, has deployed a large number of conventionally armed surface-to-surface missiles, including the 300 kilometer-range DF-11 (CSS-7) and the 600 kilometer-range DF-15 (CSS-6) short-range missiles. This is in addition to China's growing arsenal of sophisticated long-range nuclear-tipped ballistic missiles, including the DF-31 (CSS-9) road-mobile, solid-fuel intercontinental ballistic missile (ICBM), with a range of 8,000 kilometers, and the submarine-launched JL-2 (CSS-N-4) missile. India, meanwhile, has developed the short-range Prithvi and medium-range Agni missiles as nuclear delivery vehicles, and it is currently field-testing an SLBM. North Korea, of course, has deployed its notorious Nodong-1 medium-range ballistic missile, and the intermediate-range (6,000 kilometer) Taepodong-2 is under development. Other tactical missile systems in use in the region include the MGM-140 Army Tactical Missile System (ATACMS), in service with the South Korean army, the U.S.-built HIMARS multiple rocket launcher system in Singapore, and the Brazilian ASTROS-II artillery rocket in Malaysia.

Command, Control, Communications, Computers, Intelligence, Surveillance, and Reconnaissance (C4ISR)

Finally, many Asia-Pacific militaries are engaged in greatly expanding and upgrading their capabilities for C4ISR.[58] For example, China, Japan, Singapore, and Taiwan all currently possess airborne early-warning and command (AEW+C) aircraft, while Australia, India, South Korea, and Thailand intend to acquire AEW+C aircraft in the near future. Both Japan and South Korea have the Aegis naval sensor and combat system deployed on their largest surface combatants, and Taiwan is buying long-range early-warning radars for ballistic missile detection and tracking.

In addition, nearly every major military in the region is acquiring unmanned aerial vehicles (UAV), while China, India, Japan, South Korea, and Taiwan have all launched satellites for surveillance, communications, or navigation/target acquisition. Moreover, these countries and others in the region are also able to exploit imagery provided by a host of commercial earth-observation satellite operators, such as IKONOS, EROS, and QuickBird.

Several countries in the region—namely, Australia, China, Japan, Singapore, South Korea, and Taiwan—have also made or are presently making considerable investments in new types of information processing, command and control, and communications and datalinks. Australia, for example, is currently engaged in its "Hardened and Networked Army" effort, which seeks enhanced firepower and survivability, improved jointness and interoperability (particularly with U.S. forces), and superior network-enabled capabilities.[59] The South Korean military, for its part, is developing an integrated tactical communications system, while Taiwan is spending billions of dollars on a new military-wide C4ISR network that will link sensors, computers, and communications across the services.[60] The Singapore Armed Forces already possesses a secure C4I network, utilizing microwave and fiber-optic channels and linked to air and maritime surveillance systems. In addition, as part of its new "Integrated Knowledge-based Command and Control" (IKC2) concept, Singapore is putting considerable focus on expanding its capabilities for network-centric warfare.[61]

---

[58] Jason Sherman, "Digital Drive: Focus, Funding Shifts to C4ISR, Precision Weaponry," *Defense News*, February 16, 2004, 23–24.

[59] "The Hardened and Networked Army."

[60] Sherman, "Digital Drive"; and Jason Sherman, "Taiwan To Build Military-Wide C4ISR Network," *Defense News*, October 7, 2003.

[61] Bernard Fook Weng Loo, "Transforming the Singapore Armed Forces: Problems and Prospects" (paper presented at the conference "Defense Transformation in the Asia-Pacific: Meeting the Challenge," Honolulu, March 30–April 1, 2004), 5; and Tim Huxley, "Singapore and Military Transformation" (paper presented at conference "The RMA for Small States: Theory and Application," Singapore, February 25–26, 2004), 2.

China, in particular, has put considerable emphasis on upgrading C4ISR assets, according to its concepts of "informationalized" warfare. Consequently, the PLA is expanding the use of satellites for communication, surveillance, and navigation, exploiting its manned space program for military purposes, and reportedly experimenting with digitizing its ground forces (similar to the U.S. Army's "Land Warrior" program). Moreover, the PLA has invested considerable resources in creating a separate military communications network that uses fiber-optic cable, satellites, microwave relays, and long-range high-frequency radio. The PLA has also focused on developing its capacities for "integrated network electronic warfare," such as electronic defenses and countermeasures, computer network attacks (that is, disrupting the enemy's computer networks), and physical attacks on the enemy's C4ISR network, such as with antisatellite (ASAT) weapons.[62]

Assessing the Impact of Modernization on Military Capabilities

The arms build-up in the Asia-Pacific over the past ten to fifteen years is undeniably significant. In the first place, recent acquisitions by regional militaries constitute something more than mere modernization; rather, the new types of armaments being procured and deployed promise to significantly affect regional warfighting capabilities. Local militaries are acquiring greater lethality and accuracy at longer ranges. Stand-off precision-guided weapons—such as land-attack cruise missiles, tactical ballistic missiles, and a variety of smart munitions, some carried by fourth-generation-plus fighter aircraft—have greatly increased these militaries' firepower and effectiveness, making them capable of longer distance and yet more precise attack. Additionally, militaries in the Asia-Pacific are acquiring new or increased capabilities for force projection, operational maneuver, and speed. Modern submarines and surface combatants, amphibious assault ships, aircraft carriers, air-to-air refueling abilities, and transport aircraft have all extended these militaries' theoretical range of action. Regional militaries are also more survivable, due to the increased use of stealth and active defenses, particularly missile defense. Finally, these

[62] U.S. Department of Defense, *Annual Report on the Military Power of the People's Republic of China 2009* (Washington, D.C., 2009), 25–28; You Ji, "China's Emerging National Defense Strategy," Association for Asian Research, January 12, 2005; Wendell Minnick, "China Shifts Spending Focus to Info War," *Defense News*, September 11, 2006; Bill Gertz, "Inside the Ring: China Info Warfare," *Washington Times*, June 2, 2010; and Richard Bitzinger, "China's RMA: Good Enough?" International Relations and Security Network, August 29, 2007, http://www.isn.ethz.ch/isn/Current-Affairs/Security-Watch/Detail/?ots591=0C54E3B3-1E9C-BE1E-2C24-A6A8C7060233&lng=en&id=53705.

forces are improving their capabilities for battlefield knowledge, situational awareness, and command and control. New platforms for reconnaissance and surveillance, especially in the air and in space, have considerably expanded these militaries' capacities to look out over the horizon and across all five areas of the future battlespace: ground, sea, air, space, and the electromagnetic spectrum.

More importantly, many Asia-Pacific militaries—notably Australia, China, and Singapore—are acquiring the types of military equipment that could fundamentally transform their forces along the lines of the IT-led RMA. This embrace of network-enabled warfare—known in Australia as the "Hardened and Networked Army," in China as "wars under conditions of informationization," and in Singapore as the "Integrated Knowledge-based Command and Control" concept—is a potentially historic shift. Regional militaries could be on the cusp of bundling together sensors, computers, communications, command and control systems, munitions, and platforms that would greatly improve the synergy of their fighting effectiveness. Such emerging capabilities, particularly on the part of China, could in turn greatly affect strategy and operations in future military endeavors in the Asia-Pacific.

On the other hand, most discussions of military modernization tend to revolve around absolute gains in capabilities. Certainly most Asia-Pacific militaries in 2010 are a vast improvement over their predecessors of 1990 or even 1995, given the addition of fourth-generation-plus combat aircraft, new classes of warships and submarines, precision-strike weapons, and so on. In China, for example, the J-10 and Su-30 fighters have replaced MiG-19s and MiG-21s. Likewise, F-15s are replacing F-4s in the ROKAF and A-4s in the RSAF, and India is supplementing vintage Jaguars, MiG-27s, and Mirage-2000s with Su-30s and the Tejas LCA. Additionally, beyond-visual-range, active radar-guided air-to-air missiles (AAM), such as the AMRAAM and AA-12, are replacing or supplementing older generation AAMS, such as the short-range AIM-9 Sidewinder or the semi-active AIM-7 Sparrow. Moreover, Australia and Singapore are likely to acquire the F-35 fifth-generation fighter, which is perhaps the most capable fighter available on the global arms market. South Korea and Japan are also potential customers for the JSF. In terms of surface combatants, countries such as China, Japan, South Korea, and Australia are acquiring advanced destroyers with sophisticated radars, surface-to-air missiles, and combat systems that provide their militaries with long-range air defense at sea—and even missile defense—capabilities that they did not earlier possess. In the past fifteen years, countries such as South Korea, Malaysia, Singapore, and Vietnam that never possessed much in the way of submarine forces, or, indeed, any submarines at all, are being equipped with modern boats. In the case of Japan, India, the ROK, and Singapore, these submarines are outfitted with air-independent propulsion that permits them to remain submerged for much longer periods of time. China and India, for their part, have highly ambitious nuclear-powered submarine (both SSN and SSBN) programs. Finally, many Asia-Pacific militaries are being equipped for the first time with a variety of stand-off precision-strike weapons, including JDAMs (Japan, South Korea, and Singapore), JSOW (Australia and Singapore), and the AGM-142 air-to-surface missile (Australia and South Korea). Just as importantly, South Korea and Taiwan have developed their own land-attack cruise missiles, while China and India have gained new capabilities for using ballistic missiles as battlefield strike weapons.

At the same time, these forces are certainly better equipped than in the past with systems for communications, command and control, intelligence, and surveillance. For example, Australia, China, India, Japan, and Singapore (and soon South Korea) have all acquired airborne early-warning and command aircraft, while UAVs have proliferated throughout the region.

Absolute gains in capabilities do not tell the whole story, however. Military power is much more about relative gains—that is, how forces stack up against each other and where their respective comparative advantages and disadvantages lie. Most regional militaries, even China's, pale in comparison with U.S. military forces—which possess sophisticated weapons platforms such as the Nimitz-class nuclear-powered aircraft carrier, Virginia-class nuclear-powered attack submarines, the fifth-generation F-22 fighter jet, and perhaps the most advanced C4ISR infrastructure in the world. Just one Nimitz-class nuclear-powered aircraft carrier, for example, can project airpower equal to the size of many Asia-Pacific countries' entire air forces. As a result, although China may be gaining an edge over militaries in the Asia-Pacific, particularly Taiwan and perhaps even Japan,[63] the PLA remains vastly inferior to U.S. forces. Systems such as the J-10 fighter jet, the Song-class submarine, and the Luyang II-class destroyer, though advanced for the PLA, are basically 1980s-era weapons systems. The J-10, for instance, is equivalent to the F-16C fighter, which entered service in the mid-1980s. Even equipment that China has acquired from Russia—such as Su-30MKI fighters, Sovremenny-class destroyers, and Kilo-class submarines—are hardly cutting-edge, transformational systems. Finally, PLA expeditionary capabilities are still extremely limited due to a shortage of rapid mobility assets, such as amphibious assault vessels, transport aircraft, and utility helicopters. Overall, barely 20% of the PLA's air force, 25% of its surface

---

[63] China now outspends Japan on defense by a factor of nearly two to one, and the PLAN has more destroyers, frigates, and attack submarines than the MSDF.

combatants, and 50% of its submarine fleet are deemed by the U.S. Defense Department to be "modern."[64]

At the same time, the U.S. military is adding to its Pacific forces. The military build-up on Guam, for example, is a significant development, as is the deployment of a sixth aircraft carrier to the region and the basing of a nuclear-powered carrier at Yokosuka, Japan, for the first time. Additionally, the U.S. military is increasingly engaged with the Japanese MSDF in the area of cooperative missile defense, with Australia in the area of signals intelligence, and with Singapore in establishing the island as a forward-operating site for the U.S. Navy, including the maintenance of the COMLOG WESTPAC (Commander, Logistics Group Western Pacific) facility at Sembawang and the expansion of the Changi Naval Base for use by U.S. aircraft carriers.[65] Consequently, U.S. forces in the region are likely to retain their qualitative edge for some time to come.

In addition, qualitative improvements may mean little if the quantities procured remain small. This point is particularly apropos in the case of Southeast Asia: though Indonesia, Malaysia, Thailand, and Vietnam are acquiring some relatively modern pieces of equipment, such as fourth-generation-plus fighter jets, surface combatants, and submarines, the numbers are so small as to have little impact on these countries' warfighting capacities. For example, Thailand is buying just twelve Gripens; Malaysia, only eighteen Su-30MKMs; and Indonesia, just two Su-27s and eight Su-30s.

It has also been argued that any increase in Australia's expeditionary capabilities might still be too small to make any real difference to U.S. forces in contingency operations. Even after acquiring new Canberra-class LHDs, the ADF will still only be capable of lifting one armored battalion, even though its new doctrine calls for moving a 3,000-man brigade. In addition, the RAAF has no capacity for providing air cover to any expeditionary forces beyond a few hundred kilometers from Australia. All in all, the ADF could end up spending a lot of money without contributing much to coalition operations.[66] The same questions can also be raised regarding the expeditionary warfighting capacities of South Korea and Japan, both of which still possess only a relative handful of amphibious assault ships. Likewise, whether Japan possesses a sufficient number of Aegis-class destroyers to provide an adequate missile defense shield for

---

[64] U.S. Department of Defense, *Annual Report on the Military Power of the People's Republic of China 2009*, 36.

[65] The author is grateful to an anonymous reviewer for pointing out the significance of these developments.

[66] Ian Bostock, "Country Briefing: Australia—Offshore Interests," *Jane's Defence Weekly*, January 25, 2006.

the country is questionable, as is whether India's "two-carrier navy" will be operationally effective.

Finally, hardware gains can also mean very little if they are not matched by accompanying developments in the software areas of military modernization, such as doctrine, tactics, training, and systems integration. The evidence, though admittedly thin, suggests that most Asian-Pacific militaries have not embraced this side of force modernization as enthusiastically as the hardware element, thereby undermining the very effectiveness of hardware acquisitions. In particular, there is little to suggest that concepts such as inter-service jointness have really taken hold operationally in many Asia-Pacific militaries. In India, South Korea, and Taiwan, for instance, ground forces still tend to dictate military thinking and decisionmaking, which in turn often limits integrated joint operations. The Indian military, in particular, remains an army-heavy force largely oriented toward a ground war with Pakistan; consequently, the Indian air and naval forces have traditionally had less influence on military operational thinking (although this may now be changing).[67] Japan's land, air, and naval command districts have no commonality, complicating intra-SDF joint operations.[68] Consequently, with a few exceptions (such as Singapore, which has established an integrated command structure and also combined its inter-service special operations forces) very little is being done so far to promote jointness as an operational concept in terms of training or doctrine. Most Asia-Pacific militaries are nowhere near as far along in this regard as U.S. forces.

Particularly with respect to embracing network-centric warfare, few militaries in the region (excepting perhaps Australia and Singapore) have moved beyond the theoretical or speculative phase, and fewer still are experimenting with new unit structures (such as the U.S. Army's brigade units of action) or operational strategies. Even then, no country in the region has yet revised its doctrine or fielded reorganized force structures in line with transformational concepts of an RMA based on network-centric warfare.[69] In some countries—particularly India, Japan, and South Korea—even the debate has been rather thin, and any tangible movement toward true force transformation would appear to be far on the horizon. For instance, after a flurry of research activity in the late

---

[67] Bedi, "Getting in Step."

[68] In fact, it is often said that the MSDF does a better job cooperating with the U.S. Navy than it does with the Ground or Air SDF.

[69] Thomas G. Mahnken, "Conclusion: The Diffusion of the Emerging Revolution in Military Affairs in Asia: A Preliminary Assessment," in Goldman and Mahnken, *The Information Revolution in Military Affairs in Asia*, 213.

1990s and early 2000s, Japan's Ministry of Defense quietly rolled up its RMA office around 2002.

Even the PLA, which is arguably the furthest along among the larger Asia-Pacific militaries in introducing concepts of jointness and integrated operations, overwhelmingly remains a ground-based army—one that is made up largely of infantry troops and, despite the lip-service paid to informationization, still heavily oriented toward a linear, attrition-based "people's war."[70] According to an article in *Jane's Defence Weekly*, the PLA "has yet to promulgate a definitive military doctrine to guide the development of capabilities and operations" according to the principles of "Limited Local Wars under Conditions of 'Informatization.'"[71] The PLA's hierarchical and top-down command structure and interservice compartmentalization do not seem to have changed significantly, and even the Pentagon acknowledges the PLA's deficiencies in concepts such as jointness.[72] This sentiment is echoed by China analyst David Finkelstein. Even while asserting that China is pursuing a "revolution in doctrinal affairs," Finkelstein nevertheless admits that there is still very little substance when it comes to operational guidance and that China's overall national military strategy has not changed much beyond a greater stress on as-yet undefined "integrated joint operations."[73] Overall, he states that "it is uncertain at this point how much the theoretical informs the actual application of the operational art."[74]

Conclusions

That the Asia-Pacific nations have added considerably to their military arsenals over the past fifteen years or so is not in doubt. Nor does the process of military modernization—propelled by regional geopolitical forces, enabled by robust defense spending and a buyer's market in the international arms market, and stirred by the transformative promise of network-centric warfare—seem to show any signs of abating. Moreover, countries in the region are acquiring hardware that, on the surface at least, imbues their militaries with new capacities for warfighting when it comes

---

[70] Dennis J. Blasko, *The Chinese Army Today: Tradition and Transformation for the 21st Century* (New York: Routledge, 2006), 95, 101.

[71] Timothy Hu, "China—Marching Forward," *Jane's Defence Weekly*, April 25, 2007.

[72] U.S. Department of Defense, *Annual Report on the Military Power of the People's Republic of China 2009*, viii, 15.

[73] David M. Finkelstein, "Thinking about the PLA's 'Revolution in Doctrinal Affairs,'" in *China's Revolution in Doctrinal Affairs*, ed. James Mulvenon and David Finkelstein (Washington, D.C.: Center for Naval Analyses, 2005), 14–18.

[74] Ibid., 19.

to mobility, speed, precision strike, firepower, battlespace intelligence, communications, and command and control.

Yet hardware alone does not automatically translate into military capability. Certainly most Asia-Pacific militaries are better equipped now than they were ten or fifteen years ago, and certainly they possess new weapons systems—modern combat aircraft, beyond-visual range air-to-air missiles, stand-off precision-guided munitions, amphibious assault ships, large multirole warships, quieter submarines capable of longer submerged operations, AEW aircraft, UAVs, and so forth—that provide their forces with options to engage in roles and missions that they previously lacked. Nevertheless, these potential capabilities are at the very least tempered by possible deficiencies in numbers, training, doctrine, and other software factors. Bean-counting only goes so far, and the true value of new weapons systems will be undermined if not accompanied by skilled personnel and sufficient numbers of associated systems (e.g., air-launched weapons to work with a new combat aircraft), or if militaries fail to take advantage of the full potential of these systems by also engaging in organizational or doctrinal changes.

There are both positives and negatives in such circumstances. On the one hand, the military power of certain states in the region, such as China, to challenge the United States and the regional security calculus could be much less than it appears, subsequently making these states much less potentially threatening or destabilizing to the regional status quo. On the other hand, these circumstances could also mean that U.S. allies and friendly nations are limited in their ability to contribute to U.S.-led contingency and stabilization operations or to play a significant role in regional security-building.

Of course, the question of capacity and capability is ultimately unanswerable because it is, in the end, subjective. Each country must decide for itself what is an affordable and effective military force, and it may be that perfection is the enemy of good enough. Certainly the hardware acquisitions of the past fifteen years have increased the capabilities of several Asia-Pacific militaries, and will continue to do so. As a result, some countries have gained relative military power over their regional rivals. Notwithstanding a full-scale force transformation, many local militaries have derived benefits from their modernization efforts. While the end result may be only a partial one—and certainly not revolutionary in scope or structure—it could be more than adequate in terms of generating new capabilities and comparative advantages. In other words, military modernization in Asia could still be sufficient, in certain cases, to get the job done.

are beginning to affect markets for and investments in other key raw materials. For example, concerns over supplies of rare earth minerals have begun to intensify competition to lead the way in high-tech clean energy products while heightening the potential national security consequences of shortages of materials necessary for critical military applications. Consequently, energy security and security of supplies of other key raw materials have increasingly become a matter of the "high politics" of national security rather than just the "low politics" of domestic energy and economic policy.[1]

Energy and national resource security are now vital concerns on the strategic and economic agendas of all the major Asia-Pacific powers. Although energy security has been a critical issue since the oil shocks of the 1970s, today's anxieties have been further fed by the extraordinary run-up in prices for energy and industrial commodities beginning in 2003 and culminating in 2008. The global energy and raw materials sector was gripped by what many called a "super-cycle" of long-term secular commodity price increases.[2] The onset of a severe global recession led to a collapse in energy and raw material prices in 2009, but rising prices and supply insecurity have re-emerged as major economic concerns in 2010 as the global recovery, led by Asia (and, in particular, China), drives a resumption of the super-cycle.[3] While major regional powers seek to ensure access to key commodity supplies, energy and resource nationalism and a "zero-sum" atmosphere over controlling future oil, energy, and commodity supplies have become a source of regional rivalry, tensions, and potential conflict. Competition and national suspicion over control of energy and other resources is spilling over and affecting the tenor of the region's most important strategic rivalries—most importantly, the rivalry between the United States and China. There have been some efforts to improve regional and multilateral cooperation in order to maintain open markets and access to energy and resource supplies, but for the most part cooperation has been in relatively short supply.

The United States, as the traditional hub and guarantor of stability in Asia and the key energy-exporting regions of the world, has major stakes in how Asia and China respond to energy and resource insecurities. Driven by needs for energy and raw materials, China is destined to become a significant

---

[1] For an earlier look at the geopolitics of energy security in Asia, see Mikkal E. Herberg, "Asia's Energy Insecurity: Cooperation or Conflict?" in *Strategic Asia 2004–05: Confronting Terrorism in the Pursuit of Power*, ed. Ashley J. Tellis and Michael Wills (Seattle: The National Bureau of Asian Research, 2004), 349–78.

[2] Alan Heap, "China: The Engine of a Commodity Super Cycle," Citigroup/Smith Barney, Global Equity Report, March 31, 2005.

[3] John Morrissy, "China Will Drive Commodities Super-Cycle: Scotiabank," *Financial Post*, June 29, 2009.

player in key energy- and resource-exporting regions, such as the Middle East, Central Asia, Africa, and Latin America. India is also rapidly becoming an important investor in these regions. China's and India's new involvement in these regions could have a powerful impact on U.S. diplomatic, nonproliferation, human rights, and strategic goals. Moreover, given that Asia lacks a regional architecture and the institutions to manage conflict, such competition has the potential to destabilize the region. Asian stability is central to U.S. prosperity and security; thus, the potential for conflict driven by energy competition and resource insecurity must become a conscious and carefully crafted dimension of Washington's regional strategy.

The goal of this chapter is to analyze Asia's energy and resource security challenges and their impacts on U.S. geopolitical and energy security interests. The discussion will be divided into four sections. The first section will focus on Asia's energy prospects and the energy security dilemmas that condition the behavior of the major Asian powers. The second section will discuss how the key Asian countries are addressing their energy security concerns, the roots of their energy strategies, and the impact of these strategies on regional relations. The third section will examine the implications of Asia's energy security challenges for the United States and will consider what must be done to try to shape Asia's competitive energy security dynamics into more cooperative channels that would contribute to, rather than undermine, regional stability and economic security. The fourth section will discuss another resource security issue emerging in Asia that could affect regional rivalries—namely, the growing controversy over control of rare earth minerals.

Asia's Energy Fundamentals

Asia is now ground zero for growth in global energy demand as a result of the region's remarkable economic ascent over the past two decades. Energy consumption is closely tied to population growth, industrial production, urbanization, rising per capita income, and motorization, all of which are rising dramatically in the region, especially in China and India. From 1990 to 2008, total Asian energy demand grew by 123%, while total world energy demand outside of Asia grew by just 16% (see **Table 1**).[4] Excluding

---

[4] All of the historical energy data in this section is drawn from "BP Statistical Review of World Energy 2009," BP plc, June 2009. There are other good sources of energy data and forecasts, including the annual *World Energy Outlook* by the International Energy Agency (IEA), the U.S. Department of Energy's annual *International Energy Outlook (IEO)*, and an annual forecast from ExxonMobil. These, however, are primarily forecasts with limited historical and country-by-country data. BP's annual publication is the only consistent and detailed annual country-by-country, fuel-by-fuel source of historical data, and it is also the most widely available.

TABLE 1   Total energy demand, 1990–2008 (million tons oil equivalent, mtoe)

	1990	2000	2005	2008	Growth, 1990–2008	% change, 1990–2008	% share of world growth
World	8,095	9,263	10,555	11,295	3,200	40	100
World, excluding Asia	6,307	6,690	7,125	7,313	1,006	16	31
Asia	1,788	2,573	3,430	3,982	2,194	123	69
Developing Asia	1,115	1,654	2,441	2,986	1,871	168	58
China	697	983	1,595	2,026	1,329	191	42

SOURCE: "BP Statistical Review of World Energy 2009."

NOTES: Data for developing Asia excludes OECD members Japan, Korea, Australia, New Zealand, and Taiwan. Data for China includes Hong Kong.

the mature markets of industrial OECD (Organisation for Economic Co-operation and Development) Asia, energy demand in developing Asian countries grew by an astronomical 168%, while Chinese energy demand nearly tripled. Asia's share of global energy demand rose from 22% to 35% and accounted for an astonishing 69% of the entire growth in total world energy demand over this period.

Although Asia's energy demand grew across the spectrum of fuels, demand for oil has provoked the most acute security and geopolitical issues. Oil demand nearly doubled from 1990–2008, whereas oil production among Asia's producers and exporters rose only slightly. Indonesia has traditionally been Asia's largest oil exporter, but oil production leveled off in the early 1990s and began a gradual decline since the late 1990s at the same time that domestic oil demand was rising. By 2003, Indonesia had become a net oil importer. Malaysia's modest oil exports also have diminished as production has leveled off since the 1990s and rising domestic demand has reduced exports. China remains Asia's largest oil producer, but demand has outpaced production since the early 1990s. As a result, oil imports from outside Asia rose dramatically from 7 to over 17 mmdb (millions of barrels per day), driven by dynamic industrial and transportation growth (see **Figure 1**). The shift has been most dramatic in China, where demand for oil nearly

FIGURE 1   Asia's booming demand for crude oil imports

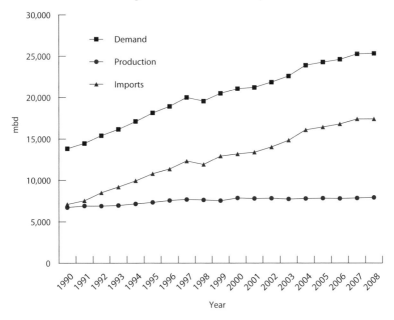

SOURCE: "BP Statistical Review of World Energy 2009."

quadrupled from 2.3 mmbd in 1990 to 8.0 mmbd by 2008.[5] In 1985, China was a net oil exporter of over 700 mbd (thousands of barrels per day), but after becoming a net oil importer in 1993, oil imports reached 4.2 mmbd in 2008, making China 53% import-dependent (see **Table 2**). Four of the world's top five oil importers are currently in Asia (China, Japan, India, and South Korea).

Asia's dependence on oil imports is certain to become even more acute in the future. The International Energy Agency (IEA) forecasts that if Asia continues to develop on its current trajectory, the region is likely to account for nearly three-quarters of the growth in global oil demand from 2008 to 2030 (see **Table 3**).[6] Oil imports from outside the region will approach 30 mmbd, or 80% of total oil demand, only slightly less than the entire current production capacity of the Organization of the Petroleum Exporting

---

[5] For 1990 data, see "BP Statistical Review of World Energy 2009." For 2009 data, see "Medium-Term Oil Market Report 2009," IEA, June 2010, http://www.iea.org/papers/2009/mtomr2009.pdf.

[6] IEA, *World Energy Outlook 2009* (Paris: OECD/IEA, 2009), 81.

TABLE 2 Asian crude oil supply, demand, and imports, 1990–2008 (mbd)

	1990	2000	2005	2008	Change, 1990–2008
Demand	13,837	21,073	24,283	25,339	11,502
China	2,323	4,772	6,984	7,999	5,676
India	1,211	2,254	2,569	2,882	1,671
Japan	5,258	5,557	5,343	4,845	-413
South Korea	1,038	2,229	2,308	2,291	1,253
Other Asia	4,007	6,261	7,079	7,322	3,315
Production	6,726	7,874	7,845	7,928	1,202
China	2,774	3,252	3,627	3,795	1,021
Indonesia	1,539	1,456	1,087	1,004	-535
Malaysia	634	735	744	754	120
India	715	726	738	766	51
Australia	651	809	580	556	-95
Other Asia	413	896	1,069	1,053	640
Imports	7,111	13,199	16,438	17,411	10,300
China	-451	1,520	3,357	4,204	4,655
Japan	5,258	5,557	5,343	4,845	-413
South Korea	1,038	2,229	2,308	2,291	1,253
India	496	1,528	1,831	2,116	1,620
Southeast and South Asia	770	2,365	3,599	3,955	3,185

SOURCE: "BP Statistical Review of World Energy 2009."

NOTES: Data for China excludes Hong Kong.

Countries (OPEC). China's oil imports would rise from the current 4.5 mmbd to nearly 13 mmbd, making China 75%–80% dependent on oil imports and likely the largest oil importer in the world. India's oil demand is expected to more than double over this same period, from 3 mmbd in 2008 to nearly 7 mmbd in 2030, with dependence on imports rising from 70% today toward 90%. For China, India, and Asia as a whole, imports from the Persian Gulf are likely to account for 70%–80% of total oil imports, with other significant increments coming from Africa, Central Asia, and Russia. Hence, Asia's mushrooming oil demand, along with the region's stark and growing dependence on oil imports from many unstable parts of the world

TABLE 3   Projected growth in world oil demand (mmbd)

	2000	2008	2015	2030	Increase, 2008–30	World growth (%)
OECD	44.7	43.2	41.2	40.1	-4.6	-22
Non-OECD	26.6	35.0	40.2	56.2	21.2	103
Developing Asia	11.2	15.8	19.6	30.7	14.9	73
China	4.6	7.7	10.4	16.3	8.6	42
India	2.3	3.0	3.8	6.9	3.9	19
ASEAN	3.0	3.5	3.8	5.3	1.8	9
World	76.5	84.7	88.4	105.2	20.5	100

SOURCE: IEA, *World Energy Outlook 2009*.

and across numerous maritime bottlenecks, is a critical source of anxiety, particularly for China and India.

Asia's rising demand for natural gas presents somewhat less stark energy security dilemmas, but dependence on imported natural gas is expected to increase dramatically over the next two decades. Gas use in Asia has traditionally been very limited—making up just 4% of energy consumption in China, for example—largely because transporting natural gas across Asia's long distances is relatively expensive. Consumption is rising rapidly, however, as both China and India seek to boost gas use to fuel electricity generation, reduce air pollution, and diversify their energy slate. The IEA forecasts that natural gas demand is likely to triple in China and India by 2030, while doubling in Asia as a whole.[7] To meet this demand, roughly two-thirds of Asia's natural gas imports will come from outside the region, with gas-import dependence likely growing to 40%–50% of consumption in both China and India. Japan, Korea, and Taiwan have been 100% dependent on natural gas imports for decades.[8]

Asia's coal consumption increasingly dominates global demand, as Asia, especially China and India, strives to keep up with booming electricity demand. China and India, which accounted for only one-fifth of global coal consumption in 1980, now account for nearly one-half, and by 2030 are likely to account for two-thirds of global consumption. The two countries combined are expected to account for 80% of the entire

---

[7] IEA, *World Energy Outlook 2009*, 366.

[8] Ibid., 434.

global increase in coal use between now and 2030.[9] China, with the world's third-largest coal reserves behind the United States and Russia, has historically been a modest exporter of coal; however, as of 2009, the torrid pace of coal and electricity consumption turned China into a net importer of coal for the first time. It now appears likely that China will surpass Japan as early as 2010 as the largest importer of thermal coal.[10] Chinese dependence on imported coal is expected to continue to rise with strong economic growth. India is already a substantial importer of coal, despite large reserves and domestic production, and this dependence on imports is also likely to grow dramatically. Even though both China and India are moving to promote cleaner sources of renewable electricity, such as nuclear, wind, and solar power, the pace of growth in electricity demand means that both countries will continue to depend fundamentally on coal for the huge majority of their electricity needs.

In sum, growth in energy demand is driving two critical dimensions of Asia's energy security angst. First, the sheer scale and pace of growth is severely testing the ability of governments to simply provide adequate energy supplies fast enough to prevent energy from becoming a critical bottleneck to continued economic growth and job creation. Second, rising dependence on imported energy supplies across the fuel spectrum is also shaking the confidence of regional governments in their ability to secure imports to meet demand. In terms of import dependence, each of the various energy sources involves different market and geopolitical implications. Oil presents the most striking geopolitical challenges, given the highly politicized nature of global oil markets and the stark concerns over the potential for future supply and price shocks. Asia is most actively seeking to manage its oil import dependency, and it is thus in the oil markets that the sense of national competition to gain secure access to future supplies is most acute. Asian governments, from Beijing to Tokyo to New Delhi to Seoul, are deeply involved in promoting the overseas investments of their national oil companies (NOC) and are actively engaged in energy and pipeline diplomacy in the Middle East, Africa, Central Asia, Southeast Asia, and even far away Latin America.

Asia's dependence on natural gas imports was until recently largely internal to the region. Japan, South Korea, and Taiwan were dependent mainly on imported gas from Southeast Asian suppliers of liquefied natural gas (LNG), such as Indonesia, Malaysia, Brunei, and increasingly Australia. The intraregional nature of this trade reduced the politicization

---

[9] IEA, *World Energy Outlook 2009*, 89–90.

[10] Javier Blas and Leslie Hook, "China Set to Overtake Japan as Largest Importer of Thermal Coal," *Financial Times*, June 24, 2010, 24.

of gas-import dependence. Moreover, global gas markets have traditionally been somewhat less politically driven than oil markets. Yet as Asia's dependence on imported gas grows—necessitating that countries import gas from long distances along transportation routes as uncertain as oil routes—anxiety over access to and the reliability of global gas supplies is likely to reinforce the region's energy security angst. Japan and South Korea have long been heavily involved in promoting their national companies' investments in LNG abroad. LNG exports from the Middle East to Asia have risen significantly with the huge expansion of natural gas exports from Qatar. Asian countries are importing LNG from Russia, where the large Sakhalin-2 project went online in 2009, and LNG from West Africa is beginning to move to Asia as well. China has been developing major gas pipeline projects to import gas from Central Asia and Myanmar, while India has so far unsuccessfully sought to develop gas pipeline projects from Iran, Afghanistan, and Myanmar. Moreover, some of the large gas-exporting countries are increasingly promoting the idea of a gas-based production management organization along the lines of OPEC in order both to reduce the potential for damaging price competition among big suppliers and to support higher gas prices. Although such an organization seems unlikely to emerge any time soon, the mere discussion of this possibility is increasing Asia's concerns about the security of future imported gas supplies.

Coal import dependence has long been critical for Japan and South Korea, who are fully dependent on imported coal, but has only recently begun to grow on a large scale elsewhere in Asia, as India and China become substantial importers. Nonetheless, like natural gas, coal markets have been less politicized than oil markets and less a source of intense energy security anxieties. As dependence on imported coal grows, however, it remains to be seen whether governments intent on securing future supplies of critical determinants of their economic prosperity and standard of living will increasingly focus on coal markets. Beijing, for example, has become increasingly active in promoting overseas coal resource acquisition by the country's large, state-owned coal companies in the name of energy security.

The Rise of Energy Nationalism in Asia

The profound increase in energy demand and import dependence in Asia has converged with two other underlying developments to strongly reinforce an increasingly nationalistic and competitive approach to energy security in the region. First, state-owned NOCs increasingly dominate the global oil and gas industry, which has further politicized the industry and accentuated the state-to-state strategic dimensions of the search for energy security. This situation has been evolving since the rise of OPEC in the early 1970s and the creation of large, state-owned NOCs in countries that produce and export oil and gas, such as Saudi Arabia's Aramco, Russia's Gazprom, Venezuela's PDVSA (Petroleos de Venezuela, SA), and Iran's NIOC (National Iranian Oil Company). Presently, the ten largest oil- and gas-reserve holding companies in the world are producer NOCs. Furthermore, NOCs in producer countries control over 75% of existing proven oil reserves globally. Although the role of the traditional international oil companies (IOC), such as ExxonMobil, BP, Royal Dutch Shell, and Total, remains important in many of the world's largest and most technically complex oil and gas projects, the rise of producer-state leviathans has gradually eroded the dominance of IOCs.[11] More recently, NOCs have also risen among the large consuming and importing countries, a trend led by Asia's large oil and gas importers.[12] As Asia's oil and natural gas demand and import dependence have accelerated over the past decade, each of the major regional powers has increasingly subsidized and promoted its own NOCs to invest in and access oil and gas supplies abroad as an important instrument in a range of national energy security strategies. These expanding Asian NOC investments—most importantly from China but also from India, Japan, and South Korea—are gradually reshaping the competitive landscape of the global oil and gas industries while reinforcing the impulse among Asia's major powers toward an increasingly politicized, competitive, and nationalistic approach to energy security.

The second development driving an increasingly nationalistic and competitive approach to energy security in Asia is the economic and strategic rise of China in tandem with that country's enormous impact on global energy markets. It is axiomatic that for the United States, Japan, India, South Korea, and other countries in the Asia-Pacific region, the rise of China promises to profoundly reshape the region's geopolitical, economic, and strategic order. But in the realm of energy geopolitics and markets, China's rapidly growing energy demand and increasing dependence on imported energy, combined with its active, state-centered reach outward to secure control of supplies through its NOC investments, financial largesse, and various trade and aid emoluments in key energy-exporting regions,

---

[11] For the best recent work on this, see Valerie Marcel and John V. Mitchell, *Oil Titans: National Oil Companies in the Middle East* (London: Chatham House, 2006); and see also "The Changing Role of National Oil Companies in International Energy Markets," James A. Baker III Institute for Public Policy, Baker Institute Policy Report, no. 35, April 2007.

[12] On Asia's NOCs, see Mikkal E. Herberg, "Energy Security Survey 2007: The Rise of Asia's National Oil Companies," National Bureau of Asian Research, NBR Special Report, no. 14, December 2007; and John V. Mitchell and Glada Lahn, *Oil for Asia: The Rise of Asian National Oil Companies*, (London: Chatham House, 2007).

promise to reshape the global energy security order as much as the global and strategic economic order. China's emergence as a major force in global energy investment and markets has reinforced and intensified the energy security angst of other Asian powers as well as of the United States. These powers are reacting with their own competitive efforts to secure future supplies or, in the case of the United States, are seeking to shape mercantilist Chinese policies on energy security toward cooperation and collaboration in multilateral energy security institutions such as the IEA and group of twenty (G-20).[13]

The net impact of Asia's rising energy insecurity, the increasingly state-dominated shape of the global petroleum industry, and the shifting geopolitical outlook in Asia in the shadow of China's geopolitical ascent is that the mercantilist, zero-sum atmosphere toward energy security in Asia has intensified. Energy competition and suspicions are spilling over into strategic competition and aggravating broader strategic relations among the region's major powers. Conversely, strategic suspicions spill back into energy competition, adding a toxic element to any efforts to promote a more cooperative regional approach to energy security. As the next section will show, energy competition among the key Asian powers tends to mirror perfectly and aggravate the existing major strategic rivalries in the region between the United States and China, China and Japan, and China and India. These rivalries are being played out across a range of arenas of energy investment, trade, and maritime and pipeline transportation.

Energy Insecurity and the Competition to Secure Future Supplies

Rising dependence on oil imports and a growing sense of vulnerability to external supply disruptions have catalyzed an intense focus on energy security as a key national strategic and industrial goal among all the major powers of Asia. The catalyst for much of the region's focus on state solutions to energy security challenges derives from China's enormous rush to secure future oil supplies following the country's rapid transition from self-sufficiency to the role of a major oil importer. As suggested earlier, China will become ever more heavily dependent on OPEC and the major

---

[13] For a full discussion of these issues, see Mikkal E. Herberg and David Zweig, "China's 'Energy Rise,'" Pacific Council on International Policy, April 2010, http://www.pacificcouncil.org/Document.Doc?id=94. For a Chinese perspective, see Zha Daojiong, "Oiling the Wheels of Foreign Policy? Energy Security and China's International Relations," S. Rajaratnam School of International Relations (RSIS), Asia Security Initiative Policy Series, Working Paper, no. 1, March 2010.

Persian Gulf exporters for future oil needs, and the vast majority of this oil will need to be transported long distances through vulnerable maritime chokepoints from Africa, by pipeline and rail from Russia, and by pipeline from Central Asia. Within fifteen years, two-thirds of China's total oil needs will likely need to pass through the Malacca Straits and the sea lanes of the Indian Ocean and Southeast Asia. China's pursuit of energy security thus has important implications for the shape and competitiveness of energy diplomacy in Asia.

Beijing's energy security angst is rooted in the leadership's concerns that disruptions of oil supply could undermine the economic growth and job creation that underpin social and political stability and support the government's ruling mandate.[14] Beijing has worked closely with its three NOCs on a statist and mercantilist set of policies and coordinated efforts for both promoting future national access to oil supplies and reducing the impact of price shocks. This "go-out" strategy is embodied in energy, commercial, and financial diplomacy by Beijing's leaders along with the commercial growth of equity investments by Chinese NOCs in overseas oil and gas fields. China's NOCs have now acquired a range of large equity oil stakes, long-term crude oil and LNG supply contracts, and oil and gas pipeline projects in virtually every major energy-exporting region. Most recently, China has also put its large foreign exchange reserves to use by providing investment capital to its NOCs and cheap loans to cash-strapped oil producers in return for guaranteed oil supplies over the long term.

Beijing's energy strategy has focused heavily on the ownership and physical control of barrels along with future access; mistrust of global energy markets is deeply ingrained. There is a prevailing view among Beijing's leadership that oil markets are controlled by the United States and that Washington seeks to exploit China's energy weakness as part of U.S. strategy to contain China. This sense of vulnerability to U.S. pressure is accentuated by the United States' strategic power in the Persian Gulf, the U.S. Navy's control over sea lanes that are critical to energy transport, and what is thought to be U.S. power over the global oil industry and institutions. The 2005 CNOOC-Unocal episode reinforced this perception of energy as an arena of strategic competition and that the United States was working to undermine China's access to energy supplies.

---

[14] This section draws heavily from Herberg and Zweig, "China's 'Energy Rise.'"

At the level of political leadership, these factors explain the strongly mercantilist character of Beijing's energy security concerns.[15] China's energy strategy has also promoted an image of "China Energy, Inc." in Tokyo, Seoul, New Delhi, and Washington. The reality, however, is much more complex. Beijing leads less and takes a far less strategic approach than is commonly portrayed. Most investments abroad by China's NOCs have strong commercial and competitive roots. Moreover, it is often unclear who is leading whom—that is, whether it is the state or the NOC that is in charge. The situation is probably better viewed as collaboration based on the convergence of the commercial interests of China's NOCs in global expansion with a view among Beijing's leadership (rightly or wrongly) that state financial and diplomatic support for such NOC investments abroad serves national energy security interests. Thus, in many ways, this is as much industrial policy as energy security policy. Other countries in the region, however, feel as though they are competing with a coordinated and very formidable Chinese energy investment package comprising China's three NOCs and extensive state economic, financial, and diplomatic support.

China has pursued its energy security strategy in a wide range of areas. Most importantly, Beijing has strongly supported large investments and supply contracts by China National Petroleum Corporation (CNPC), Sinopec, and China National Offshore Oil Corporation (CNOOC) in nearly all the major oil-exporting regions. Most of the large investments and contracts have been supported by extensive diplomacy from Beijing, a wide array of cheap financing, a range of trade and aid deals, and, most recently, huge government-to-government loans from Chinese state banks. All three companies have become important players in the Middle East. Until recently, China's major relationships in the Persian Gulf have been with Iran and Saudi Arabia. Iran has become China's third-largest source of oil imports; CNPC and Sinopec are considering new oil field investments in Iran, while CNOOC is considering partnering in a large LNG venture. Although China has no significant opportunities to invest in the Saudi Arabian upstream oil industry, Saudi Arabia is now China's largest single source of imported oil, recently surpassing one million barrels per day.

---

[15] There is a wide range of literature on the roots of China's energy security policies. For some of the best work, see Bo Kong, *China's International Petroleum Policy* (Santa Barbara: Praeger, 2010); Trevor Houser, "The Roots of Chinese Oil Investment Abroad," *Asia Policy*, no. 5 (January 2008): 141–66; David Zweig and Bi Jianhai, "China's Global Hunt for Energy," *Foreign Affairs* 84, no. 5 (September/October 2005): 25–38; Erica Downs, "China," Brookings Institution, Energy Security Series, December 2006; and Zha Daojiong, "China's Energy Security: Domestic and International Issues," *Survival* 48, no. 1 (Spring 2006): 179–90. For an overview of China's energy security policies from a Chinese perspective, see Gao Shixian, "China's Perspective on National Energy Security," in *Energy Security in the North Pacific*, ed. Fereidun Fesharaki, Nam-Yll Kim, and Yoon Hyung Kim (Kyonggi-Do: Korea Energy Economics Institute, 2009): 149–79, along with commentaries by Xia Yishan and Kang Wu, in Fesharaki, Kim, and Kim, *Energy Security in the North Pacific*, 180–207.

The relationship is burgeoning as Aramco is partnering with Sinopec in two large Chinese refinery projects fed by Saudi crude. In an important symbolic development in early 2010 Aramco began exporting more oil to China than to the United States, something unthinkable just a few years ago in view of the long history of the U.S.-Saudi strategic alliance.[16] Kuwait is also looking to partner with Sinopec on a large refinery project. Furthermore, Chinese NOCs have become the largest national group of oil companies in Iraq by investing in three enormous projects in newly opened oil field development.[17]

Beijing and Chinese NOCs have also expanded their activities rapidly in Central Asia and Russia by developing large equity investments and new pipeline projects to import Eurasian oil and natural gas. China's NOCs are now significant oil producers in Kazakhstan and have built a large oil pipeline, which is currently being expanded to bring Kazakh oil to western China. Beijing continues to strengthen China's position in Kazakhstan with two recent multibillion dollar loans from state banks to Kazakhstan and the Kazakh state oil company KazMunaiGas. In December 2009, China and Turkmenistan inaugurated a new natural gas pipeline financed by China to bring Turkmen gas to western China. The pipeline eventually will import gas from fields being developed by Chinese NOCs in Turkmenistan and, later, in Kazakhstan and Uzbekistan. Energy relations with Russia have been less productive, even though the resource and commercial potential for moving Russian oil and gas resources to the Chinese market is enormous. Russia has been shipping 250 mbd of oil to China by rail. However, a proposed pipeline to bring much larger levels of oil supplies from East Siberia's Angarsk region to China was delayed for years as Russia dithered over development of the pipeline and as Japan sought to use its own financial diplomacy to alter the planned route to the Pacific coast rather than to northern China. Finally, in late 2009, in the wake of China's state banks providing $25 billion in cheap loans to Russia's cash-strapped companies Transneft and Rosneft, Russia agreed to complete the pipeline, which will bring 300 mbd to Daqing in northern China. Yet the efforts of China's NOCs to invest equity in development of Russian oil fields remain modest.

Beijing has also used extensive state diplomacy, aid, and cheap loans to support its NOCs in building a growing oil investment position in

---

[16] Jad Mouawad, "China's Growth Shifts the Geopolitics of Oil," *New York Times*, March 19, 2010.

[17] Stanley Reed and Dexter Roberts, "Red Star over Iraq: China's Ambitions in the Iraqi Oil Fields Could Change the Landscape," *BusinessWeek*, January 20, 2010.

Africa.[18] China's largest operations are in Sudan, where investment and production continue to rise. But China's NOCs are also increasingly active in highly productive West Africa, with major new investments in large offshore fields in Angola and Nigeria, Africa's two biggest oil producers. These investments have been anchored by Beijing's energy diplomacy and by cheap loans from Chinese state banks.

China's NOCs have also become very active in Latin America. CNPC has sizeable investments in Venezuela and is moving to dramatically expand operations into Venezuela's Orinoco heavy oil belt. The company has also planned joint refinery projects in China to process Venezuelan crude. Venezuela has received two multibillion dollar loans from China to support expanded heavy oil development—the latest one for $20 billion in mid-April 2010.[19] Likewise, with Brazil now poised to become a significant oil producer and exporter following the recent discovery of huge new oil fields offshore, China has quickly moved to secure several future long-term guaranteed supply contracts from Petrobras. State banks in China provided $10 billion in cheap loans at a time in early 2009 when global credit markets had seized up and Brazil's financial ability to fund new offshore fields was in question.[20] In North America, Beijing's NOCs have become major investors in heavy oil development in western Canada.[21]

In Southeast Asia, CNPC and CNOOC have invested substantial equity in oil production in Indonesia, while CNOOC has bought an equity stake in BP's Tangguh LNG project in West Papua along with a long-term LNG supply contract. Moreover, both CNOOC and CNPC have bought into several large LNG projects in Australia. Most notably CNOOC has invested in Shell's huge North West Shelf project, and CNPC holds an equity stake in partnership with Shell in buying out Arrow Energy and developing its coal-bed methane-to-LNG projects. The importance that the Chinese government attaches to the various components of its international oil and gas strategy is illustrated by the $30 billion loan facility that the China Development Bank agreed to provide CNPC for its global investment needs in September 2009.[22]

---

[18] On China's African energy activities, see Erica S. Downs, "The Fact and Fiction of Sino-African Energy Relations," China Security 3, no. 3 (Summer 2007): 42–68; Henry Lee and Dan Shalmon, "Searching for Oil: China's Oil Strategies in Africa," in China into Africa: Trade, Aid, and Influence, ed. Robert I. Rotberg (Washington, D.C.: Brookings Institution, 2008), 109–36; Ian Taylor, "China's Oil Diplomacy in Africa," International Affairs 82, no. 5 (2006): 937–59; and Spencer Swartz and Simon Hall, "Nigeria, China Sign Major Oil Deal," Wall Street Journal, May 15, 2010.

[19] Daniel Cancel, "China Lends Venezuela $20 Billion, Secures Oil Supply," Bloomberg News, April 19, 2010.

[20] "Brazil Sells Oil to China, Expects $10 Billion Loan," China Daily, February 20, 2009.

[21] Jeffrey Jones, "Sinopec Makes China's Biggest Canada Oil Sands Deal," Reuters, April 12, 2010.

[22] "China: Energy Companies Change Strategic Tack," Oxford Analytica, Daily Brief, April 26, 2010.

Combined with Beijing's coordinated energy and financial diplomacy, the overall scale of overseas investments by China's NOCs in 200 projects located in 50 countries and with estimated investments of $50 billion have contributed to a more politicized, competitive, and zero-sum environment.[23] Yet other Asian countries, as well as the United States, have also fueled and fed this atmosphere of energy nationalism. Japan, which is fully dependent on imported oil, natural gas, and coal supplies, has long pursued a broadly mercantilist approach to its energy security, although the country has also joined in Western multilateral energy security institutions such as the IEA and APEC (Asia-Pacific Economic Cooperation) (see **Table 4**). In response to the early oil shocks in the 1970s, Japan rapidly boosted direct state support for Japan National Oil Company (JNOC) in order to secure control of overseas oil supplies. JNOC funded a number of smaller oil exploration companies, including Inpex and Japex, to expand Japan's oil acquisition capabilities.[24] Though the historical results of Japan's efforts have been disappointing, Tokyo has continued to support this strategy by increasing funding for state-sponsored companies and by more aggressively seeking nationally controlled oil supplies (so-called Hinamoru oil).[25] The record has been mixed, and in several cases Tokyo's efforts have brought Japan into direct competition with China over access to new resources.[26]

The most prominent recent example of Japan's frustrations is its long struggle to secure development rights to Iran's Azadegan oil field. Inpex negotiated with Iran for several years to secure a development contract but was caught between the energy security goal of controlling an equity stake in such a large oil field and Japan's strategic alliance with the United States. While Japan's Ministry of Economy, Trade and Industry (METI) advocated that Tokyo ratify the deal to meet the country's strategic energy needs, the Foreign Ministry argued that a deal with Iran would seriously damage the

---

[23] "China: Energy Companies Change Strategic Tack."

[24] For further historical background see Herberg, "Asia's Energy Insecurity," 354–57.

[25] For an excellent discussion of Japan's more recent energy security policies, see Reiji Takeishi, "Japan's Energy Security Strategy," in Fesharaki, Kim, and Kim, *Energy Security in the North Pacific*, 208–56.

[26] On the state of Sino-Japanese energy security competition, see Kent Calder, "China and Japan's Simmering Rivalry," *Foreign Affairs* 85, no. 2 (March/April 2006), http://www.foreignaffairs. com/articles/61515/kent-e-calder/china-and-japans-simmering-rivalry; Kent Calder, "Sino-Japanese Energy Relations: Prospects for Deepening Strategic Competition" (report of "Japan's Contemporary Challenges" conference at Yale University, March 9–10, 2007); Wenran Jiang, "History Aside, Chinese-Japanese Conflict Now Plays Out over Gas and Oil Reserves in the East China Sea," *YaleGlobal*, April 25, 2006; Janet Xuanli Liao, "The Politics of Oil behind Sino-Japanese Energy Security Strategies," Institute for Security and Development Policy, Asia Paper, March 2008; Janet Xuanli Liao, "Sino-Japanese Energy Security and Regional Stability: The Case of the East China Sea Gas Exploration," *East Asia* 25, no. 1 (March 2008): 57–78; and Shoichi Itoh, "China's Surging Energy Demand: Trigger for Conflict or Cooperation with Japan," *East Asia* 25, no. 1 (March 2008): 79–98.

TABLE 4   Asia's energy import dependence, 2008

		Crude oil (mmbd)	Natural gas (bcm)	Coal (mtoe)
Asian region	Demand	25.3	485.3	2,031.2
	Imports	17.4	74.1	0.5
	Import share	*69%*	*15%*	*0%*
China	Demand	8.0	80.7	1,406.3
	Imports	4.2	4.6	-8.2
	Import share	*53%*	*6%*	*-1%*
India	Demand	2.9	41.4	231.4
	Imports	2.1	10.8	37.1
	Import share	*73%*	*26%*	*16%*
Japan	Demand	4.8	93.7	128.7
	Imports	4.8	93.7	128.0
	Import share	*100%*	*100%*	*99%*
South Korea	Demand	2.3	39.7	66.1
	Imports	2.3	39.7	64.8
	Import share	*100%*	*100%*	*98%*

SOURCE: "BP Statistical Review of World Energy 2009."

alliance with the United States, which was pressing Japan to withdraw from investments in Iran. In the end, U.S. pressure, combined with Iran's onerous investment terms, led Inpex to largely withdraw from the project. Much to Japan's chagrin, China's CNPC has taken on the deal, although it is still unclear how soon CNPC will proceed.

In another frustrating case for Japan, Tokyo intervened late in China's negotiations with Russia on the construction of the oil pipeline to northern China mentioned earlier. Tokyo offered Russia a large financial package to develop the East Siberian oil fields and build an oil pipeline to the Pacific coast at Nakhodka, where the oil could be shipped to Japan. Russia played China and Japan against one another for several years while Moscow waffled over various issues of the field and pipeline development. Ultimately, China secured the deal with a $25 billion loan to Rosneft and Transneft in 2009. Although Moscow has promised Tokyo that it will extend the pipeline to the Pacific coast eventually, this remains a dubious commercial proposition.

A third case involving the development of a natural gas field in the East China Sea illustrates the fraught nature of the energy security competition between Japan and China. China has been developing a modest-sized offshore natural gas field, the Chunxiao field, which lies close to the median line claimed by Japan as the boundary of its exclusive economic zone (EEZ). Moreover, the field is not far from the disputed Senkaku/Diaoyu Islands. Tokyo has argued that the gas field might extend across the median line, in which case Japan would claim a right to part of the field's production. China has rejected this claim and argued that, based on the extension of China's continental shelf, the EEZ demarcation line is much farther east, putting the field nowhere near what China defines as the EEZ line. This dispute escalated quickly to the point where Chinese gunboats were used to force Japanese seismic vessels out of the area. After several years of haggling, in 2008 Japan and China came to a general agreement to negotiate some form of joint development in the area; however, this plan has so far not been completed and negotiations continue irregularly with no conclusion.

In other areas, Japan's heightened support for its oil companies— now largely under the rubric of the Japan Oil, Gas and Metals National Corporation (JOGMEC) and Inpex—has enjoyed some success. Despite the problems with the Eastern Siberia–Pacific Ocean (ESPO) pipeline, JOGMEC has acquired significant exploration rights in East Siberia. Japan also retains a significant interest through Mitsui and Mitsubishi in the huge Sakhalin-2 LNG project put together by Shell but now majority-controlled by Gazprom. Inpex controls roughly 100 mbd of oil production in Indonesia, and a separate consortium, Jodco, holds a 200 mbd equity stake in United Arab Emirates (UAE) oil production. Moreover, Japan has been much more successful in securing control over LNG supplies on which it is 100% import dependent. Japanese companies virtually invented the LNG business during the 1960s and 1970s, and Mitsubishi, Mitsui, and Marubeni are major stakeholders in a range of LNG projects in the Asia-Pacific region, as well as in Qatar and the UAE.

South Korea's energy dilemmas closely resemble those of its neighbor Japan, and, consequently, Seoul's response to its energy security anxieties has been similar as well. Korea, like Japan, depends on imports for all of its oil and natural gas supplies, as well as to satisfy much of its coal needs (see Table 4). Korea became a member of the IEA in the early 1990s and holds a 90-day supply of strategic oil stocks as part of its IEA obligations to be able to release stocks during potential supply disruptions. Seoul has promoted overseas oil and gas supply development by the state firm Korea National Oil Company (KNOC) since 1977. Currently, KNOC has various projects underway in 37 countries. Yet, although Seoul has invested

$10 billion in efforts to control global supplies, oil controlled by Korean companies presently accounts for only about 3% of Korea's domestic oil consumption. Korea's most successful recent projects have been in Yemen, Argentina, Peru, the North Sea, and the United States, along with new fields under development in Iraq, Colombia, Kazakhstan, Venezuela, Libya, and Vietnam. Despite limited results to date, the government has aimed to raise the share of oil consumption to be met by Korean equity oil production from 10% to 24% by 2016 while raising its natural gas target to meet 39% of consumption from Korean overseas equity production.[27] To reach these targets, Seoul has set up a special government funding account for overseas resource development projects, the Energy Project Special Account.[28] Korean companies have not faced direct investment competition with Chinese companies as often as Japan has, but this is changing. In mid-2009, KNOC lost out in bidding against China's Sinopec to acquire a large, London-based oil company, Addax, which has sizeable production in Nigeria as well as in the Kurdish region of Iraq.[29] KNOC is handicapped when competing with Chinese NOCs because state financing is much more limited in Korea. Additionally, KNOC is expected to earn market returns on investments, unlike many Chinese NOCs, which are focused only on adding production.

India is the other major regional power in Asia that is caught up in the strategic competition to secure overseas energy supplies.[30] India is now over 70% dependent on imports to satisfy its oil needs, and this percentage is likely to rise toward 90% as domestic oil production remains flat and demand grows strongly. Of those oil imports, roughly three-quarters comes from the Persian Gulf. India also now imports approximately one-quarter of its natural gas, all in the form of LNG from the Gulf, as well as 16% of its growing coal consumption (see Table 4). Rising dependence on oil imports, combined with the perception that China's reach outward to secure oil supplies may undermine India's access to future supplies, has provoked a strong push by New Delhi to secure overseas oil supplies for India. Oil and Natural Gas Corporation (ONGC), India's major NOC, is moving rapidly to acquire overseas positions through its international arm, ONGC Videsh

---

[27] See Ji-Chul Ryu, "Korea's Perspective on Energy Security," in Fesharaki, Kim, and Kim, *Energy Security in the North Pacific*, 290–319; and commentaries by Kent Calder and Mikkal E. Herberg, in Ibid., 320–33.

[28] Shin Jung-Won, "South Korea Aims to Triple KNOC Assets by 2012," Dow Jones Newswires, June 12, 2008.

[29] David Winning, "KNOC Loses Race for Addax, But Has Edge on China Peers," Dow Jones Newswires, June 25, 2009.

[30] For an excellent discussion of U.S. energy security policy, see David Pumphrey, "U.S. Perspective on National Energy Security," in Fesharaki, Kim, and Kim, *Energy Security in the North Pacific*, 118–44.

regional stability and for global energy markets. The collision of the energy security strategies of the Asian powers, combined with the U.S. perception that the statist energy security strategies across the region threaten to undermine free market investment and U.S. access to oil and gas resources, has deeply politicized the region's energy security dynamics. The emergence of bilateral energy supply competition has aggravated and mirrored the major bilateral strategic rivalries in the region and contributed to regional tensions. Energy is now an important and toxic element in U.S.-China relations, adding to the complexity of an already complex relationship. Even though the United States and China have found ways to cooperate on clean energy, renewable resources, and efficiency, such cooperation has done little to reduce the strategic mistrust over energy. Energy has also become an important ingredient in the Sino-Japanese rivalry, as Japan seeks to grapple with the long-term implications of a rising China and re-evaluates its traditional alliance with the United States. Sino-Indian rivalry, pitting the two rising Asian regional powers against one another, is now being further aggravated by energy suspicions, particularly on India's side. New Delhi perceives China to be encircling India with the country's growing regional and energy ties in Pakistan, Myanmar, Sri Lanka, and Central Asia. Energy has even become a divisive issue between the United States and India as Washington presses India to abandon its traditionally close relationship with energy supplier Iran. Presently, these problems are aggravating key bilateral tensions in the region rather than threatening real open conflict. Yet Asia as a region can ill afford these toxic pressures on critical strategic rivalries, particularly as the region seeks to manage the rise of China and continually adapt regional institutions and strategic relations to adjust peacefully to China's global emergence.

In terms of energy markets, as the region continues to stumble down the path of energy nationalism, these dynamics will contribute to worsening conditions in global markets, including chronically high and volatile energy prices, unstable supplies, growing dependence on unreliable political regimes, and more politicization of energy investment. World energy markets have become increasingly globalized, integrated, efficient, and transparent over the past 35 years since the first oil shocks in the 1970s. This trend has been reflected in the development of efficient futures markets, spot markets and prices, transparent data on global supply and demand, highly flexible oil and gas supply contracts, and a widening development of new supply sources from new countries. Periods of oil supply shortages now produce higher prices, but at the same time markets rapidly sort out supply movements. There are thus no real physical shortages as happened in the 1970s—i.e., oil is always available in the market at a price and cannot be hoarded effectively on a sufficient scale by national authorities to influence market prices. The market is now too big, integrated, dynamic, and transparent for that to happen. OPEC, through its production management and quota policies, certainly can have a powerful influence on supplies and prices. With the development of an integrated, flexible, and transparent global oil market, however, OPEC's job has become much more difficult, given that the organization can only influence prices indirectly and often ineffectively. For oil-importing countries, the globalization and integration of oil markets has reduced the power of OPEC and increased the influence of market supply, demand, and investment. At the governmental level, industrial countries created the IEA to help manage supply shocks, have forged a system of strategic oil stocks and emergency management, and have put energy security regularly on the agenda of the group of eight (G-8) in order to work toward cooperative management of global energy supplies.

This trend toward flexible and transparent markets is being fundamentally threatened, however, by Asia's growing national and mercantilist efforts to control supplies, which risk the increasing balkanization of global energy markets. The growing prevalence of mercantilist practices of overlaying oil and gas investment and supply contracts with bilateral political, economic, financial, and aid components could return Asia to the nationally based, rigid, opaque market structure that predated and helped lead to the oil shocks of the 1970s. Such practices risk undermining the effectiveness of globalized markets to handle sharp changes in market conditions, and increase the politicization of oil and gas markets and investment. This balkanization is the energy market version of "beggar thy neighbor" trade practices, such as protectionism and competitive currency depreciation. At the governmental level, the reticence of China and India to engage seriously with the IEA is clear evidence that the new large oil consumers and importers see energy markets in sharply national rather than multilateral terms. To be fair, this is not Asia's problem alone; this trend is also being fed by the rise of NOCs globally and the growing encroachment of governments into energy markets since the turn of the century.

While presently the region seems headed down a troubling path, this outcome might be avoided by seeking to turn energy into a source of regional cooperation and competitive markets rather than national competition and politicized markets.[34] The major oil consumers and importers in the region have fundamental mutual interests in stable global energy markets, secure

---

[34] This section relies heavily on Mikkal E. Herberg, "Energy Security in the Asia-Pacific Region and Policy for the New Administration," in *America's Role in Asia: Asian and American Views* (San Francisco: Asia Foundation, 2008), 131–44.

and free access to supplies, reasonable prices, and reliable energy transit. The region could, alternatively, work toward building trust, managing the impulse toward competition, and encouraging cooperative efforts to promote new supplies and build new regional energy infrastructure.

This approach, however, will require stronger leadership and a reordering of strategic priorities across the region. Governments will need, first, to promote regional energy cooperation and, second, to better manage likely areas of tensions over energy. The region should approach energy cooperation at regional, multilateral, and bilateral levels. As both a strategic and an energy superpower, the United States must be at the center of any regional dialogue on common energy concerns. At the same time, China, India, and Japan must also play an important role in this dialogue. China is becoming a global energy power, India is becoming a regional energy power, and Japan is the third-largest oil importer in the world and the global superpower of energy efficiency.

Confidence-building and improving mutual trust should be the goal of energy cooperation. Governments should focus on common interests in market stability and on sustaining competition for access to supplies rather than state-led exclusive deals. In a globalized energy market, no country can achieve energy security unilaterally. Over time this dialogue could potentially strengthen regional oil and natural gas production and pipeline developments. Regional Asian forums presently are ineffective in addressing major regional security concerns related to energy.

Multilaterally, the region should aim to involve China and India more directly in global institutions such as the IEA. The IEA was established in the 1970s as a mechanism for managing supply disruptions. However, today the world's global emergency oil management system does not include China or India, two of the world's six largest oil-consuming and importing countries. Involvement in the IEA also would provide expertise on energy efficiency, demand management, technology, and policymaking that could accelerate the learning curve of energy policymakers in China and India.

Bilaterally, energy dialogues are already underway among the region's key energy-consuming countries—the United States, China, and India—but greater cooperation is needed on many issues, including demand growth, energy efficiency, energy-saving technology, and reducing pollution. As **Figure 2** shows, China and India together could account for over 40% of growth in oil consumption, 75% of coal demand growth, and 45% of growth in global carbon emissions over the next two decades. Energy dialogues by the United States with both countries need to be ambitious and raise the importance of energy in strategic cooperation. U.S. policymakers should give such dialogues higher-level political support and greater resources to meet the challenge.

FIGURE 2   China's and India's share of growth in global energy demand, 2007–30

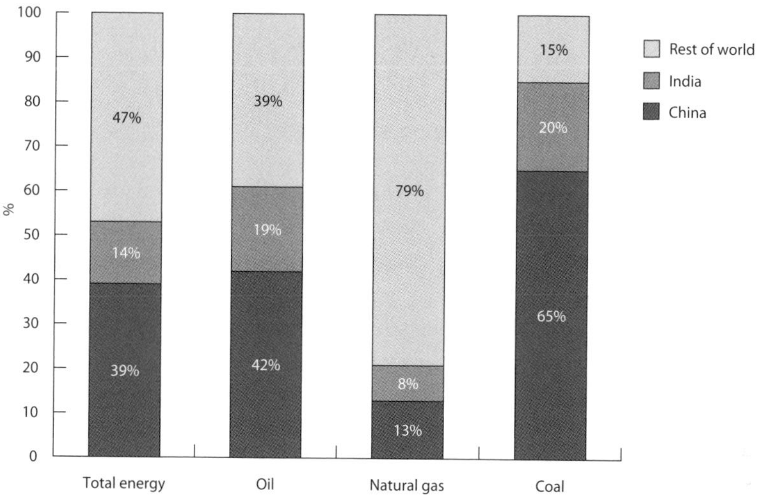

Legend:
- Rest of world
- India
- China

Total energy: China 39%, India 14%, Rest of world 47%
Oil: China 42%, India 19%, Rest of world 39%
Natural gas: China 13%, India 8%, Rest of world 79%
Coal: China 65%, India 20%, Rest of world 15%

SOURCE: IEA, *World Energy Outlook 2009*.

Managing Areas of Tension

Significantly strengthened Asian energy cooperation is unlikely to completely resolve a number of tensions that will probably continue to undermine regional relationships. These revolve around the key players' competitive energy diplomacy and access strategies to oil and gas supplies in sensitive countries. Such tensions must be carefully managed.

U.S.-China energy relations face a legacy of distrust, and China's energy relations in problem states such as Iran, Sudan, and Myanmar have only further fueled suspicions over its long-term strategic intentions. Though the current U.S.-China Strategic and Economic Dialogue includes discussion of energy, the dialogue has no significant focus on energy security in a strategic context. Energy needs to be put on the strategic agenda in these high-level executive bilateral discussions.

Although the United States has sought to use energy cooperation as a means to improve and cement stronger strategic relations with India, two issues loom in bilateral energy relations that must be managed to avoid new tensions. First, India seeks to expand energy ties with Iran. Second, India's energy investments in Sudan will remain a potential point of disagreement, although U.S. attention on energy investments in Sudan has thus far focused on China. Strategic disagreements over energy diplomacy have also emerged in U.S.-Japan relations, including a dispute over Japan's recent oil field investment plans in Iran, which provoked serious opposition from the United States. Nonetheless, the impact of these energy disagreements on bilateral relations is likely to be limited owing to the strength of the U.S.-Japan alliance.

Rare Earth Minerals and Asian Geopolitics

Although the enormous expansion in demand for energy and mineral raw materials in Asia has driven prices higher over time, energy has been the main commodity subject to strong politicization. Tight supplies for major commodities continue to be largely sorted out by markets, albeit with enormous price volatility. Recently, however, the global supply of rare earth minerals (REM) has become a new source of strategic and economic concern among regional governments—most importantly, the United States, but also Japan and Korea. The growing focus on REMs comes from two sources. First, demand is growing rapidly for minerals required for two critical energy and defense applications. REMs are very important components in many new clean and renewable energy technologies and in many communications technologies. For example, large quantities of REMs are required to manufacture hybrid electric motors and batteries for vehicles, magnets for high-tech wind turbines, computer hard drives, mobile phones, energy-efficient light bulbs, and fiber optics. Hence, the availability of REMs is becoming an important determinant of industrial competitiveness among the major economies of Asia to lead in new energy technologies. Second, REMs are critically important components of many high-tech defense products. The U.S. Defense Department has recently studied its dependence on REMs for key defense applications and has determined that REMs are critical to precision-guided munitions, lasers, communications systems, radar systems, avionics, night vision equipment, and satellites.[35]

While the importance of REM supplies for new clean energy and defense applications is growing, the availability of the raw minerals is extraordinarily concentrated, most importantly in China, which currently produces an estimated 97% of the market REMs.[36] These are located mainly in South China and Inner Mongolia. A single mine in Baotou in Inner

---

[35] See "Rare Earth Materials in the Defense Supply Chain," U.S Government Accountability Office, GAO-10-617R, April 14, 2010.

[36] Ibid.

Mongolia produces 50% of the world's REMs. Over the past three years China has been gradually reducing export quotas and raising export taxes on REMs in order to ensure that limited supplies are available to Chinese manufacturers as they ramp up production of a range of energy-efficient technologies.[37] Production has also been reduced due to government efforts to shut down small, highly polluting REM producers to reduce environmental damage.

As a result, there are growing concerns in the United States, Japan, and Korea over the availability of REMs. The United States was formerly a significant producer of REMs from the Mountain Pass Mine in California, the largest known non-Chinese ore deposit, but this mine was closed in 2002 because of high costs, low prices, and environmental constraints. Molycorp Minerals, a large U.S. mining company, is currently working to reopen the Mountain Pass Mine, but it is unlikely to be in production again before 2012. Even then, the mine does not contain many REMs that are available from China. A few small REM mines are nearing operation in Australia, and potential new supplies could likewise be available from small deposits being explored in Canada, Russia, Brazil, and India. However, the time and costs of developing the mining operation and of ore refining and processing are daunting. The U.S. Department of Defense estimates that a full-scale ore-to-product operation takes from seven to fifteen years to develop due to investments, costs, and permitting.

There are thus growing suspicions across the region that China is seeking to tighten its control over REMs and limit exports to enhance the country's competitive advantage in key energy technology industries. Beijing's Ministry of Industry and Information Technology has developed a detailed plan for the REM industry in order to ensure the availability of REMs to Chinese companies for manufacturing high-tech energy products. Many international manufacturers of these products claim that supply conditions are compelling them to consider locating their production in China in order to guarantee access to raw materials and remain cost-competitive. Both Japan and Korea are thought to have stockpiled substantial REM supplies due to concerns about availability, but there is little public information available to substantiate this, and both Tokyo and Seoul have expressed growing concern over REM availability. The U.S. Department of Defense is currently developing a study, to be completed in September 2010, of the defense and strategic implications of the potentially limited availability of REMs.

---

[37] See Keith Bradsher, "China Tightens Grip on Rare Minerals," *New York Times*, August 31, 2009.

Conclusions

Asia's rapid economic and industrial growth is driving an enormous surge in energy and industrial commodity consumption that is fundamentally altering the global market and prices for these products. In the context of Asia's strategic environment and given the lack of regional institutions to mediate tensions, an increasingly competitive and nationalistic atmosphere has developed as countries pursue control over energy and some other raw materials. These energy and commodity tensions are increasingly spilling over into regional geopolitics and aggravating key bilateral rivalries. Although the main players, including the United States, are large energy importers and, therefore, have common interests in working together to help stabilize global energy and commodity markets, cooperative regional efforts have been anemic and largely ineffective. It will take strong and courageous leadership in the region's key capitals, especially Beijing and Washington, to transform this competitive and destructive environment into a more cooperative and productive one. Without stronger and more visionary leadership, the region faces a future of greater instability in energy and commodity markets, higher and more volatile prices for key determinants of economic prosperity, greater risks of damaging supply disruptions, and deepening intraregional political tensions.

EXECUTIVE SUMMARY

This chapter assesses likely trends in nuclear energy and nonproliferation within Asia in the next two decades and examines the implications for the U.S.

MAIN ARGUMENT:

Asia's rapid growth in nuclear power use will significantly influence safe and secure operation of nuclear facilities, the global nuclear supply chain, and the potential for further nuclear weapons proliferation. Although further growth may occur in nuclear power entrant states in Southeast Asia, the spread of nuclear technologies will not necessarily lead to more proliferation as long as the U.S. and other powers can ensure security alliances and can integrate pariah states such as North Korea and Burma into the international system. Similarly, Asian powers play a major role in supporting international efforts to prevent Iran from developing nuclear weapons.

POLICY IMPLICATIONS:

- Ensuring safe and secure operations of nuclear power plants in Asia is clearly in U.S. interests because a major accident or an attack on such a facility would likely harm the prospects for further expansion of nuclear power worldwide.

- To remain economically competitive, U.S. nuclear companies must leverage corporate partnerships and demonstrate that they can build plants on time and within budget.

- Stopping further enrichment and reprocessing plants is unlikely to occur, but the U.S. should lead efforts to require more effective means of monitoring and safeguarding these facilities and to limit such plants to allies and currently nuclear-armed states.

- Shoring up security alliances will serve as an effective means of nonproliferation. In particular, redoubling coordinated efforts to eliminate nuclear weapons in North Korea will help quell the desire for such weapons in Japan and South Korea.

The Implications of Expanded Nuclear Energy in Asia

Charles D. Ferguson

Relatively rapid nuclear energy developments in Asia will significantly influence safe and secure operation of nuclear power plants, supply and demand for all components of the nuclear fuel cycle, and potential for further proliferation of nuclear weapons programs. These issues will have profound regional and global consequences. If a major accident or attack, for instance, were to occur at a nuclear power plant in Asia, such an event could quell the demand for nuclear power worldwide. The concern is that overly fast growth in nuclear power plant construction may outstrip a country's ability to train enough highly skilled personnel to operate, guard, and inspect the plants and thus ensure the highest standards of safety and security.

Concerning demand, in the past few years Asia has been the primary region for construction of new nuclear plants, and this demand is projected to continue for the next several years to few decades. The global supply chain has struggled to respond, however, because of the past two decades of comparatively stagnant global demand. Following on the heels of Asian nuclear demand is increasing interest in several Middle Eastern states for their first nuclear plants. Further, within Asia itself, Southeast Asian states such as Indonesia, Thailand, and Vietnam appear on the verge of ordering their first nuclear plants. Although meeting these demands may further stress the international supply chain, this renewed interest in nuclear power presents economic opportunities for the major Asian states that already produce nuclear power, such as China, India, Japan, and South Korea, to supply entrant states.

Charles D. Ferguson is President of the Federation of American Scientists. He can be reached at <cferguson@fas.org>.

Because nuclear technologies are inherently dual-use, in that facilities that can make fuel for peaceful reactors can also produce fissile material for nuclear weapons, increasing demand for nuclear power in Asia and the rest of the world raises the danger of further nuclear weapons proliferation. This danger will be especially acute if more non–nuclear weapon states acquire the capability to enrich uranium or reprocess spent nuclear fuel: the two dual-use technologies. The challenge thus is to ensure that the spread of the peaceful atom does not result in uncontrolled use of these technologies.

Increased peaceful nuclear energy use, however, will not necessarily lead to increased proliferation of nuclear weapons in Asia. Although enrichment and reprocessing facilities can give states latent weapons capabilities, this technological capacity is a necessary but not a sufficient condition for proliferation. The political imperative to pursue proliferation is the key driver.[1] This imperative can arise from the perceived need to protect against neighbors' or rivals' nuclear or non-nuclear military capabilities, from the influence of domestic political and bureaucratic interests, or from the view that great-power status may result from possessing the ultimate weapon.[2] Although all these factors have played a role in the decision of some Asian states to acquire nuclear weapons, the majority of Asian states have refrained from such acquisition.

Countervailing factors have consequently convinced many countries to remain as non–nuclear weapon states. For instance, U.S. security alliances have played a role in assuring allies such as Japan, South Korea, and Taiwan, which all have substantial nuclear power infrastructure. Many other Asian states, however, are not under the protection of U.S. nuclear deterrence and still have not acquired nuclear weapons. States with strongly vested interests in the international economy have tended to refrain from this acquisition.[3] Those Asian states that have acquired nuclear weapons, namely, China, India, and Pakistan, did so prior to their entry into the global economy. This observation is especially important for several Southeast Asian states with rapidly developing and globalizing economies and with interest in building their first nuclear power plants. Here again, U.S. policy can shape these states' security decisions by helping to ensure access to the international economy.

---

[1] This is shown using in-depth statistical analysis in Stephen M. Meyer, *The Dynamics of Nuclear Proliferation* (Chicago: University of Chicago Press, 1984).

[2] See, for example, Scott D. Sagan, "Why Do States Build Nuclear Weapons? Three Models in Search of a Bomb," *International Security* 21, no. 3 (Winter 1996/97): 54–86.

[3] Etel Solingen, *Nuclear Logics: Contrasting Paths in East Asia and the Middle East* (Princeton: Princeton University Press, 2007).

The themes of cooperation and competition pervade this chapter. The next section sets the background for where Asian states fit within the increasingly globalized nature of the nuclear power industry, what has motivated these states to acquire this energy source, and what Asian states have the infrastructure for nuclear weapons production. The following section examines nuclear energy developments in more depth, paying special attention to the major nuclear power producers, including China, India, Japan, and South Korea, and to the aspirant nuclear power states in Southeast Asia. The discussion in this section focuses on the plans for nuclear power use in each country, the implications for the global supply chain, concerns about maintaining safety and security, and the potential for more proliferation. Because of the profound security consequences of increased proliferation, the succeeding section assesses nuclear weapons trends in Asia and the governmental policies that may strengthen or weaken the nonproliferation regime. The concluding section analyzes the implications of nuclear energy and proliferation trends in Asia for U.S. efforts to ensure safe and secure use of nuclear power, facilitate a well-functioning nuclear supply chain, and create a more effective nonproliferation system.

Asian States, the Nuclear Power Industry, and the Potential for Proliferation

The past ten years have been a time of astonishing upsurge in nuclear power demand in Asia, especially in China, India, and South Korea. Several Asian states, including Bangladesh, Indonesia, Malaysia, the Philippines, Thailand, and Vietnam, have proposed acquiring their first nuclear power plants. **Table 1** provides a list of currently operating nuclear plants in Asia, and **Table 2** details plants that are under construction, planned, and proposed. As of early 2010, more than two-thirds of the reactors under construction are being built in Asia. Thus, Asia has emerged as the primary growth area in the world for nuclear power. That could change with the expressed interest of several Arab states to acquire their first nuclear power plants and the new stimulus for nuclear power plants in the United States and in parts of Europe. But because of the long lead time needed to develop a national infrastructure for the use of nuclear power, Middle Eastern states will likely require ten or more years before they can handle substantial construction of nuclear power plants. For example, the United Arab Emirates (UAE), which leads the region in nuclear energy development and has recently signed a commercial agreement with South Korea for the construction of four large nuclear reactors, will most likely not have operating nuclear plants until about 2020.

TABLE 1   Nuclear power reactors in Asia as of early 2010

State or territory	Nuclear-generated electrical energy in 2008 (billion kWh)	Percentage of domestic electricity (%)	Operable reactors in February 2010	Power generation capacity in February 2010 (MWe)
China	65.3	2.2	11	8,587
India	13.2	2.0	18	3,981
Japan	240.5	24.9	54	47,102
Pakistan	1.7	1.9	2	400
Russia	152.1	16.9	31	21,821
South Korea	144.3	35.6	20	17,716
Taiwan	39.3	17.1	6	4,927

SOURCE: International Atomic Energy Agency (IAEA), Power Reactor Information System database, 2010; and World Nuclear Association (WNA), WNA Reactor database, 2010.

NOTE: The commercial Russian reactors are almost exclusively deployed in the European part of Russia.

While the United States enabled many states in Asia to acquire nuclear power by supplying them with U.S.-origin technology, China, Japan, and South Korea have made innovations to U.S. nuclear power designs to become increasingly more self-reliant. Both Japan and South Korea have become major nuclear technology exporting states by following the model of receiving foreign assistance for their first set of reactors, requiring technology transfer from these suppliers, building up domestic nuclear construction capacity, and then modifying plant designs for export as largely Japanese or Korean manufactured nuclear plants, while giving a share of the royalties and business to the original designers.

Although China began to develop commercial nuclear energy a decade or two after Japan and South Korea, Beijing is emulating the course charted by Tokyo and Seoul. If China achieves its ambitious goal of more than one hundred operating commercial reactors by 2030, it will likely become the state with the most nuclear power plants in the world unless a major surge in construction occurs in the United States. China may also emerge by then as a major supplier of nuclear technologies and may garner clients in Africa, the Middle East, and Southeast Asia.

Energy security concerns have motivated China, India, Japan, South Korea, and Taiwan to invest substantially in nuclear power. But this motivation is not monolithic. Japan, South Korea, and Taiwan decided in

TABLE 2   Reactors under construction, planned, and proposed in Asia

State or territory	Reactors under construction		Reactors planned		Reactors proposed	
	No.	MWe	No.	MWe	No.	MWe
China	20	21,880	37	41,590	120	120,000
India	5	2,774	23	21,500	15	20,000
Indonesia	0	0	2	2,000	4	4,000
Japan	1	1,373	13	17,915	1	1,300
Kazakhstan	0	0	2	600	2	600
North Korea	0	0	1	950	0	0
Pakistan	1	300	2	600	2	2,000
Russia	9	7,130	8	8,000	37	36,680
South Korea	6	6,700	6	8,190	0	0
Taiwan	2	2,600	0	0	6	8,000
Thailand	0	0	2	2,000	4	4,000
Vietnam	0	0	2	2,000	8	8,000

SOURCE: IAEA, 2010; and WNA, 2010.

NOTE: For planned reactors, funding or at least a major government or industry commitment is underway, and most of these reactors will likely be under construction or built within the next ten years. For proposed reactors, industry or the government has projected a goal number of additional reactors and may not necessarily have identified funding. Depending on availability of resources and handling of financing, political, and other hurdles, many of these reactors may begin construction within the next fifteen years. In the case of Russia, the commercial reactors are almost exclusively deployed in the European part of Russia.

the 1970s to make major commitments to nuclear power because of their relative lack of indigenous sources of coal, oil, and natural gas. These countries import practically all of their fossil fuels. In comparison, whereas China and India have relatively abundant supplies of coal for electricity generation, these countries' rapidly expanding economies and concomitant increased demand for electricity are driving their governments to devote more resources to nuclear energy in order to diversify their energy portfolios. Although China and India are not required by international law to reduce greenhouse gas emissions, Chinese and Indians are growing increasingly concerned about the harmful environmental effects of fossil fuel usage, a major contributor to such emissions. An operating nuclear power plant does not emit greenhouse gases.

Access to weapons-usable technologies, formation of security alliances, and adherence to the Nuclear Non-Proliferation Treaty (NPT) have affected the strategic development of various Asian states. While much international attention has focused lately on Iran and the greater Middle East, Asia arguably has the most complex security environment from the perspective of nuclear proliferation. The region contains two NPT-recognized nuclear weapon states (China and Russia), three nuclear-armed states outside of the NPT (India, North Korea, and Pakistan), one state with a latent nuclear weapons capability (Japan), one state with sufficient nuclear infrastructure to make nuclear weapons in a relatively short period of time (South Korea), and a political entity with similar infrastructure (Taiwan). In addition, states such as Australia, Indonesia, and Kazakhstan have research facilities that could form the starter kits of latent nuclear weapons programs.

The main technical requirement for such programs is to have either uranium enrichment or reprocessing of spent fuel facilities. The spent fuel comes from nuclear reactors, which produce plutonium, a fissile material. These two dual-use technologies provide the capacity to make either fuel for peaceful nuclear reactors or fissile material for nuclear bombs. While China, India, Japan, North Korea, Russia, and Pakistan have acquired one or both technologies, only Japan has refrained from using this capability to make fissile material for bombs. Because of Japan's status as a non–nuclear weapon state, a member in good standing with the NPT, and a close ally of the United States, it poses little or no threat of developing nuclear weapons. But that could change depending on the evolving security environment and Tokyo's relationship with Washington.

Nuclear Energy Developments

China

China's nuclear power capacity has grown considerably in the last decade. In 2001, China's nuclear power capacity was slightly less than that of Finland.[4] By 2010, China had emerged as the biggest engine for global growth in nuclear power plant construction. Beijing is also determined to become self-reliant in the entire commercial nuclear fuel cycle by leveraging assistance from France on reprocessing and Russia on enrichment. To ensure uranium supplies, China has bought substantial shares of mines in Kazakhstan, one of the top three suppliers, and in African countries with significant uranium deposits. The uranium deal that captured the

---

[4] John Moens, "China's Nuclear Industry," U.S. Energy Information Administration, http://www.eia. doe.gov/cneaf/nuclear/page/nuc_reactors/china/china.html.

most attention in the past decade was China's 2006 bilateral accord with Australia, another of the top three suppliers, that allows China to explore for uranium in Australia. Australia, which has some of the strictest nuclear export control requirements in the world, had opposed selling uranium to China unless Beijing promised not to use the plutonium derived from the uranium in weapons programs. As indicated by these deals, Beijing views uranium as a strategic resource.

Regarding nuclear reactors, China has bought this technology from Canada, France, Russia, and the United States. While this approach gives some business to nearly all the major reactor suppliers, Beijing has recently settled on a few major designs for the majority of its nuclear plants. In particular, pressurized water reactors (PWR) will predominate. A PWR keeps the hot water in the primary loop circulating through the reactor core under pressure to prevent the water from boiling. The heat is transferred to a secondary water loop in which steam is made in order to turn a turbine to generate electricity. U.S.-based Westinghouse had commercialized many of the first PWRs in the Western world, and France, Japan, and South Korea have derived their PWRs from Westinghouse's models. During the Soviet era, Russia developed its own version of the PWR, designated by the acronym VVER.

Although China has contracted with Russia's Atomstroyexport for power plants at Tianwan, Beijing has focused on French and U.S. PWRs for the largest share of new construction. Leveraging a technology transfer agreement with France, Chinese engineers have created the CPR-1000, which is a 1,000 megawatt electric (MWe) power rated PWR and has been called a replication reactor because of the large number being built. In particular, Beijing is planning on building more than a dozen CPR-1000s in the next ten years, although to export this design China would need to receive permission from France. In 2009 the Westinghouse AP1000 won the competition for China's first inland nuclear power plants, and even more Westinghouse AP1000s are on the drawing board for the coming couple of decades. Prior to this, China's nuclear plants had been confined to the coastal areas, which offered plentiful seawater for cooling the plants and were typically the locations of fastest economic growth.

Looking to the future, China is investigating high temperature gas reactors and fast neutron reactors. The former, if commercially viable, would generate hydrogen that could power buildings and vehicles by serving as an energy carrier in fuel cells. Zero-emission fuel cell vehicles would greatly reduce air pollution in China's cities. The latter reactors can provide as breeder reactors a source of fuel if uranium supplies run low and can offer as burner reactors a means to dispose of long-lived radioactive waste. Presently, fast neutron reactors are considerably more expensive than thermal reactors such as PWRs. Fast reactors have also experienced numerous technical problems despite the more than $100 billion spent worldwide on their development.[5] China, however, is projecting that these reactors may become commercially viable by mid-century, especially if the demand for nuclear power expands, drawing down readily available supplies of natural uranium.

China's centralized government has allowed Beijing to make relatively quick decisions on nuclear plant construction. Large foreign cash reserves have also helped Beijing finance the plants. The China Atomic Energy Authority is primarily responsible for planning nuclear power projects but is controlled by the Commission for Science, Technology and Industry for National Defense under the State Council of Ministers. In March 2008, China established the National Energy Commission (NEC) to replace the National Energy Leading Group, an advisory body to the State Council. The NEC drafts China's national energy development strategy. With respect to nuclear energy development, the China National Nuclear Corporation, which was formed by the State Council as a self-supporting firm in 1988 and has ties to the Chinese military, manages the development of most of China's nuclear sector. China has five state-owned electrical power generation companies. In the nuclear sector, the main generation, distribution, and construction firms include China Power Investment Corporation, China Guangdong Nuclear Power Corporation, China Huaneng Group, China Uranium Corporation, China Overseas Uranium Holding, and China First Heavy Industries. In addition to these state-affiliated firms, China has formed joint ventures with foreign firms such as Areva of France and Doosan Heavy Industries of South Korea.[6]

China's massive nuclear construction has raised safety concerns. One major nuclear accident could halt global nuclear power expansion. After the Chernobyl accident in 1986, the industry is well aware of the chilling effects such an accident could have. Incidents such as lead contamination in children's toys, melamine-tainted milk, and accidents at coal mines have called into question China's ability to maintain high nuclear safety standards. In October 2009, Prime Minister Wen Jiabao ordered a quintupling of safety personnel. Although this action is encouraging, new inspectors will not be ready soon because of the long time needed for training. China must also train tens of thousands of highly skilled workers to build and operate the plants.

[5] Thomas B. Cochran et al., "Fast Breeder Reactor Programs: History and Status," International Panel on Fissile Materials, Research Report, no. 8, February 2010.

[6] WNA, "Nuclear Power in China," Country Brief, February 2010.

Pakistan

While China has yet to emerge as a significant power plant exporter, it has assisted Pakistan in building a few modestly sized nuclear reactors. China formed this deal prior to its 2004 entry into the Nuclear Suppliers Group (NSG), which requires a recipient state to have full-scope safeguards on its nuclear program. Pakistan, a non-NPT state, does not meet that requirement. In light of the U.S.-India nuclear deal and the NSG exemption for India, Islamabad has expressed interest in receiving outside support for its peaceful nuclear program. The NSG will likely withhold such support, however, because Pakistan has a poor record in controlling nuclear technology, as demonstrated by the A.Q. Khan network that was centered in Pakistan. Pakistan is also ramping up its capability to make more weapons-grade plutonium. Despite these concerns, China has revived nuclear energy cooperation with Pakistan. In late April 2010, it was revealed that Beijing has agreed to build two more commercial reactors in Pakistan.[7]

India

Over the past ten years, India has experienced dramatic changes in nuclear energy development. Having struggled up through the 1990s with many safety problems, Indian nuclear plant operators have since made significant progress in achieving better safety performance. Assistance from the World Association of Nuclear Operators, a non-governmental group of industry experts, has in part helped its Indian counterparts through confidential peer reviews.[8] Warnings in the 1990s by A. Gopalakrishnan, former chairman of the Indian Atomic Energy Regulatory Board, also played a major role in calling attention to the need for safety improvements. Gopalakrishnan has continued to argue that the government needs to empower the regulatory agency with enough independence and authority to fully investigate potential safety hazards and to order the shutdown of unsafe plants when necessary; otherwise, India will continue to lag in meeting the highest international nuclear safety standards.[9]

India has also lagged in the proportion of electricity generated from nuclear energy, but may be headed for an upswing after the late 2008 opening of the country to the global nuclear market. In 2001, India had several

---

[7] "China to Build Two Nuclear Reactors in Pakistan," Agence France Presse, April 29, 2010.

[8] Zack T. Pate, "Nuclear Plants and WANO: A Partnership for Safety" (paper presented at the Uranium Institute 25th Annual International Symposium, London, August 30–September 1, 2000), http://www.world-nuclear.org/sym/2000/pate.htm.

[9] A. Gopalakrishnan, "India Poor Nuclear Safety," *Current Affairs*, December 21, 2009, http://thecurrentaffairs.com/india-poor-nuclear-safety.html.

modest power ratings. Such plants also have the advantage of not requiring enriched uranium; they can run on natural uranium fuel. Thus, a state need not invest in an enrichment plant or buy enriched uranium. However, such reactors raise the potential for further nuclear weapons proliferation, given that they can relatively easily be used to produce weapons-grade plutonium. Moreover, PHWRs can be refueled while operating, making it difficult to determine the amount of discharged plutonium just by outside observation of the reactor. In contrast, a light-water reactor must be shut down during refueling, which can be easily observed through satellite monitoring. Because of New Delhi's affinity for South-to-South cooperation, potential clients could emerge in sub-Saharan Africa and Southeast Asia. In April 2009, for example, India announced that it had talked with Malaysia about supplying small reactors to that developing Southeast Asian state.

The Obama administration's new policy to promote sales of small modular reactors may help India win over clients. The value of this policy, however, is that it will encourage proliferation-resistant types of reactors.[13] In particular, Secretary of Energy Steven Chu envisions that small modular reactors can be cost-competitive if many can be built to take advantage of economies of scale.[14] Such reactors with lifetime cores could be leased to a client and plugged into the grid for about 30 to 40 years. At the end of that time, the reactor would be unplugged and taken back to the supplier for disposal of the spent fuel and associated nuclear waste. Another freshly fuelled reactor would then be plugged into the grid. In principle, this deal appears attractive to the client country because it does not need to host a nuclear waste repository, but this feature will likely meet with political resistance in the supplier state unless the client agrees to pay an acceptable cost for managing the waste. Another complicating factor is that only a few of the small modular reactor designs currently being marketed have lifetime cores.

Even if India does not soon start selling small- and medium-sized reactors abroad, it has begun to leverage national manufacturing capability to form alliances with foreign firms. For example, Larsen & Toubro (L&T), India's largest engineering group, decided to venture into the export market for nuclear forgings that are needed to make reactors, pressurizers, and steam generators for nuclear plants. In 2009, L&T reached four agreements with foreign nuclear vendors, including Westinghouse, AECL, GE-Hitachi, and Atomstroyexport. The lifting of sanctions also allowed Hindustan

---

[13] "Nuclear Energy Research and Development Roadmap," U.S. Department of Energy, Report to Congress, April 2010.

[14] Steven Chu, "America's New Nuclear Option: Small Modular Reactors Will Expand the Ways We Use Atomic Power," *Wall Street Journal*, March 23, 2010.

Construction Company, which has constructed more than half of India's reactors, to form a joint venture with Britain's engineering and project management company AMEC. Moreover, in January 2009 Areva reached an agreement with Bharat Forge for casting and forging components.[15] In sum, Indian firms are becoming well placed to take part in worldwide nuclear construction.

South Korea

India may look to South Korea (also known as the Republic of Korea, or ROK) as a role model for developing nuclear export expertise, and South Korea has certainly noted India's success in reaching the agreement with the United States on reprocessing. During the past decade, South Korea has further added to its nuclear power success by becoming an exporter of power plants. The ROK has done this by using technology transfer agreements from the United States to develop the Korean standard AP1400. The AP1400 will be built in the UAE within the next ten years. The UAE selected South Korea's bid because it was the lowest price and because of South Korea's recent experience in constructing a reactor in just over four years.[16] South Korean engineers have developed methods to speed up construction through use of special quick-drying, high quality concrete and management techniques that allow more work to be performed in parallel. While South Korea has been forging ahead in domestic and international nuclear power plant construction, Seoul has felt stymied by restrictions in the U.S.-ROK nuclear energy cooperation agreement, a so-called 123 agreement named after the relevant section in the U.S. Atomic Energy Act of 1954. The U.S.-ROK 123 agreement comes up for renewal in 2014, and U.S. and Korean officials are already discussing the framework for the new agreement.

The present 123 agreement prohibits South Korea from reprocessing spent nuclear fuel. Because this activity is proliferation-prone, and because of the volatile situation on the Korean Peninsula, the United States has denied South Korea permission to reprocess. South Korea, however, has sought to do a form of reprocessing called pyroprocessing, which offers proliferation-resistance compared to the PUREX (plutonium-uranium extraction) technique that is practiced in France, India, Japan, Russia, and the United Kingdom. Pyroprocessing does not completely separate out plutonium and thus is, at least in principle, not very desirable for producing

---

[15] WNA, "Nuclear Power in India," Country Brief, February 15, 2010.

[16] Ann Maclachlan, "Lauvergeon: French Lost UAE Bid Because of Expensive EPR Safety Features," *Nucleonics Week*, January 14, 2010.

nuclear weapons. Nonetheless, the concern is that pyroprocessed material may be converted to pure plutonium in a clandestine PUREX reprocessing plant. Several U.S. nonproliferation experts have sought to discourage South Korea from undertaking any type of reprocessing because of the security risks.[17]

South Korea has expressed interest in pyroprocessing as a way to mitigate the build-up of nuclear waste. By 2016, the spent nuclear fuel pools at the power plant sites will have reached their capacities. Many South Koreans oppose the establishment of a high-level waste repository. Seoul already paid an exorbitant amount of money for a low-level waste facility and thus worries that a high-level storage center would cost an astronomical sum. Pyroprocessing, if it works commercially, could reduce the waste burden by forming fuel out of long-lived fissionable material. To consume this material, South Korea would need a fleet of fast reactors, which are likely decades away from commercialization because of their expense and technical challenges. Even though there is no immediate solution for nuclear waste, many in the South Korean nuclear establishment believe that U.S. permission to perform pyroprocessing would signal a willingness to help South Korea manage nuclear waste and give the South Korean public confidence to allow the government to site and eventually open up an interim high-level waste storage facility. In addition to reprocessing restrictions, the 123 agreement does not permit South Korea to enrich uranium. In 1991, North and South Korea signed a denuclearization of the Korean Peninsula agreement that prohibited both countries from enrichment and reprocessing. However, some South Korean officials believe that they should not have to adhere to this agreement because North Korea has already violated both terms of the accord.[18]

Because of these restrictions on its nuclear program, South Korea feels that it is treated as a second-class state as compared to Japan. In the 1970s, Japan received permission from the United States to reprocess spent fuel, but the permission was contingent on Japan opening up its facility to rigorous safeguards inspections. Japan's desire for reprocessing arose from concerns about energy security. South Korea has similar concerns, and with the projected major growth in nuclear power plants, Seoul can argue that enrichment would be cost-effective, although the economics of reprocessing appear unfavorable compared to the price of enriched uranium. Following

---

[17] See, for example, Frank N. von Hippel, "South Korean Reprocessing: An Unnecessary Threat to the Nonproliferation Regime," *Arms Control Today*, March 2010.

[18] Kwan-Kyoo Choe, "ROK's Contribution to Global Nuclear Nonproliferation," Nautilus Institute, http://www.globalcollab.org/Nautilus/programs/east-asia-science-and-security-collaborative/ civil-society-monitoring-verification-network/korea.

the 2010 agreement allowing India to reprocess U.S.-origin spent fuel, South Korea believes it should receive the same privilege—especially given the country's close relationship with the United States, having literally shed blood in defense of U.S. interests during the Vietnam War and more recently having committed the third-largest deployment during the first few years of the 2003 Iraq War. Nonetheless, Ellen Tauscher, the undersecretary of state for international security and arms control, stated at an April press briefing that her mind has not changed on the matter of allowing pyroprocessing by South Korea.[19]

The terms of the renewed U.S.-ROK 123 agreement in 2014 will likely influence the future course of other U.S. nuclear energy cooperation agreements. If South Korea does not receive permission for pyroprocessing, Seoul may decide to decouple its nuclear program from the United States, although a complete decoupling will be hard to achieve because U.S. firms still hold rights on some equipment. But South Korean engineers could redesign these plant components so that eventually South Korea would have essentially indigenous types of plants to sell. Pulling away from the United States in nuclear commercial interests may also affect South Korea's willingness to buy other U.S. commercial products.

New Nuclear Power States

While China, India, Pakistan, Japan, South Korea, and Taiwan will continue to expand their nuclear power programs, new nuclear power entrant states will most likely be located in Southeast Asia, where Indonesia, Thailand, and Vietnam appear to be closest to acquiring such capabilities. Although the Philippines had gone the furthest in the past with nuclear power development, corruption in the Marcos administration resulted in the closure in the mid-1980s of the essentially completed Bataan nuclear power plant. Because of this experience, many people in the Philippines remain skeptical about nuclear power. The Indonesian government has also faced public opposition to nuclear plants. In addition, seismic experts have raised concerns about the potential sites for Indonesian plants, given the intense earthquake activity in the region. Table 2 shows projections for the leading Southeast Asian states' plans for nuclear power.

Countries in Southeast Asia have taken steps to improve nuclear safety and security. They have focused their multinational nuclear safety activities by working with three organizations: the Asian Nuclear Safety Network (ANSN), the Association of Southeast Asian Nations (ASEAN), and the

---

[19] Ellen Tauscher in response to a question from a *Chosun Ilbo* reporter at the foreign correspondents' press briefing, Washington, D.C., April 20, 2010.

International Atomic Energy Agency (IAEA). ANSN facilitates the pooling and sharing of information and experiences in East Asia to further improve nuclear safety practices. This network consists of countries with extensive nuclear power experience as well as those IAEA advising countries with an interest in acquiring their first nuclear power plants. The former group includes China, Japan, Germany, South Korea, and the United States, while the latter group includes Indonesia, Malaysia, the Philippines, Thailand, and Vietnam. The ANSN could play an important role in the future as a forum for senior officials to share strategies and experiences that could enhance nuclear safety in the region.

Established in 1987 to promote development and stability in Southeast Asia, ASEAN includes ten Southeast Asian states: Brunei Darussalam, Cambodia, Indonesia, Laos, Malaysia, Myanmar (Burma), the Philippines, Singapore, Thailand, and Vietnam. Of these states, Indonesia, Malaysia, the Philippines, Thailand, and Vietnam have recently expressed new or renewed interest in commercial nuclear power. Because of this growing interest in commercial nuclear power and increasing concerns about nuclear security, ASEAN officials announced a new initiative to focus on improving the security of nuclear materials in the region at the ASEAN Regional Forum (ARF) on August 2, 2007. The United States as well as some ARF members had urged earlier in 2007 for ASEAN to take this step toward better security. As part of this initiative, ASEAN members are working toward finding ways to better enforce the Southeast Asia nuclear weapon–free zone. The timeline set in mid-2007 focused on developing more effective compliance mechanisms in the next five years, including improving methods to detect and interdict shipments of nuclear weapons or nuclear weapons–usable materials through the region, strengthening national laws to prevent the rise of nuclear black markets, and calling on the nuclear weapon states to respect the region's nuclear weapon–free zone.

In a parallel initiative, the ASEAN +3 Forum convened its first conference on nuclear energy safety in June 2008. ASEAN +3 includes the ten ASEAN states plus China, Japan, and South Korea. Thailand initiated the idea of the nuclear safety conference and hosted the event in Bangkok. Drawing on the experiences of the established nuclear energy states of China, Japan, and South Korea, ASEAN +3 members discussed development of a regional nuclear safety regime. This proposed safety regime is still in its formative stages, but, like ANSN, it can serve as another mechanism for sharing experiences between more developed nuclear energy users and those that are still in the early stages of nuclear energy development.

Furthermore, in partnership with the IAEA, twelve Asian states established the Asian Network for Education in Nuclear Technology

(ANENT) in 2004. The organization intends to develop human resources, facilitate knowledge management, and build up research and training for the nuclear power field. The network has involved universities, research centers, government agencies, and other institutions focused on nuclear education and training. The creation of this network is evidence of a growing recognition that the region will need to devote significant resources in order to ensure enough highly trained personnel to build, operate, and inspect the projected large number of nuclear plants.

Nonproliferation in Asia

During the past decade, the prospects in Asia for a strengthened nonproliferation regime have been both discouraging and encouraging. This section first examines the relatively bad news of North Korea's emergence as a nuclear-armed state and the daunting challenge of dismantling North Korean nuclear weapons programs as well as the possibility of Burma developing nuclear weapons. Both North Korea and Burma are isolated states with regimes that feel under siege. The section next discusses the relatively good news of China providing more rhetorical, diplomatic, and export-control support for nonproliferation and of U.S. security alliances helping to provide needed assurances to Japan, South Korea, and Taiwan, which all have the infrastructure to develop nuclear weapons in several months to years. This part of the section also highlights the role and influence of Asian powers in helping to prevent Iran from making nuclear weapons. At the same time, the section cautions that many of these states will be reluctant or opposed to exerting substantial pressure on Iran because of their significant use of Iranian oil and gas.

Pariah States, Discouraging Trends, and Threshold Nuclear Weapon States

In 2001, North Korea (also known as the Democratic People's Republic of Korea, or DPRK) was not producing plutonium for nuclear weapons, having frozen its 5 MWe reactor at Yongbyon under the terms of the 1994 Agreed Framework. But not all nuclear weapons–related activities in North Korea had been stopped during the latter half of the 1990s. In a meeting in October 2002, Bush administration officials confronted their North Korean counterparts with the allegation that North Korea had reneged on its agreement to refrain from enriching uranium, a weapons-usable technology. Though at first North Korean officials denied this charge, the next day they reportedly confirmed it. A couple of years later it was revealed that nonproliferation regime. Yet even after joining the NPT, Chinese state-owned firms have at times continued to assist states of proliferation concern, while the government has gradually been strengthening export controls; overall the record has been mixed.[31] Beijing has been more receptive, however, to helping the United States stop nuclear weapons development in North Korea, especially after the October 2006 nuclear test. But Beijing would not want to precipitate the collapse of North Korea, which would likely result in millions of refugees streaming into China.

As mentioned earlier, China has recently renewed nuclear energy cooperation with Pakistan. The timing of this new agreement follows closely with the U.S.-India civilian nuclear energy deal. It remains to be seen what terms Beijing will apply to the deal with Islamabad. If China insists on those facilities being safeguarded and thus outside of Pakistan's military program, then the deal may not significantly harm the nonproliferation system. Such a deal could also assuage Pakistan's concerns that it was treated unfairly. More positively, if China could be convinced to apply diplomatic pressure on Pakistan to exert more effective controls on nuclear technologies, the new deal may help nonproliferation.

Continued Chinese military pressure on Taiwan could precipitate further proliferation. In the 1970s, when the Taiwanese leadership doubted the alliance with the United States as Washington tilted toward Beijing, Taiwan began exploring a nuclear weapons program and started operating a heavy-water reactor of the type that later provided plutonium for India's nuclear weapons. By 1978, Taiwanese nuclear specialists had separated about 30 kilograms of plutonium, enough for about four or five first-generation nuclear bombs.[32] Although political pressure from Washington and reassurances via the Taiwan Relations Act and other military assistance turned back this nuclear weapons program, the effort to do so took considerable time. Furthermore, nine years transpired before the United States discovered this program. Similarly, four years elapsed before South Korean nuclear weapons activities were discovered in the 1970s, when that country also doubted the U.S. security alliance.[33] These observations underscore the possibility for nuclear surprise and that the United States plays an essential role in preventing allies from developing nuclear weapons.

---

[31] Joseph Cirincione, "China's Proliferation and the Impact of Trade Policy on Defense Industries in the United States and China," testimony before the U.S.-China Economic and Security Review Commission, Washington, D.C., July 12, 2007.

[32] David Albright and Corey Gay, "Taiwan: Nuclear Nightmare Averted," *Bulletin of the Atomic Scientists*, January/February 1998.

[33] Rebecca K. C. Hersman and Robert Peters, "Nuclear U-Turns: Learning from South Korean and Taiwanese Rollback," *Nonproliferation Review* 13, no. 3 (November 2006): 539–53.

Implications for the United States

Further nuclear power use in Asia will undoubtedly occur. This should not alarm Washington, however, as long as the United States remains engaged in ensuring the highest international standards of nuclear safety and security, maintaining access to all components of the fuel cycle, upholding adequate controls on enrichment and reprocessing components of this cycle, shoring up security alliances, and working to bring pariah states into the international system. Rather than an alarming prospect, more nuclear power plants in Asia would offer environmental and energy security benefits. Nuclear power plants do not emit greenhouse gases when operating, and the fuel cycle as a whole emits a proportionally small amount of these gases compared to other energy sources. If nuclear power plants further displace coal and other fossil fuel plants, air quality will tend to improve. Regarding energy security, more nuclear power use will reduce the demand for foreign sources of fossil fuels for electricity generation. The United States should welcome these developments.

Balancing these benefits are the risks of accidents at and attacks on nuclear facilities, the erosion of U.S. economic competitiveness, and the threat of proliferation. To effectively engage in reducing the likelihood of accidents, the United States has led and should continue to lead by example. In particular, states that possess or want to possess nuclear power plants look to the U.S. Nuclear Regulatory Commission as the gold standard because of its independence, authority to order the shutdown of unsafe plants without too much pressure from industry, and technical capacity. Similarly, it is important for the United States to support financially and technically the capability of the IAEA to provide safety and regulatory assistance, especially to nuclear power entrant states. The IAEA also has been offering security advice to nuclear facility operators. The United States and all other states using nuclear power have a vital interest in preventing major accidents and attacks because such events could put the brakes on a potential global nuclear energy revival.

The rise of Asian nuclear energy competitors should not overly alarm the United States, but neither should it call for complacency. For instance, although China's deals to secure uranium supplies may appear threatening, the fact is that uranium is an abundant element, and reserves estimates forecast that the world will have many decades worth of uranium based on current demand for nuclear power and the current price range of uranium. A large increase in demand would tend to increase the price, but this will create an incentive for more uranium prospecting and mining. The price of uranium fuel is a relatively small fraction of the total cost of nuclear

EXECUTIVE SUMMARY

[handwritten: Q: What are the global commons?]

This chapter examines the importance of the global commons to the Asia-Pacific region and U.S. interests, and analyzes the implications of the emergence of new Asian powers in the global commons.

MAIN ARGUMENT:

[handwritten: A:]

[handwritten in left margin: how do they acquire this influence?]

Asia's rise and America's geopolitical preeminence have been dependent on the physical openness of the global commons—the seas, air, space, and cyberspace—which has been sustained by U.S. military dominance since the end of World War II. Yet the emergence of new Asian military powers is creating pivotal states—states with a significant degree of influence over the security of the commons. The emergence of these pivotal states is simultaneously driving both cooperation and competition throughout the Asia-Pacific region. Shared interest in the openness and stability of the global commons will compel like-minded states to cooperate in security operations and diplomatic initiatives. Yet uncertainty about China's rise, combined with distrust over the region's many simmering territorial disputes, will also drive the region's new powers to compete militarily with one another.

POLICY IMPLICATIONS:

- Given the rise of pivotal Asian states, Washington's ability to build a regional consensus on sustaining the openness and security of the global commons will largely determine if regional security is to be defined by cooperation or competition.

- If Washington fails to respond to the fundamental challenges posed by adversarial capabilities within the global commons, U.S. access to the Asia-Pacific during times of conflict will be in doubt. The presence of the U.S. in the region, and regional confidence in its will and ability to act, will be central to the maintenance of peace and stability.

Asia's Security and the Contested Global Commons

Abraham M. Denmark

The rise of Asia has been enabled by the region's ability to access and utilize the global commons. Since the end of World War II, and especially since the end of the Cold War, the openness and security of the global commons has been sustained by U.S. military dominance. Yet the Asia-Pacific's emerging economic powers are beginning to translate their newfound prosperity into military power, with profound implications both for regional stability and for military balances within the global commons. This chapter will explore these implications and suggest a way for the United States to preserve the security of the global commons and the stability of the Asia-Pacific region.

The global commons are an essential, though often overlooked, component of today's globalized international system. Free trade agreements and liberal exchange arrangements would be largely useless without the ability to freely access and utilize the world's common spaces for commercial, informational, and personal interactions. Open commons allow large container ships to connect manufacturers to customers all over the world, like-minded individuals to share information and ideas, and global militaries to coordinate movements over vast distances. These capabilities did not happen by accident; rather, they are the result of decades of effort by governments and private corporations to build a "system of systems" allowing for global commerce. These systems exist within and between the global commons: the seas, air, space, and cyberspace.

The U.S. military's ability to utilize the global commons is similarly fundamental to its global dominance. Geography made the United States

Abraham M. Denmark is a Fellow with the Center for a New American Security. He can be reached at <adenmark@cnas.org>.

a natural sea power, and the successful exploitation of air and space, along with U.S. technological prowess, made the United States a power in the air, space, and cyber commons as well. The commons, in turn, serve as a key enabler of the U.S. military and its ability to project power globally. U.S. armed forces demonstrated their conventional military dominance in the 1991 Persian Gulf War, the 1994 air war over Yugoslavia, and the 2003 invasion of Iraq. The utilization of satellites and advanced communications technologies empowered the U.S. military to operate with overwhelming speed, coordination, efficiency, and destructiveness. For example, as former secretary of the Air Force Michael Wynne explained, "in World War II, it took 1,500 B-17s dropping 9,000 bombs to destroy a given target. Today, one B-2 can strike and destroy 80 different targets on a single mission using weapons guided by space-based USAF global positioning system signals."[1] Today, the world's largest corporate intranet is operated by the U.S. Navy.[2]

The open and stable commons previously guaranteed by U.S. military dominance have been a tremendous benefit to Asia's rising powers. Instead of the competition that defined previous ages in the region, U.S. military dominance allowed states to peacefully compete economically and politically.

The rise of Asia's economic powers has gradually enabled the emergence of new Asian military powers, some of whom will become pivotal states—states with a significant degree of influence over the security of a commons. The emergence of these pivotal states within the global commons will simultaneously drive two countervailing trends: cooperation and competition. Shared interest in the openness and stability of the global commons will compel like-minded states to cooperate in security operations and diplomatic initiatives. Yet uncertainty about China's rise, combined with distrust over the region's many simmering territorial disputes, will drive the region's new powers to compete militarily with one another.

Pivotal states wielding newfound military capabilities within the global commons will signal the end of long-standing U.S. dominance of the global commons in the Asia-Pacific. The status quo, in which the United States ensures the stability of the global commons and other states enjoy a free ride, is unsustainable. This chapter will advocate that the United States adopt a proactive strategy to lead a cooperative effort among like-minded states to

---

[1] Michael Wynne, "Space: The Ultimate High Ground Creating Strategic and Tactical Conditions for Victory," *High Frontier* 3, no. 4 (August 2007): 4.

[2] Carrol Chandler, "Contested Commons: The Future of American Power in a Multipolar World" (presentation at the Center for a New American Security, Washington, D.C., January 26, 2010), available at http://www.cnas.org/node/3864.

preserve the openness of the global commons. At the same time, the United States must adjust its regional basing structure to account for emerging challenges within the commons. Sustaining a credible U.S. military presence in the region will not only ensure U.S. access during a time of conflict; it will also maintain the country's long-standing role as a maritime balancer and preserver of regional stability.

The chapter will begin with a discussion of Asia's economic expansion and the importance of the global commons in enabling that rise. The next section will then describe how the military investments of Asia's new powers will fundamentally change military balances within the global commons, followed by discussions of the implications of this phenomenon for the Asia-Pacific and the United States. The chapter will conclude by offering policy recommendations for the United States to adjust to these new realities.

Asia's Rise and the Global Commons

Ongoing shifts in geopolitical power from West to East have made the Asia-Pacific region increasingly important to U.S. interests. The region's rise over the past 30 years has been nothing short of miraculous and will define the dynamics of the emerging multipolar world. The region is already an engine of the global economy, accounting for 33% of the world economy in 2007 (compared to 21% and 23% for the United States and Western Europe, respectively). Asian countries are also becoming global political and military actors, playing decisive roles in issues such as climate change, nonproliferation, and counter-piracy. This rise has led several adroit strategic observers to opine that the 21st century will be Asian, just as the 20th century was supposedly American and the 19th century was British.[3]

Economic data and trends at the beginning of this young century support the hypothesis of a rising Asia. Asia-Pacific economies[4] generated 24% of global GDP in 1992, which rose to 33% in 2007 and is projected by the International Monetary Fund (IMF) to account for almost 37% of

---

[3] See, for example, Jeffrey Sachs, "Welcome to the Asian Century," *Fortune*, January 12, 2004, http://money.cnn.com/magazines/fortune/fortune_archive/2004/01/12/357912/index.htm; Doug Bandow, "The Asian Century," *National Interest*, February 17, 2009, http://www.nationalinterest.org/Article.aspx?id=20844; and H.D.S. Greenway, "An Asian Century," *New York Times*, January 29, 2009, http://www.nytimes.com/2008/01/29/opinion/29iht-edgreenway.1.9574945.html.

[4] In this case, the Asia-Pacific economies are defined as a combination of developing Asian states (Afghanistan, Bangladesh, Bhutan, Brunei Darussalam, Cambodia, China, Fiji, India, Indonesia, Kiribati, Laos, Malaysia, Maldives, Myanmar, Nepal, Pakistan, Papua New Guinea, Philippines, Samoa, Solomon Islands, Sri Lanka, Thailand, Timor-Leste, Tonga, Vanuatu, and Vietnam), newly industrialized states (Hong Kong, Singapore, and Taiwan Province of China), and developed states (Japan, South Korea, Australia, and New Zealand). Definitions derived from the International Monetary Fund (IMF), World Economic Outlook Database, October 2009.

Instead of assuming continued U.S. dominance, it is far more likely that in the coming years and decades the global commons—especially within the Asia-Pacific—will be defined by simultaneous trends of cooperation and competition. The following section details the effects of Asia's rise on the global commons, as well as the implications of this rise for the future of U.S. military strategy and presence in the region.

The Changing Asian Balance of Power in the Global Commons

The rise of Asia's economies is funding an unprecedented explosion in regional military procurement. According to the Stockholm International Peace Research Institute (SIPRI), defense expenditures by major developing Asian states overtook those of developed Asian states in 2001 and are on track to double the expenditures of the latter shortly (see **Figure 3**).[14] The emergence of new military powers within the global commons, potentially with a wide variety of intentions and priorities, will fundamentally change the regional balance of military power and have profound implications for the United States. Indeed, in a relatively short period of time, Asia's common spaces may quickly evolve from areas dominated by the United States to domains in which several states—often with differing interests—operate in close proximity to one another. How these new military powers use their newfound capabilities will simultaneously drive the region to engage in two divergent modes of behavior that will define the global commons in the Asia-Pacific for the foreseeable future: cooperation and competition.

It is important to note that the motivations behind military investments vary greatly by country. China, for example, has invested in advanced naval, air, space, and cyberspace capabilities following analysis of U.S. and coalition warfighting practices in the 1991 Persian Gulf War and subsequent operations in Yugoslavia, Afghanistan, and Iraq. Chinese strategists acknowledged the force-multiplying effects of U.S. dominance of the global commons; they also saw a potential vulnerability in U.S. dependence on the commons for military operations. These observations drove the People's Liberation Army (PLA) to procure and develop capabilities to operate within the commons while contesting

---

[14] In this case, the major developing Asian states are China, India, Indonesia, Malaysia, Russia, Sri Lanka, Thailand, and Vietnam. See Stockholm International Peace Research Institute (SIPRI), http://www.sipri.org/databases/milex.

FIGURE 3   Shifts in Asian defense spending, 2000–08

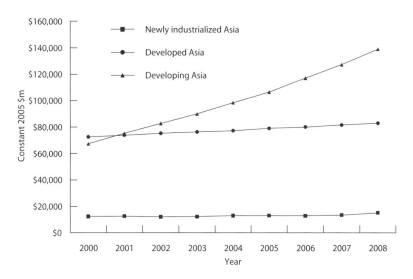

SOURCE: Stockholm International Peace Research Institute (SIPRI), http://www.sipri.org/databases/milex.

U.S. dominance via a layered anti-access/area-denial strategy.[15] Yet observations about the importance of naval power projection, air dominance, space-based C4ISR (command, control, communications, computers, intelligence, surveillance, and reconnaissance), and computer networking have also driven the PLA, as well as other advanced militaries in the region, to see the ability to operate within the global commons as a necessary capability of any modern military.

The protection of vital sea lines of communication (SLOC) is also driving states such as Australia, India, Indonesia, Japan, the Republic of Korea (ROK), Singapore, and increasingly China to pursue capabilities within the global commons. Given that all states in the region (except perhaps North Korea and Burma) have an interest in protecting the

---

[15] U.S. Department of Defense, "Military Power of the People's Republic of China 2009." "Anti-access/area-denial" is an American term intended to describe a military focused on challenging an opposing force's ability to enter, or operate within, a given geographical area. Such a strategy usually focuses on attacking regional bases, logistics, and long-range platforms that support extended-range military power projection. For more information, see Andrew Krepinevich, Barry Watts, and Robert Work, "Meeting the Anti-Access and Area-Denial Challenge," Center for Strategic and Budgetary Assessments (CSBA), 2003, http://www.csbaonline.org/4Publications/PubLibrary/R.20030520.Meeting_the_Anti-A/R.20030520.Meeting_the_Anti-A.pdf.

commons from pirates and terrorists, several Asian states have contributed to the multinational effort to combat piracy off the coast of Somalia. While promoting national status is another factor driving this cooperation, this joint effort to combat piracy is nonetheless a promising model for future collaboration in the global commons against a shared threat.

However, the global commons will also be the venue for significant military competition within the Asia-Pacific for two somewhat related reasons. The first is an emerging military competition between China, on the one hand, and the United States and its allies, on the other. China's 30-year military modernization program—which has acquired and produced advanced maritime anti-access capabilities such as the anti-ship ballistic missile (ASBM), a direct-ascent anti-satellite missile, and a reportedly robust cyber warfare capability—has been geared toward presenting the United States and its allies with a layered anti-access/area-denial challenge during a Taiwan-related conflict. The harassment of U.S. ships in international waters of the South China Sea by Chinese vessels, reports of computer network intrusions emanating from China and targeting governments and corporations around the world, and the unannounced destruction of satellites in orbit have reinforced concern within the region about China's intentions.

The second related driver of competition in the maritime commons is the ongoing disputes between several states over islands in the South and East China seas (see **Figure 4**). Vietnam, for example, sees disputes within the South China Sea as a major potential source of conflict within the region.[16] Indeed, several states with claims in the region have recently invested in advanced military capabilities in the air and maritime commons, portending a future when sovereignty disputes are waged with more than rhetoric.

Regardless of the motivation for investments in advanced military capabilities by Asian states, U.S. strategists should realize that the global commons will soon become significantly more crowded, complex, and contested. As new entrants begin to operate on the high seas, field advanced air and anti-air capabilities, launch and control satellites, and operate within cyberspace, military calculations within the commons will inevitably change. Following are short descriptions of recent developments within the global commons.

---

[16] Carlyle A. Thayer, "Vietnam's New Defence White Paper," Thayer Consultancy, December 8–9, 2009, http://www.scribd.com/doc/23918915/Thayer-Vietnam-s-New-Defence-White-Paper.

FIGURE 4 Disputes in the South China Sea

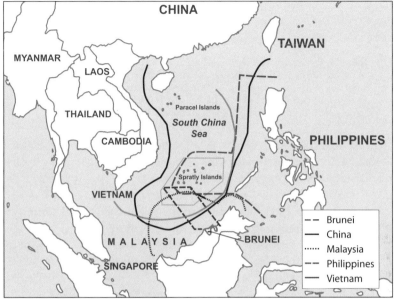

SOURCE: Abraham Denmark and James Mulvenon, "Executive Summary," in Denmark and Mulvenon, *Contested Commons*, 21.

Maritime Commons

Several states in the Asia-Pacific region are heavily investing in naval and maritime capabilities, portending a time in the near future when several blue water navies[17]—potentially from Australia, China, India, Indonesia, Japan, the Republic of Korea (ROK, or South Korea), Singapore, and the United States—will operate simultaneously on the high seas in the Western Pacific, South China Sea, Indian Ocean, and within critical littoral waters.[18] Although these states have a shared interest in sustaining maritime trade, uncertainties regarding intentions and disagreements over the means of SLOC protection—as well as enduring sovereignty disputes over islands within the East and South China seas—mean that the maritime commons in the Asia-Pacific will probably be defined by states cooperating in the short term while simultaneously competing in the long term.

[handwritten margin note: Sea lines of communication]

---

[17] The term "blue water navy" is a generic label for a maritime force capable of operating in deep ocean waters far from shore for extended periods of time. While some attribute the label to a navy with useable aircraft carriers, it is more a colloquialism than a clearly defined attribute.

[18] See Robert Kaplan, "China's Two Ocean Strategy," in Abraham Denmark and Nirav Patel, eds., "China's Arrival: A Strategic Framework for a Global Relationship," Center for a New American Security, September 2009, 43–58.

All states in the Asia-Pacific (discounting North Korea) recognize the centrality of maritime power in defending this commons. Singapore's Ministry of Defense, for example, made the following observation about the country's location:

> The strategic location of Singapore at the meeting point of the Indian Ocean and South China Sea has made Singapore one of the world's busiest ports, with more than 1,000 vessels plying the Singapore Strait daily. While that may be an economic boon for the Republic, it can also translate into its sea lines being lucrative hunting grounds for sea robbers, pirates and terrorists.[19]

Likewise, the Indian Navy's most recent strategy document, entitled "Freedom to Use the Seas," clearly recognizes the implications of the maritime commons to India's security. Even China has highlighted the protection of vital sea lanes as a major future challenge.[20]

Military acquisitions have matched the rhetoric. Singapore's Ministry of Defense cited protecting the Strait of Malacca, the importance of SLOCs, and the threats of terrorism and piracy when announcing the entry of its final two Formidable-class frigates into active service in January 2009.[21] Indonesia, Singapore, and Vietnam have acquired diesel-electric submarines, though all three states face challenges in integrating these capabilities into existing strategies and doctrine. Australia has also committed to acquiring twenty offshore combatant vessels, eight new future frigates, and twelve new future submarines over the next three decades, which is Australia's largest-ever single defense project.[22]

Air Commons

Several states in the Asia-Pacific are developing or procuring advanced air and surface-to-air platforms. These capabilities, combined with the ability to attack air bases using advanced ballistic and cruise missiles, will significantly affect U.S. military planning and posture and could have profound implications for regional stability.

---

[19] Sheena Tan, "Guardians of the Sea," *Cyberpioneer*, Singapore Ministry of Defence, March 26, 2009, http://www.mindef.gov.sg/imindef/publications/cyberpioneer/features/2009/mar09_cs.html.

[20] See Ian Storey, "China's 'Malacca Dilemma,'" Jamestown Foundation, China Brief 6, no. 8, April 12, 2006, http://www.jamestown.org/programs/chinabrief/single/?tx_ttnews[tt_news]=31575&tx_ttnews[backPid]=196&no_cache=1.

[21] Sherlyn Quek, "A Truly Formidable Squadron," *Cyberpioneer*, Singapore Ministry of Defence, March 3, 2009, http://www.mindef.gov.sg/imindef/publications/cyberpioneer/features/2009/feb09_fs.html.

[22] Department of Defence of Australia, *Defending Australia and the Asia-Pacific Century: Force 2030*, (Canberra: Commonwealth of Australia, 2009), 70–73, available at http://www.apo.org.au/node/14278.

The proliferation of advanced combat aircraft is largely the result of exports from Russia, with China playing an increasing role in cooperative research and development. Of the advanced combat aircraft in service and on order, there is a wide presence of Russian-made or license-produced Sukhoi aircraft. Described as "generation 4.5" and superior in many ways to the current fourth-generation F-15, F-16, and F/A-18 fighters in U.S. service, the Sukhoi aircraft represent a potent technical competitor to the current generation of U.S. combat aircraft. As part of China's Taiwan-focused military modernization program, the PLA has acquired a robust and layered military capability in the air commons. The purchase of advanced Russian Su-27, Su-30, and Su-33 fighters; the development of the J-10 and J-11 fighters; and the acquisition of the SA-20 surface-to-air missile have greatly improved China's ability to contest the air commons during a time of crisis. Indeed, a recent RAND study concluded that China would be able to establish air dominance in a Taiwan contingency regardless of U.S. intervention.[23]

Russia and China are also developing fifth-generation fighter aircraft, and both states are heavily involved in cooperative research with other countries. In November 2009, India and Russia announced an expansion of their cooperative work on the PAK-FA fighter, and industry sources believe that 2017 will be the target date for an Indian prototype.[24] Additionally, China is clearly moving toward an indigenously developed, next generation combat aircraft. Although U.S. Secretary of Defense Robert Gates has predicted that China will have no fifth-generation aircraft comparable to the F-22 by 2020, the deputy commander of the PLA Air Force publicly declared that China will in fact have such an aircraft in service by that date.[25] Beyond the debate over specific dates, the larger issue is the broad pursuit of capabilities that outclass current U.S. fighters and compete directly with the next generation of fighter aircraft. With expertise and technology flowing out of China and Russia, U.S. control of the air likely will be more vigorously contested. Even if the United States never directly confronts Russia or China, the proliferation of advanced air platforms around the world suggests that the United States may eventually fight against Russian

[23] David A. Shlapak et al., *A Question of Balance: Political Context and Military Aspects of the China-Taiwan Dispute* (Santa Monica: RAND, 2009), http://www.rand.org/pubs/monographs/MG888/index.html.

[24] Siva Govindasamy, "Russia, India to Advance Deal on PAK-FA Fighter Variant," *Flight International*, November 12, 2009, http://www.flightglobal.com/articles/2009/12/11/335995/russia-india-to-advance-deal-on-pak-fa-fightervariant.html.

[25] Siva Govindasamy, "China Expects Fifth Generation Fighter in 10 Years," *Flight International*, December 11, 2009, http://www.flightglobal.com/articles/2009/11/12/334680/china-expects-fifth-generation-fighter-in-10-years.html; and Robert M. Gates, "Economic Club of Chicago" (speech presented at Economic Club of Chicago, July 16, 2009), U.S. Department of Defense, http://www.defense.gov/speeches/speech.aspx?speechid=1369.

and Chinese equipment. Given the small size of the F-22 fleet and recent concerns over cost growth and delays in the $300 billion F-35 program, the ongoing proliferation of advanced combat aircraft should be cause for significant concern.

In addition to states pursuing traditional military capabilities in the air, U.S. control of this commons has pushed state and nonstate actors to develop asymmetric methods of contesting U.S. air capabilities, primarily through the development and acquisition of advanced Russian "double-digit" surface-to-air missiles (SAM), which feature long ranges, mobile launchers, and advanced radars. As a system, these weapons were designed to defeat stealth aircraft and target U.S. stand-off command, control, and refueling assets. Double-digit SAMs not only decrease the survivability of non-stealth combat and support aircraft but are also more difficult to defeat using current tactics. In fact, Russian SA-20 SAM deployments reportedly caused NATO to elect not to deploy the airborne warning and control system (AWACS) aircraft during Russia's conflict with Georgia in 2008.[26]

Though the primary source of advanced SAM technology is Russia, the number of operators is growing. In early 2009 the director of the U.S. Defense Intelligence Agency noted that China possesses sixteen SA-20 battalions and an equivalent number of shorter-range, but still lethal, SA-10 systems.[27] Other reported customers of the SA-10 and SA-20 include Iran and Vietnam.[28] In addition, China is developing an indigenous variant of the SA-10, the HQ-9, which is now available for export, repeating the trend of proliferation seen with combat aircraft.[29]

The third emerging threat to U.S. air dominance in the Asia-Pacific is the proliferation of capabilities designed to penetrate U.S. air defenses and strike fixed and mobile air bases in the region. The United States routinely operates from secure sanctuaries on land and at sea in order to achieve control of the air. Since the Cold War, these runways, taxiways, hangars, fuel bunkers, air operations centers, carrier battle groups, munitions ships, and oilers that enable control of the air commons have rarely been systematically

[26] David A. Fulghum and Douglas Barrie, "Russia Sells SA-20 to Iran," *Aviation Week*, December 12, 2008, http://www.aviationweek.com/aw/generic/story_channel.jsp?channel=defense&id=news/aw121508p2.xml.

[27] Michael D. Maples, "Annual Threat Assessment," statement before the Committee on Armed Services, U.S. Senate, March 10, 2009, 2, http://armed-services.senate.gov/statemnt/2009/March/Maples%2003-10-09.pdf; and U.S. Department of Defense, "Military Power of the People's Republic of China 2009," 50, 66.

[28] Carlo Kopp, "Proliferation of Advanced Surface to Air Missiles," Air Power Australia, June 2009, http://www.ausairpower.net/APA-S-300-Proliferation.html.

[29] Andrei Chang, "China Exports New Surface-to-Air Missile," United Press International, March 18, 2009, http://www.upi.com/Business_News/Security-Industry/2009/03/18/China-exports-new-surface-to-air-missile/UPI-30271237410000/.

threatened. Faced with a variety of ballistic missiles, cruise missiles, rockets, and artillery capable of striking airbases and aircraft carriers, the threat to the air commons lies as much in challenges to these bases, aircraft carriers, and logistics on the surface as in challenges to aircraft. Destroying bases is more effective and efficient than facing a dispersed, maneuvering, and armed opponent in the air.

While China's developments and acquisitions have the most profound implications for U.S. military strategy and posture (see **Figure 5**), the proliferation of advanced air and anti-air capabilities will fundamentally alter the military calculations informing regional territorial disputes and bilateral competitions. Vietnam has recently purchased the Su-MK2 multi-role fighter from Russia, Japan is examining options for modernizing its fighter capabilities, India has already acquired the Su-30 fighter from Russia and has plans to procure an advanced multi-role combat aircraft as well as the PAK-FA, Australia plans to purchase the F-35 once available,

FIGURE 5   Chinese anti-access/area-denial missile capabilities

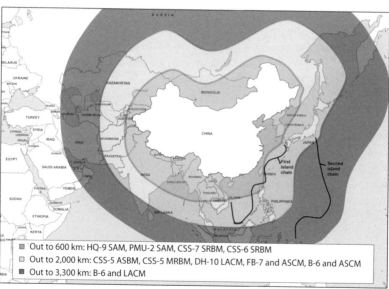

Out to 600 km: HQ-9 SAM, PMU-2 SAM, CSS-7 SRBM, CSS-6 SRBM
Out to 2,000 km: CSS-5 ASBM, CSS-5 MRBM, DH-10 LACM, FB-7 and ASCM, B-6 and ASCM
Out to 3,300 km: B-6 and LACM

SOURCE: Kelly Martin and Oliver Fritz, "Sustaining the Air Commons," in Denmark and Mulvenon, *Contested Commons*, 95; and U.S. Department of Defense, "Military Power of the People's Republic of China 2009."

and Malaysia has twelve operational Su-30 fighters, with an additional six on order.[30] Indeed, some analysts believe Vietnam's purchase of the Su-MK2 was motivated in part by a desire to assert and defend its claims in the South China Sea.[31]

Space Commons

Beginning with the advent of high-thrust rocketry in the late 1940s, space was primarily a venue for Cold War competition between the United States and the Soviet Union. Yet the proliferation of advanced rocketry and missile technologies has enabled the rise of new space powers, most of which reside in the Asia-Pacific. China, Japan, and India are the world's three most significant rising space powers, with the ROK and North Korea (DPRK) pursing nascent space efforts.

Several states are developing civilian space capabilities, including space launch, remote sensing communications, and science and robotics (see **Table 1**).[32] Astronauts from the Asia-Pacific have participated in multinational space missions, and China in 2007 became the third country to develop a manned space program. China, India, and Japan all maintain robust civilian space infrastructures, with the ability to both design and build satellites and rockets. All three countries also have ambitions to eventually land astronauts on the moon, though China appears to be further along than India or Japan in that regard and also plans to build a space station. The emergence of these civilian space capabilities and ambitions promises a new era of space collaboration and cooperation, in which more states are able to substantively contribute to space exploration for the greater benefit of humankind.

The emergence of new space powers also has major implications for the future stability of the global commons. Recognizing that space operations bring capabilities that cannot be replicated elsewhere, several states in the Asia-Pacific are deploying satellites to assist in reconnaissance,

---

[30] "Directory: World Air Forces," *Flight International*, November 11–17, 2008, 52–76, http://www.flightglobal.com/assets/getasset.aspx?ItemID=26061.

[31] Carlyle A. Thayer, "Vietnam: New Order for Su30MKs," Thayer Consultancy, February 2010, http://www.scribd.com/doc/26686992/Thayer-Vietnam-Buys-12-More-Su30-MK2s.

[32] It should be noted that the entirety of China's space activity is controlled and managed by the PLA. China's civilian space agency, the Chinese National Space Agency, is primarily a civilian liaison organization and does not have any operational, budgetary, or strategic oversight of China's space efforts. For the purposes of this chapter, however, Chinese space activity that would normally be considered civilian by the West, such as orbital research and space exploration, will be treated as civilian activity. For more on China's space policy, see Jeffrey Lewis and Gregory Kulacki, *A Place for One's Mat: China's Space Program, 1956–2003* (Cambridge: American Academy of Arts and Sciences, 2009), http://www.cissm.umd.edu/papers/files/a_place_for_ones_mat.pdf.

TABLE 1   Space capabilities in the Asia-Pacific

	Launch	Remote sensing	Communications	Science/ robotics
Australia	–	Yes	Yes	Yes
China	Yes	Yes	Yes	Yes
India	Yes	Yes	Yes	Yes
Indonesia	–	–	Yes	–
Japan	Yes	Yes	Yes	–
Malaysia	–	–	Yes	–
North Korea	Developing	Developing	–	–
Philippines	–	–	Yes	–
Russia	Yes	Yes	Yes	Yes
South Korea	Developing	–	Yes	Developing
Thailand	–	–	Yes	–
United States	Yes	Yes	Yes	Yes
Vietnam	–	–	Yes	–

SOURCE: Eric Sterner, "Beyond the Stalemate in the Space Commons," in Denmark and Mulvenon, *Contested Commons*, 110; "The Space Report 2009: The Authoritative Guide to Global Space Activity," Space Foundation, April 2009; and Robert D. Newberry, "Latin American Countries with Space Programs: Colleagues or Competitors?" *Air & Space Power Journal* XVII, no. 3 (Fall 2003): 39–45. For useful websites, see the James Martin Center for Nonproliferation Studies (CNS) at the Monterey Institute of International Studies, http://cns.miis.edu/pubs/ missiles.htm; and SpacePolicyOnline, http://www.spacepolicyonline.com/pages/.

NOTE: A more detailed and rigorous survey would likely find that each of these states possesses some ability to utilize remote sensing and communications applications and had participated in some form of space-related research because anyone can purchase satellite phones and terminals and remote sensing data on the commercial market.

navigation, timing, and communications. In 2007, Japan adopted a law allowing for the use of space for military purposes, and India in 2008 announced plans to "optimize space applications for military purposes." A senior Indian military officer candidly stated that "with time we will get sucked into a military race to protect our space assets, and inevitably there will be a military contest in space."[33]

More disconcerting is that China is developing multiple types of anti-satellite (ASAT) weapons, including jammers and direct-ascent missiles,

---

[33] Gavin Rabinowitz, "Indian Army Wants Military Space Program," Associated Press, June 17, 2008.

such as the SC-17 that was tested in January 2007.[34] Less famously, China conducted another test with ASAT implications in January 2010, although China described this as a test of a ballistic missile defense system. China's development of ASAT military capabilities, along with the proliferation of satellite-jamming technologies to several militaries in the developing world, suggests a future in which space becomes a vital battleground and U.S. access to space is contested.

Cyber Commons

The veil of secrecy that conceals states' cyber capabilities makes a thorough analysis of the cyber commons in the Asia-Pacific impossible. Yet the region's emergence as a technological hub of the global economy, along with the nascent discussion in the international community about the nature of the cyber commons and the threats confronted within it, strongly suggests that the Asia-Pacific will be at the forefront of the international effort to understand and protect the cyber commons.

Asia's economic rise has created technological hubs throughout the Asia-Pacific. Since 2000, the region has become a world leader in information and communication technology.[35] The region is home to the world's largest share of Internet users (39%), and four of the world's top ten economies with household broadband access are from the Asia-Pacific (the ROK, Singapore, Hong Kong, and Macao).[36] In 2008, China surpassed the United States as the world's largest fixed broadband market.[37]

Due to their indigenous technological capabilities, infrastructure, and expertise, China, India, South Korea, Japan, Taiwan, and the United States are all potential centers of cyberpower in the coming years. Russia reportedly also has developed a robust ability to deny its adversaries access to cyberspace.[38] In April 2007, during an imbroglio surrounding the removal of a Soviet-era monument, the websites of the Estonian Parliament, ministries, media outlets, and banks were attacked and defaced. Although the Estonian government immediately blamed Russia, Tallinn could not definitively link the attack to Moscow.[39] Georgia faced similar

---

[34] U.S. Department of Defense, "Military Power of the People's Republic of China 2009."

[35] "Information Society Statistical Profiles 2009: Asia and the Pacific."

[36] Ibid.

[37] Ibid.

[38] See, for example, Timothy L. Thomas, "Nation-state Cyber Strategies: Examples from China and Russia," in *Cyberpower and National Security*, ed. Franklin D. Kramer, Stuart H. Starr, and Larry Wentz (Dulles: Potomac Books, 2009), 465–90.

[39] Bright, "Estonia Accuses Russia of 'Cyberattack.'"

attacks during its war with Russia over South Ossetia in 2008.[40] China has likewise reportedly developed several types of computer network operations. According to the U.S. Department of Defense's annual report to Congress "Military Power of the People's Republic of China 2009," China's military has "established information warfare units to develop viruses to attack enemy computer systems and networks, and tactics and measures to protect friendly computer systems and networks."[41] Indeed, according to the Pentagon, China's military has integrated cyberattacks into its exercises, using such measures as first strikes against enemy networks.

As in other commons, the Asia-Pacific region's approach to the cyber commons will be defined by a simultaneous move toward cooperation and competition. The biggest threat to the cyber commons emanates not from states but from the anarchic and decentralized nature of the cyber commons itself.[42] Thus, in the coming years several states will attempt to develop international cooperative efforts, "rules of the road," and global regimes.[43] Due to the region's technological significance, the role of Asia-Pacific states in these efforts will be fundamental to their success or failure. Yet mutual suspicion about the strategic intentions and motives of some states, primarily China, will also drive increasing regional competition in the cyber commons. Recognizing the importance of cyberspace to economic survival and military power, states will be reluctant to fully cooperate with other states they fear may grow hostile.

Implications for the Asia-Pacific

As this chapter has discussed, the rise of several new Asia-Pacific powers within the global commons will fundamentally alter regional military power balances, with profound implications for regional peace and stability. The anarchic international system, concern over the rise of China, long memories of historical grievances, and simmering territorial disputes will drive states toward competition. Yet shared interests in the openness and stability of the global commons, enabled by U.S. leadership, will at the same time drive states in the region toward cooperation. It is this complexity—simultaneous competition and cooperation—that will define the nature of the global commons in the Asia-Pacific for the coming years and decades.

---

[40] John Markoff, "Before the Gunfire, Cyberattacks," *New York Times*, August 12, 2008.

[41] U.S. Department of Defense, "Military Power of the People's Republic of China 2009," 27–28.

[42] See Rattray, Evans, and Healey, "American Security in the Cyber Commons," 137–76.

[43] See Denmark and Mulvenon, eds., *Contested Commons*.

The Rise of China

Beijing's 30-year military modernization program has made China a significant military power in the global commons, yet the implications of this power remain unclear. The PLA's efforts to develop a robust anti-access/area-denial capability, though originally intended to undermine traditional U.S. military advantages in the global commons, would, if employed, threaten the openness and stability of the commons for the entire region and potentially on a global scale. In every commons, a decision by Beijing to actively enforce an exclusionary, zero-sum approach would profoundly undermine the broader open nature of the global commons. Yet, simultaneously, a decision by Beijing to use its military capabilities to defend and sustain the global commons would go a long way toward ensuring the commons' stability. This dichotomy, as well as the persistent uncertainty surrounding China's long-term intentions, will in many ways define the cooperation and competition that are likely to characterize the region's approach to the global commons in the coming years.

For example, China has rhetorically claimed that the South China Sea is included within its territorial waters and not subject to the laws governing international seafaring. If Beijing were to decide to enforce this rhetoric with military action, it would in effect undermine centuries of international maritime custom and establish China as the sole guardian of one of the world's most important waterways. Yet at the same time, if China were to use its navy to combat piracy and ensure the fair use of international waterways, it would promote openness and stability in the region's maritime commons.

Space provides another useful example. Satellites are highly vulnerable—they are susceptible to kinetic and directed energy attacks, as well as to jamming from the surface of the earth. Even modest damage to satellite subsystems, such as to optics or solar arrays, can prove disastrous. The high speeds and amount of debris in orbit—hardware and spacecraft fragments that have broken up, exploded, or been abandoned—render the space commons itself inherently fragile. There are 19,000 objects in space as small as ten centimeters across, including 1,300 active payloads and 7,500 pieces of debris.[44] These objects in orbit make for a crowded, dangerous commons. A tiny speck of paint that had broken off a satellite once dug a pit in a space shuttle window nearly a quarter-inch wide, causing a near catastrophe.[45] It is estimated that a pea-sized ball moving in orbit would

---

[44] Larry James, "Keeping the Space Environment Safe for Civil and Commercial Users," statement before the Subcommittee on Space and Aeronautics, Committee on Science and Technology, U.S. House of Representatives, April 28, 2009.

[45] Timon Singh, "Space: The Final Junkyard," *EU Infrastructure*, August 24, 2009, http://www.euinfrastructure.com/news/Space-The-Final-Junkyard/.

cause as much damage to a satellite or manned spacecraft as a 400-pound safe travelling at 60 mph.[46] Spacecraft are frequently maneuvered to avoid debris, thereby burning up fuel and shortening their lifespan. In 2008, for example, U.S. and French officials admitted moving spacecraft eight times just to avoid debris.[47] The destruction of satellites thus threatens the space commons, with explosions in orbit creating millions of small pieces of debris, some of which can remain for decades.

China's 2007 test of an anti-satellite missile produced about 2,400 pieces of known debris, and a 2009 collision between an Iridium communications satellite and a defunct Russian communications satellite produced more than 870 pieces of cataloged debris.[48] Most disconcertingly, China has publicly taken a nonchalant approach to orbital debris; four months after the 2007 test, the vice chairman of China's Central Military Commission, General Guo Boxiong, laughed off the seriousness of space debris and told PACOM commander Admiral Keating that the test had no serious consequences.[49] A broad kinetic anti-satellite campaign, alluded to in several Chinese military writings,[50] could create an environment in orbit that would be analogous to fighting World War II without gravity, in which stray bullets, mortars, and bombs would not simply fall to earth but would continue to circle the world for decades, rendering much of the surface of the earth uninhabitable. Orbits littered with debris from a kinetic anti-satellite campaign would render useless satellites on which the global economy depends.

Conversely, support from China for realistic and constructive efforts to ensure the prevention of orbital debris and the security of the global commons would be a major bulwark for the security of the space commons. As a nation with a burgeoning space program, an expanding economic and military reliance on access to a secure space commons, and ambitions to be seen as a responsible global power, working with the United States to secure the space commons would be in China's interest.

Bearing in mind these concerns, it should be noted that China's eventual approach to the global commons is unclear. The United States has for several years employed a strategy to engage China while hedging against

---

[46] Singh, "Space: The Final Junkyard."

[47] Robert Lee Hotz, "Harmless Debris on Earth Is Devastating in Orbit," *Wall Street Journal*, February 27, 2009, http://online.wsj.com/article/SB123568403874486701.html.

[48] James, "Keeping the Space Environment Safe."

[49] "U.S. Questions on China's ASAT Met with Laughter," *Voice of America*, May 17, 2007.

[50] As described in Christopher Griffin and Joseph E. Lin, "China's Space Ambitions," *Armed Forces Journal*, April 2008, http://www.afji.com/2008/04/3406827/.

other possibilities.[51] This approach has generally required economically and politically integrating China into the international system and forthrightly discussing issues of concern and disagreement, while maintaining the military capability to deter, dissuade, and defeat Chinese hostility or coercion. As China has become an increasingly important economic and political power in the Asia-Pacific, other states are pursuing a similar hedging strategy—engaging China economically and politically while maintaining a military hedge, often in the form of a military alliance or partnership with the United States.

To address regional concerns vis-à-vis the global commons, an "engage-and-hedge" strategy continues to be most prudent. Engagement, through diplomacy but most importantly via frank and transparent military-to-military discussions about the global commons, would go a long way toward addressing regional anxieties and uncertainties. By developing a robust military capability to ensure the openness and stability of the commons in the face of a potential threat from the PLA, hedging would address U.S. and allied military requirements while also dissuading China from pursuing disruptive or confrontational policies toward the commons.

In many ways, this engage-and-hedge strategy toward China is already in effect throughout the Asia-Pacific, given that China's military modernization and unclear intentions toward the global commons are fueling concerns. Once a taboo subject, now regional governments regularly discuss their apprehension publicly and privately about the long-term strategic ramifications of China's rise. Though China's economy has been well-integrated into the rest of the international system to the point of some referring to a "shared balance of economic terror,"[52] some states in the region are beginning to adapt to the potential for conflict with China in the global commons. Japan's pursuit of a next generation fighter capability is driven by concerns over a Chinese attack, as are several U.S. programs to counter Chinese technological advances, including the Pentagon's decision to pursue an "Air-Sea Battle" concept to respond to anti-access challenges.[53]

Maritime Flashpoints

U.S. dominance of the global commons has enabled a remarkable era of peace and stability. Indeed, the peaceful simultaneous rise of several

---

[51] National Security Council, *The National Security Strategy of the United States of America* (Washington, D.C., March 2006), 42.

[52] Jim Hoagland, "The Lukewarm War with China," *Washington Post*, April 16, 2006.

[53] "US Moves to Counter Chinese Military Modernization," *Voice of America*, January 27, 2009, http://www1.voanews.com/english/news/a-13-2009-01-27-voa58-68666362.html; and "Quadrennial Defense Review."

new regional powers, many with long-simmering territorial disputes and historical animosities, is largely unprecedented in the region's history. However, the emergence of new military powers within the global commons, combined with the end of the United States' monopoly of military power in the region's common spaces, may undermine the factors for stability that have kept these forces of regional conflict largely at bay—and thus may provoke territorial or historical disputes—while equipping states to militarily assert their interests in aggressive and potentially destabilizing ways.

The Asia-Pacific region is rife with long-simmering territorial disputes, mostly over islands in the East and South China seas. The Pinnacle Islands (also known as the Senkaku Islands or Diaoyutai Islands), located northeast of Taiwan and west of Okinawa, are controlled by Japan but also claimed by mainland China and Taiwan. Various parts of the Spratley Island chain are claimed, in part or in whole, by six countries and Taiwan. The Liancourt Rocks (also known as the Dokdo or Takeshima Islands), located between Korea and Japan, are controlled by South Korea but claimed by Japan. Both Japan and Russia claim ownership of the Kuril Islands northeast of Hokaido, though the two sides have recently signaled an interest in resolving the dispute. Lastly, the final status of Taiwan can be understood as a territorial dispute between Beijing and Taipei.

Even the long-standing dispute between China and India over areas of their shared border has a significant maritime component, even though the dispute itself does not involve any bodies of water. During a China-India conflict, China's access to vital resources from Africa and the Middle East would be highly vulnerable to Indian interdiction in the littoral waters of Southeast Asia or the Indian Ocean.

It is important to note that these disputes all involve territories located in bodies of water—the Western Pacific, the South China Sea, and the Indian Ocean—that some strategists believe will be the most strategically significant waters of the 21st century. The potential for a conflict in the Western Pacific between the United States and China over Taiwan is well-understood, as are the multiple disputes within the East and South China seas. Further, Robert Kaplan, a senior fellow at the Center for a New American Security, has argued persuasively that the Indian Ocean will be "the center stage for the challenges of the 21st century" because of the presence of unstable states (Pakistan and Burma) and maritime competition between Asia's two great powers (China and India).[54]

---

[54] Robert Kaplan, "Center Stage for the 21st Century: Rivalry in the Indian Ocean," *Foreign Affairs* 88, no. 2 (March/April 2009): 16–32.

This combination of factors—rising powers in the global commons, diminishing factors for stability, simmering territorial disputes, and conflict in strategically significant locations—has profound implications for maintaining the commons spaces in the Asia-Pacific. At every maritime flashpoint, a state's ability to exert power in the maritime and air commons will determine its ability to assert claims of sovereignty.

The common denominator in every such flashpoint is the United States. Kaplan argues that it will be up to Washington to maintain peace and protect the global commons. Yet instead of acting as a sheriff between China and India as if between the Hatfields and McCoys, as Kaplan implies, the United States can only keep the peace in these flashpoints if it maintains a presence as the region's maritime balancer while working with the region toward the shared objective of preserving the global commons.

The Emergence of the Pivotal States

In 1999, the historian and strategist Paul Kennedy and his colleagues called for a U.S. strategy that focuses attention on "pivotal states" whose futures are "poised at critical turning points, and whose fates would significantly affect regional, and even international, stability."[55] In the Asia-Pacific, size, geography, economic capacity, and military capability will define the emergence of pivotal states having an inordinate amount of influence in the future openness and stability of the global commons (see **Table 2**). Several states have already indicated an interest in playing major roles in the global commons. For example, in addition to the 2010 U.S. Quadrennial Defense Review and National Security Strategy, India's national security advisor made the global commons a major theme of his remarks to the 2010 Shangri-La dialogue in Singapore. Likewise, Japan's acting secretary-general Goshi Hosono informed an American audience that the global commons would be a major element of Japan's future approach to regional security issues and will be codified in an upcoming review of his country's future defense policy guidelines.[56]

---

[55] Robert Chase, Emily Hill, and Paul Kennedy, *The Pivotal States: A New Framework for U.S. Policy in the Developing World* (New York: W. W. Norton & Company, 1999), 5.

[56] U.S. Department of Defense, *Quadrennial Defense Review*; National Security Council, *The National Security Strategy of the United States of America*; Shivshankar Menon, "Second Plenary Session Remarks to the 9th IISS Asia Security Summit" (remarks presented at the 9th International Institute for Strategic Studies Asia Security Summit, Singapore, June 5, 2010), http://www.iiss.org/conferences/the-shangri-la-dialogue/shangri-la-dialogue-2010/plenary-session-speeches/second-plenary-session/shivshankar-menon/; and Goshi Hosono, "Remarks to the Center for a New American Security Conference on the U.S.-Japan Alliance" (remarks made at the conference "150 Years of Amity & 50 Years of Alliance," Center for New American Security, Washington, D.C., June 18, 2010).

TABLE 2   Pivotal Asia-Pacific actors in the global commons

Maritime	Australia, China, India, Indonesia, Japan, South Korea, Malaysia, Singapore, and the United States
Air	Australia, China, India, Japan, South Korea, and the United States
Space	Australia, China, India, Japan, Russia, and the United States
Cyberspace	China, India, Japan, South Korea, Russia, and the United States

Pivotal maritime states. A pivotal state's geography and economic capacity will determine its ability to influence the maritime commons. The geographic significance of Indonesia, Malaysia, and Singapore—sitting in a vast arc between the Indian Ocean and the South China Sea, between Asia's two greatest developing powers, and astride the world's most vital sea lane—inherently makes them pivotal to the preservation of the maritime commons in the Asia-Pacific. U.S. and Australian support of a cooperative effort by these three states to maintain the openness of the littoral waters has been a tremendously important development for the region's maritime commons and provides a significant precedent for regional cooperation.

It is significant that several of the pivotal maritime actors are U.S. allies, and most others have substantive military-to-military relationships with the United States. Developing and sustaining strong and cooperative security relationships with pivotal maritime states should be an integral element of the broader U.S. effort to maintain the openness and stability of the maritime commons. The United States should engage pivotal maritime states who share an interest in maintaining open access to the global commons, build their capacity to promote and protect those interests, and engage their support in efforts to build a lasting set of institutions and norms to protect the commons. Assistance provided to the littoral states surrounding the Strait of Malacca, which enhances responsible local control of a strategic chokepoint without increasing U.S. or foreign military commitments, could be an important model for future efforts to engage pivotal actors in securing the global commons.

Pivotal air states. As much of the threat to the U.S. military's ability to utilize the air commons stems from China, the Pentagon's efforts to protect the commons should likewise be primarily geared toward addressing the PLA's anti-access/area-denial challenges. Given that U.S. allies and partners will remain key to ensuring access to the air commons of the Asia-Pacific, the United States should focus on building up the air forces of allies and like-minded partner countries. For the United States, new partnerships mean production contracts and the development of capable air forces that are interoperable with the U.S. military. For the pivotal actor, partnering with the United States means gaining access to advanced technologies and building a relationship with the world's only global air power. In addition to building military air capabilities, engaging pivotal actors in the air commons should include assistance in the construction of robust civilian air infrastructure, which has proven to be an effective mechanism for economic development in the developing world.[57] The United States should work with its partners to encourage public assistance and private investments in order to build airports and supporting facilities, secure this infrastructure, improve navigation systems networks, and train network operators and managers.

Pivotal space states. Most pivotal space states in the Asia-Pacific are U.S. allies or partners, offering ample opportunities for positive engagement. As an experienced space power and the world's leader in space technologies, the United States can leverage its superior position in space to encourage the responsible behavior of pivotal space actors. This means encouraging the use of space for scientific exploration and collaboration, instead of as a theater for nationalistic chest-thumping.

The United States should work with like-minded pivotal space states to preserve the openness of the space commons and promulgate space situational awareness (SSA), or the ability of a space power to know what objects are in orbit and identify potential problems before they emerge. SSA information is currently a closely held secret, but it need not be. The United States could, and should, develop a version of SSA that can be shared with responsible space-faring nations. Another potential area for the engagement of responsible space actors is the tracking and eventual mitigation of space debris. The Inter-Agency Space Debris Coordination Committee (IADC)—composed of space agencies from the United States, the EU, Russia, Japan, Italy, the UK, France, China, Germany, India, and Ukraine—has already been established to facilitate cooperation by exchanging information on space debris research activities. Yet further cooperation to limit the creation of additional orbital debris and to mitigate existing debris is needed and will be a major challenge in the coming decades.

The United States should also engage its partners to ensure that international agreements on space are responsibly conceived and enacted. China and Russia have already proposed a treaty intended to ban space weapons, though their proposal was fundamentally flawed because it only focuses on space-based weapons (conveniently ignoring ground-based

---

[57] "Aviation Economic Benefits," International Air Transport Association, 2008, http://www.iata.org/ps/Documents/8907-00_Aviation_Economic_Benefits_Summary_Report.pdf.

ASAT weapons), lacks rigorous provisions for verification, and does not adequately define what would constitute a "space weapon." Despite these flaws, however, the proposed treaty's stated goal—"keeping outer space from turning into an arena for military confrontation, in assuring security in outer space and safe functioning of space objects"—is laudable. To accomplish this objective, the United States should work with its partners to pursue an international "no first use" agreement for all kinetic ASAT weapons and an international agreement prohibiting harmful interference with space objects that would encompass a prohibition against the jamming, blinding, and hacking of satellites during peacetime. With these agreements in place, the United States would be able to research kinetic and non-kinetic military capabilities for use in extremis while developing defenses against a condensed range of threats. The international community would also benefit: the use of kinetic weapons would be restrained, as would the creation of destructive orbital debris. Moreover, prohibiting harmful interference with space systems in peacetime would offer better protection while labeling interference more clearly as an act of hostility.

Pivotal cyber states. There is a great deal of conceptual work that remains to be done on the nature of cyber warfare. Foundational issues such as deterrence, proportional response, escalation, and norms of behavior remain undefined. The United States should work with pivotal cyber states in the Asia-Pacific to explore these topics. Further, identifying such states should make Washington realize that its allies and partners possess significant expertise. Engagement and an exchange of ideas and capabilities with U.S. allies would improve the quality of cyber capabilities for all involved.

The United States should also work with pivotal Asian allies and partners to pursue international agreements that preserve the openness of the cyber commons. The U.S. Computer Emergency Readiness Team Coordination Center (CERT/CC), other national CERTs, and international organizations such as the Forum of Incident Response and Security Teams (FIRST) perform some of the same functions for cybersecurity as the World Health Organization (WHO) and the Centers for Disease Control do for public health. However, these organizations are not nearly as comprehensive. As an example, the U.S. CERT/CC provides risk management and threat awareness at the system and software levels, assists in vulnerability reporting to vendors, and facilitates information-sharing.

The United States should work with like-minded states in the Asia-Pacific to make international organizations such as FIRST more comprehensive. Moreover, Washington should give these organizations the same level of legitimacy and capacity to address shared cybersecurity concerns as the WHO has in the realm of global health. Because of the lack of a global consensus on cybersecurity approaches, the United States would initially have to build a coalition of similar-minded actors (including states and corporations) to promote the health and openness of the cyber commons.

Implications for U.S. Strategy, Policy, and Regional Military Posture

Maintaining the global commons as open and stable arenas will be increasingly complex and challenging as new powers within the commons emerge. The status quo, in which the U.S. military guarantees the stability of the global commons and other states receive a "free ride," will become increasingly unsustainable. The development of military capabilities by potential adversaries of the United States will have significant implications for the future regional presence of the U.S. military, as well as for the ability of the U.S. military to project and sustain power in the region during times of crisis or conflict.

Ultimately, what is required is a shift in the United States' approach to the global commons in Asia from a uniform policy of dominance across the spectrum of warfare and at all times against all possible threats to one that is more tailored, more nuanced, and more sustainable. Though the United States should maintain the ability to deter, dissuade, and defeat any adversary during a time of crisis or conflict, basic deterrence and stability capabilities could be multilateralized through a deft mix of military adjustments and cooperation with pivotal like-minded states. This strategy shift would ensure U.S. presence and military dominance for a potential regional conflict while also engaging states that can responsibly contribute to the openness of the commons, and thus would begin to reduce the burden of that role on the U.S. military.

U.S. Military Shifts

When examining the future of U.S. presence in the face of anti-access threats, it is important to recall the reasons for the country's presence in the region. As the security guarantor for its allies, the United States deters and dissuades conflict and instability. Indeed, the period of U.S. military dominance in the Asia-Pacific has been a time of unprecedented peace and stability, especially given the simultaneous rise of several Asian states with long-brewing historical animosities. Without the United States, these long-dormant conflicts and rivalries would probably boil over and herald a new era of instability and conflict. By retaining a credible presence in the region, however, Washington can encourage the peaceful resolution of disagreements while dissuading and deterring hostility.

The U.S. regional military presence in the Asia-Pacific is founded on a network of bases that house aircraft, soldiers, sailors, and marines. These bases also provide logistical support to U.S. Navy ships by ensuring that expeditionary forces remain armed, fed, and fueled. China's development of medium-range ballistic missiles armed with precision-guided conventional warheads poses a significant threat to the U.S. network of forward bases in the region and, with the addition of anti-ship ballistic missiles, to U.S. power projection in the Asia-Pacific writ large.[58] China's Joint Anti-Air Raid operational strategy incorporates aircraft, ballistic missiles, cruise missiles, and space and air-breathing intelligence to comprehensively degrade the ability of an adversary to deploy into the region and sustain operations.[59] In 2009, Secretary Gates noted that these "investments in cyber and anti-satellite warfare, anti-air and anti-ship weaponry, and ballistic missiles could threaten America's primary way to project power and help allies in the Pacific—in particular our forward air bases and carrier strike groups."[60] The main operating bases in Okinawa, the main islands of Japan, and South Korea are already well within striking distance of Chinese missile systems, as are the likely operating areas for a U.S. carrier group during a Taiwan-related crisis (see Figure 5).[61]

Without the use of air bases in the region, the United States would lose the ability to generate a sortie rate that is sufficient to maintain dominance of the air commons in the Western Pacific. Thus, China's use of a high number of precise ballistic missiles fundamentally challenges Washington's traditional reliance on fixed regional forward bases. Furthermore, if China gained the capacity to successfully employ the much-discussed anti-ship ballistic missile (ASBM), U.S. air power in the region would be limited to long-range penetrating strike capabilities, which are far from sufficient to establish air dominance over a battlefield.

As the U.S. base network comes under increasing threat, the United States should pursue the creation of a more flexible network of smaller bases and supply stations around the world that support the military's

---

[58] This is capably described in Andrew Krepinevich, Robert Work, and Robert Martinage, "The Challenges to U.S. National Security," Center for Budgetary Assessments, August 21, 2008.

[59] U.S. Department of Defense, "Military Power of the People's Republic of China 2009," 13.

[60] Robert M. Gates, "Air Force Association Convention" (speech given at the Air Force Association Convention, National Harbor, September 16, 2009), http://www.defense.gov/speeches/speech.aspx?speechid=1379.

[61] U.S. Department of Defense, "Military Power of the People's Republic of China 2009," 23.

logistical needs yet require a smaller geographic and political footprint with the host nation. This will require moving away from the Cold War model of large, overtly military bases to dual-use civil-military facilities based on more implicit bilateral agreements. Supporting this should be a sustained effort to cultivate strong diplomatic and economic ties with strategically located states. An example is Singapore's Changi Naval Base, which can accommodate the largest of ships, including an aircraft carrier.

The Unites States should focus on adjusting its forward-basing posture to account for the threat of Chinese precision ballistic missiles. Theater missile defense and hardening will be necessary but far from sufficient. Making fixed bases invulnerable to ballistic missile strikes is both cost-prohibitive and unlikely to succeed. Therefore, the Pentagon should pursue alternative basing strategies that emphasize distribution, movement, and deception. Such a "nomadic" approach would entail quickly and regularly shifting operations to undermine threats against fixed points.[62]

Leading Cooperation and Building Partner Capacities

In addition to shifts in military capabilities, the United States should drive cooperation among like-minded states to share the burden of keeping the commons stable and open. Each state will naturally have its own unique interests and capabilities, and the U.S. approach should be carefully tailored for each state the United States engages. Although Asian allies will naturally be the first likely collaborators in the commons, other partners should also be approached as their intentions are clarified and areas of cooperation are identified. Collaboration and cooperation can take several forms, depending on the status of U.S. relations with the given partner as well as on the interests and capabilities of the cooperating state. With the most capable of allies, the United States should pursue joint operations and encourage policy collaboration across the commons. With countries whose interests in maintaining the openness of the commons are less clear, dialogue and confidence-building measures should be utilized to emphasize shared interests, build trust, and identify areas of cooperation. In this way, even China could become a partner in securing the global commons, should mutual interests be sufficiently identified and mutual trust sufficiently developed.

There is a third category of Asian states that the United States cannot afford to ignore if it wishes to engage partners in securing the commons: states whose interests toward the global commons largely match those of

---

[62] Robert Kaplan, "The Geography of Chinese Power," *Foreign Affairs* 88, no. 3 (May/June 2010): 22–41.

the United States, but who lack the capability to substantially contribute to cooperative security efforts. In order to build a network of like-minded states that will work to preserve Asia's commons, the United States must carefully and responsibly develop the capabilities of these states by utilizing dialogue, training, professional military education, and responsible military aid. Clearly, any arms sales must be carefully calibrated to ensure that regional animosities are not aggravated. Yet targeted and responsible military aid can help like-minded states contribute to the health and success of the global commons.

An example of this dynamic can be seen in U.S. and Australian assistance to the littoral states in improving maritime security in the Strait of Malacca. By providing radars and other types of military equipment, the United States and Australia built the capacities of similar-minded states and successfully improved security in one of the world's most important waterways while simultaneously reducing the burden on the U.S. Navy of providing security. This can in many ways be a model for future partner capacity-building.

The key for the United States will be to build a group of like-minded states and drive their cooperation in a constructive and pragmatic fashion. As a public good, it will be easy for states to continue to free ride on U.S. power or make diplomatic noises of cooperation while contributing little of substance. For a cooperative approach to work, real collaboration must take place, and that will require sustained U.S. leadership. Appealing to mutual interests, leading multinational military exercises, and driving international diplomatic efforts will all be essential for building a consensus on the openness of the commons. For states who decide they share interests with the United States, cooperation can be a major benefit for all sides. For those who reject cooperation, U.S. military shifts and the improved capabilities of U.S. allies and partners will ensure that the commons remain secure.

Conclusion

U.S. power and the stability of the existing international order depend on the openness and stability of the global commons. Goods flow, ideas promulgate, militaries operate, and people travel through these commons with little thought to how and why they are kept open. Ensuring the openness and stability of the global commons is in the mutual interest of all states with a stake in economic development; the openness of the commons has enabled Asia's dramatic rise to be the most important region of the 21st century. Ironically, however, the region's economic rise has funded the development of military capabilities that have fundamentally changed the dynamics of the global commons. While the United States will certainly remain the most militarily capable state in the region, Washington must recognize that the emergence of Asia-Pacific powers within the global commons will make the United States unable to secure the commons on its own.

The rise of China is a defining characteristic of every commons. A 30-year military modernization effort has made China the region's largest potential threat to the stability of the commons while, ironically, also making it more dependent on those commons. While the region can hope that Chinese strategists will recognize this dependence and begin to use the country's military to support rather than undermine the commons, hope is not enough. A hedging strategy, in which states encourage China to act responsibly while developing military capabilities to deter, dissuade, and defeat Chinese hostility, is prudent.

Yet the rise of China is not the only story of the global commons in the Asia-Pacific. The United States should not forget the rise of other states in the region that are developing the ability to operate within the commons. There is the potential for these new capabilities to enable a more aggressive enforcement of several long-dormant rivalries and territorial disputes, while potentially broadening the scope of other conflicts that were previously ground-focused. The United States has an important role to play in this challenge—primarily to act in its traditional role as a maritime balancer.

Related to the rise of other states in the region with the ability to operate within the global commons is the emergence of pivotal states, many of which are U.S. allies. The pivotal states will be an essential component of the United States' ability to adapt to the challenges posed by China's rise while developing and enlisting a responsible and capable cadre of like-minded states that can share in the responsibility of sustaining the commons.

Lastly, the emergence of Asia-Pacific powers in the global commons will have significant implications for the future of U.S. presence and power projection in the region. The threat posed by precise ballistic missiles will force the U.S. military to re-examine the way it projects and sustains military power. Alternative basing concepts and flexible basing options will supplement the traditional network of regional forward bases.

As with most strategic developments in the Asia-Pacific, the dynamics of the global commons in the region will not be straightforward. Suspicion, history, and diverging interests will drive states to compete with one another in order to prepare for a possible future conflict. Yet mutual interests in preserving the openness and stability of the commons will drive states together, forcing states to cooperate with other states that may well be hostile adversaries in a short period of time.

In the end, however, protection of the global commons in the Asia-Pacific will depend on the United States' presence and will to lead. Despite the rise of new powers, no other country has the ability to lead a global effort to protect and sustain the commons. No other country can challenge the U.S. legacy of building global institutions and enabling friends to advance shared goals.

EXECUTIVE SUMMARY

This chapter focuses on the real and potential impacts of climate change in Asia.

MAIN ARGUMENT:
Climate change models predict significant climate effects throughout the region. Dry areas will become drier and wet areas will become wetter. Coastal storms will increase in frequency and intensity. The monsoon may transform in dramatic ways. This situation is driven by many factors, including rapid population growth, urbanization, and economic growth. The likely social impacts of climate change include challenges to public health, increased population movement, diminishing state capacity, obstacles to development, and environmental damage. In this context, the potential for violent conflict ranging from riots to war is real, although there are also considerable opportunities for cooperation. In particular, with China's acknowledgment of the seriousness of climate change and its emergence as the world's leading investor in clean energy, the U.S. should deepen engagement in the region on climate change and related issues.

POLICY IMPLICATIONS:
- Take a leadership position on mitigating climate change and urge China to do the same.
- Develop a better understanding of the region by encouraging study abroad and similar programs.
- Fund research collaboration in China and throughout Asia.
- Rethink regional dynamics and consider the impact that activity at this level will have at the local level.
- Step up regional diplomacy—there are many stresses that need to be reduced.
- Help create a global humanitarian response capability.

Climate Change
and Environmental Impact

Richard A. Matthew

Since the Intergovernmental Panel on Climate Change (IPCC) published its Fourth Assessment Report (AR4) in 2007, climate change has been widely acknowledged as a phenomenon likely to have a significant and perhaps decisive impact on the prospects for development and security worldwide for many decades.

The overall picture is quite alarming for Asia, as climate change models predict significant effects throughout the region. While many factors will play a role in determining regional and local impacts, and planning will need to take place in the context of high levels of uncertainty, dry areas will tend to become drier and wet areas will tend to become wetter. Coastal storms will increase in frequency and become more intense. Disease curtains will migrate northward and southward from the equator. India and China may face unprecedented levels of water scarcity, while low-lying areas such as Bangladesh will face unprecedented levels of flooding. The timing and intensity of the monsoon, which is the single most important weather process in Asia, are likely to change, although the precise character of this transformation is not yet known. It is possible that weather patterns that are vital to the predominantly agricultural economy of much of Asia, such as the beginning of the rainy season, will become harder to predict in the decades ahead.

In the following seven sections, this chapter will provide a snapshot of the climate change situation in Asia today; examine the demographic, economic, and other factors underlying this snapshot; consider the likely

Richard A. Matthew is Founding Director of the Center for Unconventional Security Affairs and an Associate Professor of International and Environmental Politics at the University of California–Irvine. He can be reached at <rmatthew@uci.edu>.

and possible social effects of climate change within and outside Asia; explore the potential for conflict and cooperation around this issue; consider the potential for surprises in this area; and conclude with a discussion of the implications of climate change in Asia for the United States. The principal argument that emerges from this analysis can be summarized in three statements. First, poverty, geography, and demographics have combined to make much of Asia highly vulnerable to climate change, especially to drought and flooding. Second, the social effects of climate change could be disastrous—massive population displacement, chronic and rising famine, vast and aggressive health challenges, and diverse forms of misery and violence as communities struggle to survive. Finally, though this worst-case scenario is in no sense assured, it is an important benchmark for policymaking and provides a strong basis for recommending a deepening and expansion of U.S. engagement on climate change mitigation and adaptation throughout the region.

Overview of Climate Change

In very simple terms, climate change refers to an enduring change in the statistical characteristics of weather. A hot year is not climate change; a trend of global warming over decades or centuries is. Based on weather data extending back hundreds of thousands of years, scientists have concluded that we are living in a period in which the weather patterns that characterized past millennia are changing dramatically.[1] Specifically, since approximately 1850, the average temperature of the world has increased by one degree centigrade. This is scarcely the first time this has happened. As is made clear in numerous studies, the earth has been subjected to dramatic climate change since it was formed some 4.5 billion years ago. Variables that have caused climate change in the past include the intensification of solar energy, the shifting of tectonic plates into new latitudes, changes in the earth's orbit that affect the distribution of solar energy on the earth's surface, and intense volcanic activity.[2] Contemporary research suggests that none of these variables can explain current climate change, and scientists studying this issue since at least 1896 have identified and recently confirmed a new climate-forcing agent—industrialized human activity. Industrialization affects global climate through a range of factors including fossil fuel

---

[1] S. Solomon et al., eds., *The Physical Science Basis: Contribution of Working Group I to the Fourth Assessment Report of the Intergovernmental Panel on Climate Change* (Cambridge: Cambridge University Press, 2007), http://www.ipcc.ch/publications_and_data/ar4/wg1/en/contents.html.

[2] Edward O. Wilson, *The Diversity of Life* (New York: W. W. Norton, 1999).

emissions, aerosol use, and the dramatic reduction of natural carbon storage areas such as forests.[3]

It is worth noting that while the IPCC reports demonstrate strong scientific support for anthropogenic climate change, many people remain unconvinced by this claim. Although there are few skeptics within the scientific community, opinion polls show that throughout the world the general public is deeply divided on this issue. For example, a 2010 Populus poll in the United Kingdom showed skepticism rising, with only 26% of the public convinced that climate change was both real and caused by human behavior.[4] The concerns of climate skeptics can be organized into several categories:

- Concerns that climate change is not happening but has been fabricated by liberals and radicals to advance the hidden agenda of wealth redistribution

- Concerns that models are imperfect because they do not adequately take into account important variables such as cloud formation

- Concerns that climate change is real but there are alternative explanations for it that have not been adequately disproven, such as solar variation

- Concerns that while climate change may be real, the social impacts receiving attention are largely speculative and discount the possibility that impacts will be, on balance, positive, opening access to resources in the north and south and expanding growing seasons in large parts of the world such as Australia, Canada, and Russia

- Concerns that mitigation will impose higher costs than simply allowing societies to gradually adapt in response to market signals

Extensive consideration by climate experts suggests that these concerns tend to be nonscientific or highly selective in their use of science. Although there are some valid points raised about uncertainty, especially with regard to social effects, and though the possibility of a more robust alternative

---

[3] Spencer Weart, *The Discovery of Global Warming: Revised and Expanded Edition* (Cambridge: Harvard University Press, 2008).

[4] "'Climate Skepticism 'On the Rise,' BBC Poll Shows," *BBC News*, February 7, 2010. http://news.bbc.co.uk/2/hi/8500443.stm.

explanation can never be dismissed by science, counterarguments to date have garnered little support from the broad scientific community.[5]

Thus, there continues to be wide support for the AR4, which includes an entire report devoted to the social effects of climate change[6] and another on the mitigation actions that should be taken.[7] The end result is an integrated account of the causes and effects of climate change, albeit at a very high level of generality, based on averaging the outputs of climate models and aggregating large volumes of data (see **Figure 1**).Throughout the AR4 and in many other reports and studies, Asia is singled out as a region of particular importance because it (1) has almost half of the world's population, (2) is increasing its emissions, and (3) has large areas of high vulnerability where changes in temperature, precipitation, or the intensity and frequency of severe weather events could have unprecedented, and largely negative, human impacts.

Given the IPCC's authoritative rendering of climate science, it is not surprising that the 2007 IPCC reports have stimulated considerable discussion, especially in the areas of security and development. The German Advisory Council on Global Change, for example, concludes that "climate change will overstretch many societies' adaptive capacities within the coming decades," and describes how water scarcity, food scarcity, and an increase in natural disasters may "further undermine the economic performance of weak and unstable states, thereby encouraging or exacerbating destabilization, the collapse of social systems, and violent conflicts."[8] Taking this a step further, the Center for Naval Analyses (CNA), a group of retired U.S. military leaders, forecasts a future in which "climate change acts as a threat multiplier for instability in some of the most volatile regions of the world" and adds "tensions even in stable regions of the world."[9] Dan Smith and Janna Vivekananda quantify this threat, claiming that there are "46 countries—home to 2.7 billion people—in which the

---

[5] Several websites are devoted to the climate change controversy and provide an excellent overview of arguments on both sides. See, for example, "How to Talk to a Climate Skeptic: Responses to the Most Common Skeptical Arguments on Global Warming," *Grist*, http://www.grist.org/article/series/skeptics/; and Climate Change Skeptic web log, http://climatechangeskeptic.blogspot.com/.

[6] M.L. Parry et al., eds., *Impacts, Adaptation and Vulnerability: Contribution of Working Group II to the Fourth Assessment Report of the Intergovernmental Panel on Climate Change* (Cambridge: Cambridge University Press, 2007), http://www.ipcc.ch/publications_and_data/ar4/wg2/en/contents.html.

[7] B. Metz et al., eds., *Mitigation of Climate Change: Contribution of Working Group III to the Fourth Assessment Report of the Intergovernmental Panel on Climate Change* (Cambridge: Cambridge University Press, 2007), http://www.ipcc.ch/publications_and_data/ar4/wg3/en/contents.html.

[8] German Advisory Council on Global Change, *World in Transition: Climate Change as a Security Risk* (London: Earthscan, 2008), 1, 3.

[9] "National Security and the Threat of Climate Change," Center for Naval Analyses (CNA), April 16, 2007, 6–7, available at http://securityandclimate.cna.org/.

FIGURE 1   Schematic framework of climate change's anthropogenic drivers, impacts, responses, and linkages

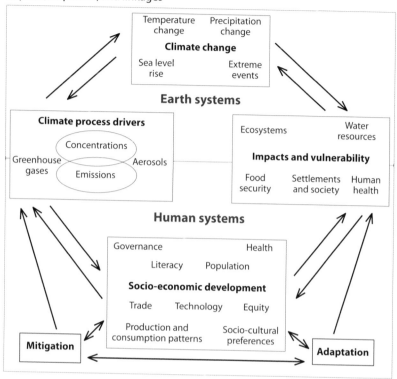

SOURCE: Core Writing Team, R.K. Pachauri, and A Reisinger, eds., *Synthesis Report: Contributions of Working Groups I, II and III to the Fourth Assessment Report of the Intergovernmental Panel on Climate Change* (Geneva: Intergovernmental Panel on Climate Change, 2007), http://www.ipcc.ch/publications_and_data/ar4/syr/en/contents.html.

effects of climate change interacting with economic, social and political problems will create a high risk of violent conflict."[10] In 2009, Achim Maas and Dennis Tanzler examined the first wave of assessments and predictions produced in response to IPCC's AR4 and concluded that "climate change is first and foremost a challenge for development and individual or human security, which could halt or reverse developmental achievements and threaten livelihoods." In their synthesis document, Maas and Tanzler also

---

[10] Dan Smith and Janani Vivekananda, *A Climate of Conflict: The Links between Climate Change, Peace and War* (London: International Alert, 2007), 3, http://www.international-alert.org/pdf/A_Climate_Of_Conflict.pdf.

underscore the significant "potential impacts of climate change on the existing armed conflicts and unstable regions or the potential for emerging conflicts and zones of turmoil."[11] In these and many similar reports, Asia has been singled out as an area of heightened concern.

Overview of the Situation in Asia

In the spring of 2010, severe floods caused havoc and took lives in China, Pakistan, Sri Lanka, and Indonesia as well as throughout Central Asia and in the Mekong River basin. Ironically, at the same time, farmers throughout the region—including in southern China, Southeast Asia, and northern Pakistan—struggled with the onset of another severe season of drought. These extreme weather events are becoming more frequent in a part of the world already highly vulnerable to natural disasters. In fact, according to the Natural Disasters Risk Index, Asia has the highest vulnerability to natural disasters in the world. Eleven of the fifteen countries considered to be most at risk are Asian nations, including Bangladesh (1), Indonesia (2), Pakistan (4), India (11), and China (12). The 2010 report, produced by the British risk analysis group Maplecroft, notes that

> over the last 30 years Bangladesh has seen 191,637 deaths as a result of major natural disasters, with storms claiming 167,178 lives. Indonesia has lost 191,105 lives over the same period, but 165,708 of these casualties were caused by the tsunami in December 2004.... India is subject to a wide variance of events and has lost 141,961 of its population to major natural disasters since 1980, including 50,000 to earthquakes, 40,000 to floods, 15,000 to epidemics and 23,000 to storms. China has suffered more losses than India, with 148,417, but a high concentration of these occurred during the 2008 Sichuan earthquake where 87,476 people lost their lives.

The authors of the report conclude that "extreme hydro-meteorological events" will increase in the region, a concern that is supported by considerable scientific evidence.[12]

In particular, using calculations from 23 different climate models, the AR4 authors have concluded that over the course of the next century, much of Asia will experience warming that is significantly above the global mean. Specifically, the average temperature is expected to increase by about 2.5 degrees centigrade in Southeast Asia, which is in line with the global average;

---

[11] Achim Maas and Dennis Tanzler, *Regional Security Implications of Climate Change: A Synopsis* (Berlin: Adelphi Consult, 2009), 3. See also Richard Matthew and Anne Hammill, "Sustainable Development and Climate Change," *International Affairs* 86, no. 6 (November 2009): 1,117–28.

[12] "BRICs and N11 Countries Top Maplecroft's Natural Disaster Risk Ranking—France, Italy, USA at 'High Risk,'" Maplecroft, May 26, 2010, http://www.maplecroft.com/about/news/natural_disasters.html.

by 3.3 degrees centigrade in South Asia and East Asia; and by 3.7 degrees in Central Asia, 3.8 degrees in Tibet, and 4.3 degrees in northern Asia—increases well above the global mean (see **Figure 2**). The IPCC describes an increase in heat waves in Central Asia as "very likely."[13] In support of this, considerable research catalogues an increase in the frequency and severity of heat waves and droughts throughout much of Asia in the recent past.[14]

FIGURE 2   Asian temperature and precipitation changes, MMD-A1B simulations

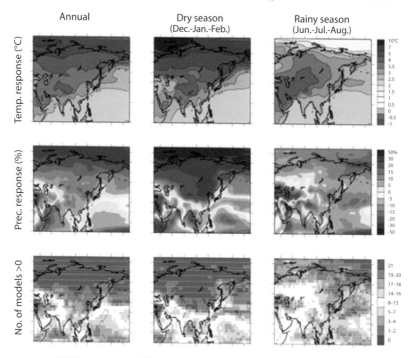

SOURCE: J. H. Christensen et al., "Regional Climate Projections," in S. Solomon et al., *The Physical Science Basis*, 883, http://www.ipcc.ch/publications_and_data/ar4/wg1/en/contents.html.

NOTE: Top row: annual mean, dry season, and rainy season temperature change between 1980 to 1999 and 2080 to 2099, averaged over 21 models; middle row: same as top but represents fractional change in precipitation; and bottom row: number of models out of 21 that project increases in precipitation.

---

[13] J. H. Christensen et al., "Regional Climate Projections," in S. Solomon et al., *The Physical Science Basis*, 850, http://www.ipcc.ch/publications_and_data/ar4/wg1/en/contents.html.

[14] Parry et al., *Impacts, Adaptation and Vulnerability*, 473.

For example, China has experienced an increase in the frequency of short heat waves in recent decades; Japan, Korea, India, and Southeast Asia have observed more hot days than in the past. The drought-affected regions of China have expanded by a million hectares since 2000.[15]

Insofar as precipitation is concerned, the IPCC projects that the dry season (December, January, and February) will become drier in South Asia, whereas the rest of the year will be wetter than in the past. East Asia is expected to experience an increase in precipitation throughout the entire year. In Southeast Asia, there is substantial uncertainty because the overlap across various climate models is less pronounced, but the IPCC projects an overall increase in precipitation, with wide regional variance. In Central Asia, models forecast an overall decrease in precipitation, whereas an annual increase is projected for Tibet and northern Asia. According to the authors responsible for the chapter on regional climate projections, "extreme rainfall and winds associated with tropical cyclones are likely to increase in East Asia, Southeast Asia and South Asia."[16] Many parts of China have observed increases in extreme rain events and flooding consistent with climate models. Record rainfalls and flooding also have occurred in many areas of South and Southeast Asia.

Driving Forces

The climate change occurring today is caused primarily by increases in the amount of greenhouse gases in the atmosphere. This in turn is related to the use of fossil fuels and aerosols as well as to the reduction of natural carbon storage, which is largely the result of the extensive modification of land cover. Both the long-term trajectory of climate change and its social effects depend on the interplay of many driving forces. These driving forces are not uniform across the planet, although there are many common causes across countries and regions. In the context of Asia, the major driving forces of climate change are linked to the urbanization of the region's growing population. Furthermore, Asia is the world's economic powerhouse and leads in energy consumption. Complicating these trends encouraging higher energy consumption are food security and governance challenges. While recognizing that drivers are interactive, this chapter seeks to provide an overview of the driving forces of climate change by discussing the following six issues:

---

[15] Parry et al., *Impacts, Adaptation and Vulnerability*, 476.

[16] Christensen et al., "Regional Climate Projections," 850.

- demographic change
- economic growth
- energy consumption
- food security
- governance capacity
- technological innovation and diffusion

The first three driving forces reflect the well-known equation for environmental impact popularized by Paul Ehrlich and John Holdren in 1971:

I(mpact) = P(opulation) x A(ffluence) x T(echnology)[17]

Demographic Change

One of the most remarkable trends in human history has been the steep increase in population growth over the past century—from 1.6 billion in 1900 to about 6.8 billion in 2010. The current rate of growth is approximately 1.1%, and the middle or average prediction of demographers at the United Nations is that the population will peak at about 9.2 billion by 2050.[18] As the population stabilizes toward the middle of the 21st century, Jack Goldstone argues that, at least in terms of security issues, outcomes

> will depend less on how many people inhabit the world than on how the global population is composed and distributed: where populations are declining and where they are growing, which countries are relatively older and which are more youthful, and how demographics will influence population movements across regions.[19]

In simple terms, more people translates into higher energy consumption and the conversion of more land cover into farms, ranches, and urban areas—all of which offer considerable potential to increase emissions and reduce carbon storage. Kerri Smith has calculated that on "a global scale, per capita carbon dioxide emissions from fossil fuels have hardly changed since 1970, hovering around the 1.2-tonne mark." She observes that "this average varies hugely from nation to nation, but the general trend is that

---

[17] Paul Ehrlich and John Holdren, "Impact of Population Growth," Science 171, no. 3,977 (March 1971): 1,212–17.

[18] UN Population Division, World Population Prospects: The 2006 Revision (New York: United Nations, 2007).

[19] Jack Goldstone, "The New Population Bomb: The Four Megatrends That Will Change the World," Foreign Affairs 89, no. 1 (January/February 2010): 31.

as the population has grown, emissions have increased in proportion."[20] Further complicating matters, as Goldstone's analysis suggests, where people live and how they produce and consume goods and services also will be of critical importance in determining climate change trends. In any case, whether one focuses on population growth or approaches the topic of demographic trends in Asia through a more complex prism, the outlook from a climate change perspective is extremely worrisome. According to the UN's 2009 data set,

> since 1990, the population of the Asia-Pacific region has been growing more slowly than that of the rest of the world. Between 1990 and 1995, it grew 1.5% annually but subsequently the growth rate declined steadily. By 2008, annual growth had fallen to 1.0%—the lowest rate among the world's developing regions.[21]

As the UN authors make clear, however, when unpacked this aggregate data discloses considerable variation across the region. For example, the population growth rate of Japan is negative, whereas the growth rate of Afghanistan is 3.5% at the time of writing. In any case, with a population of over 4 billion people, an average increase of just 1% amounts to Asia growing by roughly 40 million people per year, or 1.6 billion between now and 2050.

Asia not only is growing in numbers but also is developing a middle class with a considerable appetite for commodities. Furthermore, the region is rapidly urbanizing. According to the UN, "the Asia-Pacific urban population is growing more than twice as fast as the population as a whole—2.3% per annum compared with 1%." Moreover, "urbanization in Asia and the Pacific has also resulted in the growth of megacities—those with more than 10 million people. Of the world's 19 megacities, the Asia-Pacific region has 11, including 6 of the 10 largest."[22] One unfortunate outcome of rapid urbanization is the development of vast peri-urban areas constructed with little or no regulation, where huge populations eke out an existence in impoverished economies with little or none of the infrastructure that defines urban living in the developed world. According to the same UN report,

> as of 2005, the proportion of Asia-Pacific urban residents living in slums was around 35%. This did not differ greatly between subregions: in East and North-East Asia it was 33%; in South-East Asia it was 34% and in South and

---

[20] Kerri Smith, "The Population Problem," *Nature Reports Climate Change* 2, no. 6 (June 2008): 72–74, http://www.nature.com/climate/2008/0806/pdf/climate.2008.44.pdf.

[21] UN Economic and Social Commission for Asia and the Pacific (UNESCAP), *Statistical Yearbook for Asia and the Pacific 2009* (Thailand: United Nations, 2010), http://www.unescap.org/stat/data/syb2009/1-Demographic-trends.asp.

[22] Ibid., 13.

South-West Asia it was 37%. However in some countries it was much higher. In Bangladesh, Cambodia, the Lao People's Democratic Republic, Mongolia and Nepal, a majority of the urban populations live in slums.[23]

These slums, and other environmentally marginal areas in which the poor settle, tend to increase exposure to climate change and natural disasters. For example, "in Bangladesh and China, populations in low elevation coastal zones grew at almost twice the national rate between 1990 and 2000, exposing a growing number of people to the impacts of extreme weather like cyclones and flooding."[24]

Both Asia's vibrant middle class, aspiring to own cars and eat meat, and its desperate lower class, using vast quantities of wood and coal in a permanent struggle to stay warm and prepare food, are likely to increasingly contribute to climate change by raising emissions and reducing forest cover.

Economic Growth

Population growth has been outmatched by the rate of economic growth in Asia. The UN reports that "between 1990 and 2008, the region's aggregate GDP nearly doubled—to $17.7 trillion, and is now not far behind that of the largest region, Europe, at $19.7 trillion. In 2008, the real GDP of Asia and the Pacific grew at 3.8%."[25] As one UN commentary notes, "the region's rapid economic growth is putting a considerable burden on the environment, partly as a result of the increase in energy consumption. Asia-Pacific's carbon dioxide emissions surged from 1.9 tons per capita in 1990 to 3.2 tons per capita in 2004."[26] Today, China is the world's largest emitter of carbon dioxide, and three other Asian countries (India, Japan, and South Korea) figure among the top ten.[27]

While economic growth means more cars, larger houses, and an increase in meat consumption, wealth also creates the demand and capacity for stricter environmental standards and regulations—the so-called Kuznets curve (see **Figure 3**).

Wealth likewise increases a country's or region's bargaining position vis-à-vis great powers such as the United States. This is surely enhanced by the fact that China exports about $270 billion of goods and services to

---

[23] UNESCAP, *Statistical Yearbook*, 14.

[24] "Population and Climate Change," Population Action International, Fact Sheet, 2009, http://www.populationaction.org/Publications/Fact_Sheets/climate-datasheet/climate_datasheet.pdf.

[25] UNESCAP, *Statistical Yearbook*, 99.

[26] "Urbanization Brings Both Growth and Poverty to Asia-Pacific Region," UN News Centre, March 19, 2008, http://www.un.org/apps/news/story.asp?NewsID=26042&Cr=escap&Cr.

[27] "Population and Climate Change."

FIGURE 3   The Kuznets curve

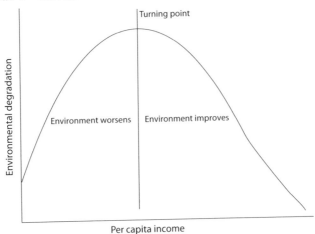

SOURCE: Ministry of Agriculture and Forestry (New Zealand), *Sustainable Development of New Zealand Agriculture and Forestry* (Wellington: Ministry of Agriculture and Forestry Policy, 2007), http://www.maf.govt.nz/mafnet/publications/agriculture-forestry-perspectives/sustainable-dvlpmt-of-nz-ag-and-forestry/page-05.htm.

the United States but imports only $61 billion. Asia's other great economic power, Japan, exports $86 billion to the United States but imports only $46 billion. This helps explain how China has accumulated $1.95 trillion in foreign exchange reserves and has thus been able to help the United States finance deficit spending by purchasing $798 billion of U.S. Treasury bonds. The comparable numbers for Japan are $1.01 trillion in foreign reserves and $751 billion in U.S. Treasury bonds.[28] Under these circumstances, it seems inevitable that U.S. bargaining capacity will erode and that the set of financial institutions Washington designed to help manage the global economy—the World Bank, the International Monetary Fund, and even the World Trade Organization (WTO)—will have diminishing capacity to steer the developing world, especially Asia, toward a given course of action. Based on past trajectories, one can anticipate that China and other economically robust regions of Asia will migrate toward stricter environmental

---

[28] These figures, which are provided by the U.S. Joint Forces Command, may be conservative. See "The Joint Operating Environment," U.S. Joint Forces Command, February 2010, 24, http://www.jfcom.mil/newslink/storyarchive/2010/JOE_2010_o.pdf. For example, China's State Administration of Foreign Exchange reports 2.447 trillion in foreign exchange in March 2010. See "Monthly Foreign Exchange Rates, 2010," State Administration of Foreign Exchange, http://www.safe.gov.cn/model_safe_en/tjsj_en/tjsj_list_en.jsp?ID=30303000000000000&id=4.

regulation, but this migration is likely to be steered more by Asian values and innovations than by Western ones.

The big question is whether the environmental impacts linked to the rising consumption pressures of the growing lower and middle classes in Asia will be offset or managed by stricter environmental standards.

Energy Consumption

China's consumption of energy has grown dramatically since 1980, with about three-fourths of its energy demand met by coal.[29] According to the U.S. Energy Information Administration's latest report,

China and India are the fastest-growing non-OECD economies, and they will be key world energy consumers in the future. Since 1990, energy consumption as a share of total world energy use has increased significantly in both countries. China and India together accounted for about 10 percent of the world's total energy consumption in 1990, but in 2006 their combined share was 19 percent. Strong economic growth in both countries continues over the projection period, with their combined energy use increasing nearly twofold and making up 28 percent of world energy consumption in 2030 in the reference case. In contrast, the U.S. share of total world energy consumption falls from 21 percent in 2006 to about 17 percent in 2030.... [Overall] Asia shows the most robust growth of all the non-OECD regions, with energy use rising by 104 percent from 2006 to 2030.[30]

Although renewable energy is the fastest-growing sector of the energy market, experts predict that fossil fuels will continue to dominate the energy mix through the next few decades; the use of coal alone is expected to double in developing countries by 2030.

The growing demand for energy could create several challenges. As noted in the 2010 Joint Operating Environment report, "the potential sources of future energy supplies nearly all present their own difficulties and vulnerabilities."[31] Concerns range from the diffusion of nuclear technology and materials out of the energy sector and into the hands of extremist groups or hostile nations to the increasingly aggressive jockeying for position that is taking place over the vast gas and oil reserves in the Arctic region.

On this latter issue, a U.S. Geological Survey assessment completed in 2008 determined that "90 billion barrels of oil, 1,669 trillion cubic feet of

---

[29] In 2010 the Chinese government announced that the renewable energy sector was now growing more quickly that the coal sector. See Patrick James, "China's Renewable Energy Growth Now Outpaces Coal," GOOD, April 9, 2010, http://www.good.is/post/china-s-renewable-energy-growth-now-outpaces-coal/.

[30] "International Energy Outlook 2009," U.S. Energy Information Administration, May 2009, http://www.eia.doe.gov/oiaf/ieo/pdf/world.pdf.

[31] "The Joint Operating Environment," 24.

natural gas, and 44 billion barrels of natural gas liquids may remain to be found in the Arctic, of which approximately 84 percent is expected to occur in offshore areas."[32] With the exception of the United States, the nations bordering the Arctic Ocean (Canada, Denmark, Norway, and Russia) have petitioned through the Law of the Sea Convention for an extension of their sovereign jurisdiction based on the physical characteristics of the continental shelf. The United States is expected to sign the treaty and follow suit shortly. This comes at a time when global warming is making the entire area more accessible to transportation and resource extraction—indeed, climate models predict complete or nearly complete ice melt as early as 2029. Since 1996, the region's environment has been governed by the Arctic Council, which consists of the five border nations plus Sweden, Finland, and Iceland. China, the European Union, France, Germany, Italy, Japan, South Korea, the Netherlands, Poland, Spain, and the UK have or will soon have observer status. These countries have been seeking a greater role in shaping the future of the region, but their efforts have been rebuffed. As access grows, tension between permanent members and observer nations may also grow.

Without a doubt, however, the single greatest concern about the growth in fossil fuel consumption is the contribution this will make to climate change, a contribution increasingly led by Asia. Asia leads the world now in emissions of the two most potent greenhouse gases, carbon dioxide and black carbon (or soot), which results from the incomplete combustion of fossil fuels and biomass.

Food Security

Food security is a major global challenge that involves addressing the impacts of trends such as population growth and demographic change, changing diets and food consumption patterns, rising food prices, concerns about food safety, and the considerable expected impacts on the global food system from climate change.[33] Clearly, the issue of food security has many dimensions, but experts tend to agree that the problem of undernutrition is largely a problem of poverty: desperately poor people cannot afford to buy enough food. This problem was aggravated following the 2008 global financial crisis when, in spite of record cereal harvests, food prices escalated and the number of malnourished rose from 854 million in 2006 to 1.02

---

[32] "Arctic Oil and Gas Report: Estimates of Undiscovered Oil and Gas North of the Arctic Circle," U.S. Geological Survey, Fact Sheet, July 2008, http://geology.com/usgs/arctic-oil-and-gas-report.shtml.

[33] Bryan L. McDonald, *Food Security* (Cambridge: Polity Press, 2010).

billion by the end of 2009.[34] The World Bank noted a 23% increase in its food benchmark index for 2009 and drew the following conclusion from this trend:

> The recent increase could aggravate the adverse effect of the food price spike of 2008 which continues to be felt in many countries in Asia and Africa. This is primarily for two reasons. First, despite the general easing of food prices in international markets after the mid 2008 food price spike, prices had been coming down very slowly in domestic markets in some of these countries. The recent upward trend in the international markets could reverse this gradual decline. Second, the global economic crisis of 2009 may have further strained the poor's already stretched coping mechanisms, though this impact varies considerably by region.[35]

Increasingly, experts are integrating climate change into analyses of the global food situation. Economists note that agriculture continues to be the principal livelihood of a majority of the people in Asia and of about two-thirds of the population of South Asia. Scientists point out that traditional forms of agriculture increase greenhouse gas emissions, reduce carbon storage, and reduce the biodiversity that protects against climate change. Against this background, a cycle is emerging that may prove devastating to parts of Asia (see **Figure 4**).

FIGURE 4   Agriculture and global warming: A vicious cycle

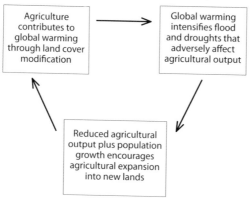

[34] "World Hunger Facts 2010," World Hunger Education Service, http://www.worldhunger.org/articles/Learn/world%20hunger%20facts%202002.htm.

[35] "Food Price Watch," World Bank, February 2010, http://siteresources.worldbank.org/INTPOVERTY/Resources/335642-1210859591030/FINAL_Food_Price_Watch_Feb2010.pdf.

As the AR4 notes, "recent studies suggest that substantial decreases in cereal production potential in Asia could be likely by the end of this century as a consequence of climate change."[36] It will not be easy for many countries to break free of this vicious cycle through which clearing land for agriculture contributes to climate change, which in turn reduces agricultural productivity and thus creates a need for more arable land.

Governance Capacity

The Failed State Index prepared by the Fund for Peace collects data on a dozen social, economic, and political indicators for every country in the world. Countries are then ranked along a spectrum, and those that fall on the "alert" (as opposed to "sustainable") end of the spectrum are classified as failed or fragile states. Such states lack the capacity to provide basic services such as security, their economies are disorganized and vulnerable, and they have severe social tensions and pressures. Pakistan, Bangladesh, Sri Lanka, and Nepal are all located at the high end of this scale; with the exception of Japan, the rest of Asia falls into the second-highest category of concern.[37]

The implication of this ranking is that South Asia, with two nuclear powers and a turbulent history that includes a considerable amount of violent conflict, may lack the governance capacity needed to fully assess climate change, optimize climate change mitigation and adaptation, and participate in climate change negotiations and the emerging carbon market.

Technological Innovation and Diffusion

Climate change has in large measure been driven by the technologies of the industrial era, which transformed the natural environment on an unprecedented scale through inventions such as the gas-powered car. Some analysts argue that this trend could be extended by Asia, which is poised to purchase an enormous number of cars and other vehicles. The authors of the Joint Operating Environment observe that "at present, the United States possesses approximately 250 million cars, while China with its immensely larger population possesses only 40 million." They add that "the Chinese are laying down approximately 1,000 kilometers of four-lane highway every year, a figure suggestive of how many more

---

[36] Cruz et al., "Asia," 479.

[37] "Failed States Index 2009," Fund for Peace, 2009, http://www.fundforpeace.org/web/index.php?option=com_content&task=view&id=391&Itemid=549.

vehicles they expect to possess, with the concomitant rise in their demand for oil."[38]

Technology is a capacity multiplier that in principle can be applied to the pursuit of a wide range of ends. Whereas some technologies amplify greenhouse gas emissions and modify land cover at alarming rates, others improve preparedness and response systems and reduce human vulnerability. Still others can mitigate climate change and facilitate adaptation to its effects. Current investment in alternative energy and other forms of green research and development in China, for example, may generate technologies that will strengthen resilience and help the economy grow by providing green goods and services to the world. Indeed, China is increasingly being described as the world leader in developing forms of alternative energy. Renewable energy is the fastest growing component of the country's energy mix, and analysts see a substantial clean energy market emerging. As a 2010 Pew report makes clear, "China has set ambitious targets for wind, biomass and solar energy and, for the first time, took the top spot within the G-20 and globally for overall clean energy finance and investment in 2009."[39]

Current and Predicted Vulnerabilities and Impacts

The increased human vulnerabilities and diverse societal impacts of climate change have been mentioned in the preceding sections, but they are worth elaborating on. Insofar as Asia is concerned, these include growing health challenges, increasing population flows, diminishing state capacity, development challenges, and resource scarcity and biodiversity loss.

Growing Health Challenges

The principal health concerns related to climate change are increased malnutrition due to reductions in agricultural productivity, higher mortality due to heat stress, more disease due to the migration of disease vectors and human movement into marginal environments resulting in exposure to new pathogens, and sickness related to water scarcity and contamination. According to the IPCC, "about 2.5 to 10% decrease in crop yield is projected for parts of Asia in 2020s and 5 to 30% decrease in 2050s compared with 1990 levels." The AR4 predicts that, absent mitigation and adaptation, an

---

[38] "The Joint Operating Environment," 24, 26.

[39] "Who's Winning the Clean Energy Race? Growth, Competition and Opportunity in the World's Largest Economies," Pew Charitable Trusts, 2010, http://www.pewtrusts.org/uploadedFiles/wwwpewtrustsorg/Reports/Global_warming/G-20%20Report.pdf.

"additional 49 million, 132 million and 266 million people of Asia…could be at risk of hunger by 2020, 2050 and 2080, respectively."[40] The IPCC authors further contend that

> climate change poses substantial risks to human health in Asia. Global burden (mortality and morbidity) of climate-change attributable diarrhea and malnutrition are already the largest in South-East Asian countries including Bangladesh, Bhutan, India, Maldives, Myanmar and Nepal in 2000, and the relative risks for these conditions for 2030 is expected to be also the largest.[41]

In the years ahead, areas that become warmer and wetter will likely be areas for the expansion of insects carrying infectious diseases. Countries with larger expanses of warm surface water will face an increased threat of phytoplankton blooms, which are ideal habitats for bacterial diseases such as cholera.[42] Moreover, malnutrition, especially involving micronutrient deficiency, weakens natural immunity and hence makes people more vulnerable to disease. Compromised public health can place enormous burdens on an economy as people require higher levels of medical care and are unable to work.

Increasing Population Flows

In 2006 Sir Nicholas Stern wrote that "200 million more people may become permanently displaced due to rising sea levels, heavier floods, and more intense droughts" by midcentury.[43] The AR4 reiterates this prediction:

> Climate-related disruptions of human populations and consequent migrations can be expected over the coming decades. Such climate-induced movements can have effects in source areas, along migration routes and in the receiving areas, often well beyond national borders. Periods when precipitation shortfalls coincide with adverse economic conditions for farmers (such as low crop prices) would be those most likely to lead to sudden spikes in rural-to-urban migration levels in China and India. Climatic changes in Pakistan and Bangladesh would likely exacerbate present environmental conditions that give rise to land degradation, shortfalls in food production, rural poverty and urban unrest. Circular migration patterns, such as those punctuated by shocks of migrants following extreme weather events, could be expected. Such changes would likely affect not only internal migration patterns, but also migration movements to other western countries.[44]

---

[40] Cruz et al., "Asia," 471.

[41] Ibid., 487.

[42] Ibid.

[43] Nicholas Stern, *The Economics of Climate Change* (Cambridge: Cambridge University Press, 2007), 56.

[44] Cruz et al., "Asia," 488.

Although there is strong agreement that drought and flooding due to climate change will add to the already significant repertoire of variables that encourage or compel people to move—such as the push factors of war and poverty and the pull factors of urban and foreign economic opportunities— some scholars underscore the high levels of uncertainty in such forecasts. Henrik Urdal, for example, claims that the

> potential for and challenges related to migration spurred by climate change should be acknowledged, but not overemphasized. Some forms of environmental change associated with climate change like extreme weather and flooding may cause substantial and acute, but mostly temporal, displacement of people. However, the most dramatic form of change expected to affect human settlements, sea-level rise, is likely to happen gradually, as are processes of soil and freshwater degradation.[45]

The volume of population movement, and the extent to which it is temporary rather than permanent, will depend on many factors. In any case, climate stress will have an impact on these complex processes and may well emerge as the single most important variable in shaping population flows.

Diminishing State Capacity

State capacity is diminished when the demand for services, such as education and health care, exceeds the growth of revenue streams, such as taxes and concession fees; when revenues shrink due to factors such as a recession; or when revenues are diverted from providing public goods due to corruption or other forces. According to the AR4,

> significantly longer heatwave duration has been observed in many countries of Asia....[The] frequency of occurrence of more intense rainfall events in many parts of Asia has increased, causing severe floods, landslides, and debris and mud flows....Increasing frequency and intensity of droughts in many parts of Asia are attributed largely to a rise in temperature, particularly during the summer and normally drier months, and during ENSO events.... Recent studies indicate that the frequency and intensity of tropical cyclones originating in the Pacific have increased over the last few decades.[46]

These trends receive support from the 2009 report of the International Federation of the Red Cross and Red Crescent Societies (IFRC):

> In terms of natural disasters and their impacts, 2008 was one of the most devastating years. While hazards are largely unavoidable, especially with the growing threat of climate change, they only become disasters when communities'

---

[45] Henrik Urdal, "Demographic Aspects of Climate Change, Environmental Degradation and Armed Conflict" (presentation at the UN Expert Group Meeting on Population Distribution, Urbanization, Internal Migration and Development, New York, January 21–23, 2008).

[46] Cruz et al., "Asia," 473.

coping mechanisms are exceeded and they are unable to manage their impacts. The world's poorest and most vulnerable people are those most at risk.[47]

As disasters grow in scale and frequency, and as the cost of relief efforts mount, government resources may be diverted away from other goods such as infrastructure, education, security, health care, and job creation. With fewer resources available to direct at the core elements of sustainable development, another type of vicious cycle could take hold in which underinvestment in development creates higher levels of vulnerability, resulting in more disasters and the continuing redirection of government resources into a sector that does not generate wealth. In this scenario, communities and even entire countries may become dependent on emergency assistance. The shifting of resources away from development and into disaster response could become a virtually permanent situation in low-lying countries such as Bangladesh.

Development Challenges

As anyone who has seen Hans Rosling's famous Technology, Entertainment, Design (TED) lectures is aware, Asia has made enormous strides in terms of improving public health and increasing per capita income.[48] This success has not been uniform, and Asia is also home to several of the poorest countries in the world, such as Afghanistan, Bangladesh, Nepal, and Pakistan. The economist Paul Collier writes that "the countries at the bottom coexist with the twenty-first century, but their reality is the fourteenth century: civil war, plague, ignorance."[49] Based on extensive statistical research, Collier has associated a distinctive pattern with these failed states: they experience high levels of violent conflict and environmental stress, they abut other unstable and violent countries, and their governments have too little capacity and too much corruption. Climate change, which is manifest through droughts, floods, and severe weather events, adds a further dampening layer to any development program.

Resource Scarcity and Biodiversity Loss

Finally, climate change also generates environmental impacts of concern to human societies. Climate change can affect the natural environment

[47] International Federation of Red Cross and Red Crescent Societies, *World Disasters Report 2009* (Switzerland: ATAR Roto Presse, 2009), 7, http://www.ifrc.org/Docs/pubs/disasters/wdr2009/WDR2009-full.pdf.

[48] "Speakers: Hans Rosling," TED, http://www.ted.com/speakers/hans_rosling.html.

[49] Paul Collier, *The Bottom Billion* (Oxford: Oxford University Press, 2007), 3.

directly—for example, through a drought that causes sand storms—or indirectly, through mechanisms such as the increased demand for water that occurs during a heat wave. Insofar as Asia is concerned, scientists are concerned about several climate-aggravated environmental trends:

- A wide range of changes to water systems and supplies, from glacial melt and permafrost thaw that have raised water levels in some parts of Asia to growing water scarcity in other areas due to increasing temperatures and demand

- Destruction of coral reefs along the coasts of Asia

- Increasing incidence of fires, especially in Southeast Asia, which destroy land cover

- A severe decline in wetlands in the major deltas of Asia in Bangladesh, China, India, and Pakistan

- Biodiversity loss

These forms of environmental degradation and damage reduce habitat and weaken the ability of Asia's ecosystems to provide invaluable services such as water and waste filtration, protection from severe weather, and carbon storage, thereby reducing the availability of some natural resources at a time when the region is growing in numbers and income.

Potential for Conflict and Cooperation

According to the 2005 Human Security Report, since the end of the Cold War there has been a "steep drop in the number of wars and international crises, [an]... even steeper decline in the number of genocides and other mass slaughters, and...[a] longer-term decline in battle-death rates."[50] Still, according to the Uppsala Conflict Data Program, there were roughly 27 violent conflicts around the world at the start of 2010, many of which have lasted years and even decades.[51] As noted above, Paul Collier has identified statistical patterns in which these persistent cases of violent conflict are associated with poverty, weak governance, conflict-prone neighbors, and environmental stress. This pattern is especially noticeable in the crescent of conflict that extends from West Africa across the continent into the Middle East and then down through South Asia and into Southeast Asia. Climate

---

[50] Human Security Report Project, *Human Security Report 2005: War and Peace in the 21st Century* (Oxford: Oxford University Press, 2005), 15, http://www.humansecurityreport.info/index.php?option=content&task=view&id=28.

[51] Uppsala Conflict Data Program, http://www.pcr.uu.se/research/UCDP/.

change is a form of environmental stress that amplifies other types of environmental stress while also placing burdens on weak governments and creating challenges for poverty alleviation and sustainable development. Given the focus of this chapter, a brief overview of the linkages between the environment and violent conflict are in order.

Since Thomas Malthus argued in the 18th century that agricultural output would not keep up with population growth, leading to a volatile condition of scarcity, many analysts have examined the social effects of environmental stress from the perspective of conflict and cooperation. In the aftermath of World War II, for example, Fairfield Osborn wrote: "When will it be openly recognized that one of the principal causes of the aggressive attitudes of individual nations and of much of the present discord among groups of nations is traceable to diminishing productive lands and to increasing population pressures?"[52]

In the post–Cold War era, and following the 1992 UN "Earth Summit" in Rio de Janerio, a number of scholars explored two theses: first, that certain forms of natural resource scarcity could trigger or amplify violent conflict; and, second, that certain forms of natural resource abundance—such as high value and easily lootable resources like diamonds, oil, and gold—could have a similar effect.[53] These intuitions have been examined statistically and through extensive case study analysis, and have contributed to the UN policy justification for integrating natural resource management into conflict prevention and peace-building.[54] The publication of the 2007 IPCC reports stimulated a flurry of activity around the possibility that climate change will intensify the linkages between the environment and violent conflict as it heightens competition for dwindling resources such as water, displaces people through drought and flooding, and weakens fragile states by overwhelming them with more frequent and intense natural disasters. As with all theories that seek to predict the incidence of violent conflict, this approach has attracted criticism. One particularly influential and fruitful vein of critique, associated with cornucopian thinkers such as Julian Simon and Bjorn Lomborg, emphasizes patterns of cooperation and innovation

---

[52] Fairfield Osborn, *Our Plundered Planet* (New York: Grosset and Dunlap, 1948), 200–201.

[53] See, for example, Thomas Homer-Dixon, *Environment, Scarcity and Violence* (Princeton: Princeton University Press, 1999); Ian Bannon and Paul Collier, *Natural Resources and Violent Conflict Options and Actions* (Washington, D.C.: World Bank, 2003); and Daniel Deudney and Richard Matthew, *Contested Grounds: Security and Conflict in the New Environmental Politics* (Albany: SUNY Press, 1999).

[54] UN Environment Programme (UNEP), *From Conflict to Peacebuilding: The Role of Natural Resources* (Geneva: UNEP, 2009).

that can also be associated with environmental stress.[55] This notion has received considerable support lately through the work of the International Institute for Sustainable Development, the UN Environment Programme's Post-Conflict and Disasters Management Branch, and scholars such as Geoff Dabelko and Ken Conca.[56]

In this regard, Collier's work could be especially useful, suggesting that the potential for conflict and cooperation may vary throughout Asia, influenced by the level of poverty, the capacity of the government, and the pressures coming from neighboring states. South Asia may be especially vulnerable to violent conflict triggered or amplified by environmental stresses related to climate change. Afghanistan has been in a state of war for three decades, and the fate of Pakistan, at least its northern part, seems closely linked to what is taking place across the border to the west. Tensions between India and Pakistan have waxed and waned since 1947, but both countries rely on water from the same sources—rivers that rely on snow and glacial melt and that could become seasonal or dry up altogether in a matter of decades.[57] Water is widely seen by experts as a resource that can cause tension and conflict, especially when it flows across borders and this flow changes significantly. Water treaties governing rivers such as the Indus and Mekong will likely require restructuring that will be very challenging politically. It is also possible that river systems that lack a joint management agreement, such as the Kabul River shared by Pakistan and Afghanistan, will become flashpoints of tension. Bangladesh, a poor country born of violent conflict, has become the poster child for the era of climate change, as massive annual flooding displaces millions of people on an increasingly regular basis. Further, Nepal is not sure what it should be doing about the country's vast water resources, given the growing needs of its much larger neighbors.

One can easily imagine enormous stresses related to the high costs of disasters, food shortages, water scarcity, population movement, and

---

[55] Bjorn Lomborg, *The Skeptical Environmentalist: Measuring the Real State of the World* (Cambridge: Cambridge University Press, 2001); and Julian Simon, *The Ultimate Resource 2* (Princeton: Princeton University Press, 1998).

[56] Ken Conca and Geoff Dabelko, eds., *Environmental Peacemaking* (Baltimore: Johns Hopkins University Press, 2002); Richard Matthew, Mark Halle, and Jason Switzer, eds., *Conserving the Peace: Resources, Livelihoods, and Security* (Geneva and Winnipeg: IISD Press, 2002); and UNEP, *From Conflict to Peacebuilding*.

[57] Although scientists agree glaciers are melting at an increased rate, predictions can be highly controversial. The IPCC recently apologized for warning of a potential full melt in the Himalayas by 2035, a claim based on anecdotal evidence. For an overview, see Bryan Walsh, "Himalayan Melting: How a Climate Panel Got It Wrong," *Time*, January 21, 2010, http://www.time.com/time/health/article/0,8599,1955405,00.html.

growing urban-rural and regional inequalities within both China and India. The authors of the Joint Operating Environment write:

> The course that China takes will determine much about the character and nature of the 21st Century—whether it will be "another bloody century," or one of peaceful cooperation. The Chinese themselves are uncertain as to where their strategic path to the future will lead. Deng Xiaoping's advice for China to "disguise its ambition and hide its claws" may represent as forthright a statement as the Chinese can provide. What does appear relatively clear is that the Chinese are thinking in the long term regarding their strategic course.[58]

All-out interstate and civil wars are costly and may not occur, but it is reasonable to predict a sharp spike in lower levels of violence and conflict such as demonstrations and riots. On the other hand, in a few years China and other Asian countries may have the technical confidence to cooperate more closely with the rest of the world on climate change mitigation and adaptation.

Potential for Surprises

Although skepticism about global warming caused by human activity has fallen sharply in recent years, there remain many areas of uncertainty. For example, climate scientists do not know what will happen to cloud cover in the years ahead as global warming continues, although they do know that cloud cover affects local weather and believe that dramatic changes in cloud cover are possible. Scientists have determined that enormous reservoirs of methane are locked in the permafrost that is extensive at high altitudes and in the polar regions, but they are not sure if these stockpiles will be released by global warming, and how quickly that could occur. Above all, scientists do not know how good—or how terrible—people will be at mitigating climate change and adapting to it. Moreover, the AR4 forecasts are derived from some 23 climate models developed in eleven countries, which generate different results that are often averaged to define trends. One large area of uncertainty, then, stems from the fact that predictions are based on assumptions and imperfect models.

Extrapolating from population and energy trends, scientists predict in the AR4 that the earth could experience an average increase in temperature of as much as 6.4 degrees centigrade by 2100. It is possible that global warming will initiate feedback mechanisms that counter this trajectory. It is also possible that climate change will drive biomes and ecosystems over critical thresholds resulting in dramatic and unforeseen knock-on effects,

---

[58] "The Joint Operating Environment," 40.

such as sudden gas release, rapid glaciation, or unprecedented microbial explosions. In addition to threshold effects (where the pace or scope of change suddenly increases or decreases significantly), scientists are also concerned about nonlinear effects—that is, effects that move along pathways that cannot be foreseen. In short, humankind could find itself surprised by conditions changing more quickly than the dates used in the AR4 suggest or by events that nobody has yet predicted.

A very different type of surprise could come from technological and political breakthroughs. From a climate change perspective, these could be highly destructive, such as a combination of powerful new technology and political will that would enable substantial resource extraction in the Arctic region. On August 2, 2007, two Russian bathyscaphes, Mir-1 and Mir-2, descended to the Arctic seabed beneath the North Pole. Russian scientists placed a Russian flag at the North Pole on the ocean floor. This symbolic gesture of claiming territory created tensions with the other Arctic nations, although the Russian government claimed that it was a harmless gesture made by scientists. Some analysts, however, believe that Russia and several other Arctic nations are moving toward increasingly aggressive competition to expand their claims to the region's natural resources and potential transportation routes. Substantial R&D investment in Arctic technologies by the militaries of these countries have been noted.[59] On the other hand, and in line with the arguments of Julian Simon and Bjorn Lomborg, technological breakthroughs could have tremendously positive effects on climate change—for example, researchers could develop a safe, clean, and cheap form of alternative energy that would rapidly reduce the demand for fossil fuels.

Finally, unforeseen disasters—events such as a third world war or the appearance of a highly transmissible and very lethal pathogen initiating a global pandemic—could reduce the human population enough to dramatically alleviate human pressures on the environment, thereby improving survival and development opportunities for the remaining population and enabling the recovery of many ecosystems.

Implications for the United States

Future Scenarios

The range of possible future scenarios is defined by two extremes, either of which would entail a massive restructuring of world affairs. The key word for the first scenario is "engagement," for the second, "turbulence."

---

[59] "Arctic Sees Military Buildup," *CBC News*, March 25, 2010, http://www.cbc.ca/canada/north/story/2010/03/25/arctic-military025.html.

China, the United States, and the EU, which account for roughly 55% of global greenhouse gas emissions, have not cooperated in trying to reduce emissions in order to mitigate climate change. The "common but differentiated responsibilities" clause of the Framework Convention on Climate Change (FCCC) relieves China, as a developing country, of the obligation to reduce emissions unless industrialized Annex 1 countries provide the funding and technology to do so. China thus far has been content to remain outside Annex 1. This is not to say, however, that China is unconcerned with the issue or has failed to take any action on the mitigation and adaptation fronts. Far to the contrary, and as noted in preceding sections, China has emerged as the world leader in clean energy investment and has made strong statements about the importance of addressing the challenges of climate change. A recent article in *Bloomberg Businessweek* notes:

> Climate change represents a threat to Chinese economic development, and laws should be strengthened to meet climate targets, the Chinese president's special envoy Xie Zhenhua wrote in the *China Economic Herald*. "The scale of economic destruction would be equivalent to that of the two world wars and the Great Depression combined" if global temperatures rise by 3 degrees (5.4 Fahrenheit) to 4 degrees Celsius, Xie said. "Human beings and the Earth cannot afford such disasters."[60]

In contrast, under the current U.S. president and his predecessor, climate change has received little attention, displaced from the policy agenda by terrorism and the financial crisis. While historically the U.S. Congress has been largely responsible for the lack of progress on climate change in the United States, there has been some promising legislative activity in the past year.[61] This comes at a time when Washington is examining ways to reduce carbon emissions by 17% compared to 2005 levels by 2020 as part of the agreements reached in Copenhagen in 2009. Clearly there are some grounds for optimism. If the three major sources of greenhouse gases were to work together to reduce emissions, united by a shared sense of responsibility and a shared level of concern about the high costs of not acting, then the next few decades could see dramatic progress toward mitigation. In the process, this novel configuration of great powers could well shape and influence many other dimensions of world affairs that are linked to the climate issue,

---

[60] Jeremy van Loon and Ben Sills, "China to Fight 'World War' Scale Climate Change Destruction," *Bloomberg Businessweek*, April 15, 2010, http://www.businessweek.com/news/2010-04-15/china-to-fight-world-war-scale-climate-destruction-update1-.html.

[61] Pew Center on Global Climate Change, "Climate Action in Congress," http://www.pewclimate.org/federal/congress.

such as sustainable development and governance capacity in much of the developing world.

On the other hand, one can imagine years and even decades of weak commitments and little coordination of effort, resulting in the erratic but steady escalation of tension, mistrust, and conflict. Flows of desperately poor Chinese into Siberia and of large volumes of Chinese funds, often in partnership with OPEC state funds, into the resource-rich, high-risk areas of Africa; a world heavily taxed and increasingly embittered by an unrelenting cascade of natural disasters; chronic food shortages and vast, crowded, parched areas in China and India as well as in large portions of Africa and West Asia; a spike in terrorism that rationalizes itself with allusions to the environmentally destructive practices of the Western world; and nuclear proliferation from South Asia into West Asia could be among the prominent features of a world headed for catastrophe.

What, then, are the trends and behaviors that would foster the latter scenario and render the former less likely? One concern is the proliferation of nuclear technology, driven by energy imperatives, into the hands of aggressive states and extremists. A related threat is the rise of political extremism linking climate change and its effects to the West. Another factor that could reduce the ability to mitigate and adapt to climate change would be a sharp increase in costly humanitarian disasters.

Many other factors could evolve in ways that support either scenario. In particular, the migration of skills and knowledge from India, Pakistan, and China to places that are far more environmentally attractive to live in—Australia, Canada, the EU, and the United States—might reduce capacity in Asia but could also deepen networks that increase mutual understanding and exchange. Similarly, the migration of labor outside Asia and into areas such as Siberia, which is experiencing a sharp population decline, and Africa could either generate tension or lay the foundation for more cooperation.

Moreover, increased competition between Asian countries, such as China and India, and Europe and the United States in various regions of the world—for example, in the resource-rich countries of Africa—could either promote an adversarial relationship or stimulate climate-sensitive innovation and exchange.[62]

Recommendations for the United States

The United States should adopt the following measures to discourage turbulence and foster engagement.

---

[62] John Ghazvinian, *Untapped: The Scramble for Africa's Oil* (New York: Harcourt, 2007).

Mitigate climate change. A UN report released in 2009 defines "a maximum temperature increase of 2°C above pre-industrial levels as the target for stabilizing carbon concentrations at a level that prevents dangerous anthropogenic interference in the climate system." According to the report, "this corresponds to a target greenhouse gas concentration (in terms of carbon dioxide equivalents) of between 350 and 450 parts per million (ppm) and to global emission reductions of the order of 50–80 per cent over 1990 levels, by 2050."[63]

There are four basic pathways to mitigation: (1) improving energy efficiency in transportation, building, agriculture, and elsewhere; (2) migrating to alternative sources of energy; (3) protecting natural carbon storage systems and developing new ways of capturing and storing carbon; and (4) reducing consumption. The United States should assume a leadership position on this issue, thereby inspiring China to follow suit. Otherwise, China may soon assume leadership on this front, as it already has in clean energy investment, making strong commitments at future conferences of the parties to the Climate Change Convention and offering the world an array of green technologies.

Encourage study abroad in China and throughout Asia. According to a 2009 article in the *New York Times*, "while India was, for the eighth consecutive year, the leading country of origin for international students— sending 103,260 students, a 9 percent increase over the previous year— China is rapidly catching up, sending 98,510 last year, a 21 percent increase."[64] In contrast, the number of U.S. students studying in China in 2008 was 19,194.[65] There is a need for the next generation of Americans to gain a higher level of global proficiency if the United States is to maintain a leadership position in world affairs and address global challenges such as climate change. To do this, many more students need to study abroad in China and throughout Asia, as well as in other parts of the world.

Encourage and fund research collaboration in China and the rest of Asia. An expansion of study abroad programs ought to be accompanied by a focused expansion of research cooperation between U.S. and Chinese universities. Climate change is an ideal research area around which to construct a global epistemic community—a group of scientists who work together, have a shared understanding of an issue and how to address it, and

---

[63] UN, *World Economic and Social Survey 2009: Promoting Development, Saving the Planet* (New York: UN Publications, 2009), vi, http://www.un.org/esa/policy/wess/wess2009files/wess09/wess2009.pdf.

[64] Tamar Lewin, "China Is Sending More Students to U.S.," *New York Times*, November 16, 2009 http://www.nytimes.com/2009/11/16/education/16international-.html.

[65] Chen Jia, "Number of US Students Set to Soar in 4 Years," *China Daily*, April 2, 2010, http://www.chinadaily.com.cn/china/2010-04/02/content_9678391.htm.

are in a position to influence policy. The AR4 provides a list of "key specific research-related priorities for Asia" that could serve as the initial platform for more extensive research collaboration:

- basic physiological and ecological studies on the effects of changes in atmospheric conditions;

- enhancing capability to establish and maintain observation facilities and to collect, and compile, climatic, social and biophysical data;

- improvement of information-sharing and data networking on climate change in the region;

- impacts of extreme weather events such as disasters from flood, storm surges, sea-level rise, heatwaves, plant diseases and insect pests;

- identification of social vulnerability to multiple stressors due to climate change and environmental change;

- adaptation researches concerning agro-technology, water resources management, integrated coastal zone management; pathology and diseases monitoring and control;

- sectoral interaction such as between irrigation and water resources, agricultural land use and natural ecosystem, water resources and cropping, water resources and livestock farming, water resources and aquaculture, water resource and hydropower, sea-level rise and land use, sea-water invasion and land degradation;

- mainstreaming science of climate change impacts, adaptation and vulnerability in policy formulation;

- identification of the critical climate thresholds for various regions and sectors.[66]

It would be useful for such collaboration to focus also on solutions—especially mitigation technologies and alternative fuels.

Rethink regional dynamics. Climate change will have dramatic environmental impacts, including the creation of new ecosystems due to drought, flooding, and ice melt. Related to this, novel social configurations are likely to emerge around new problems, something that could change regional structures and dynamics throughout Asia. For example, flooding is gradually displacing people from low-lying areas on a permanent basis. Even though displaced people, especially if they are poor, do not tend to move very far, their movements can modify the character and dimensions

---

[66] This bulleted list appears in Cruz et al., "Asia," 497.

of regional economies and politics in dramatic ways.[67] What will these new regions look like, and what sort of interventions might encourage stability—or facilitate turbulence? Similarly, it seems reasonable to assume that China and India are both contemplating their relationships with small, water-rich nations such as Nepal, something that could produce a novel form of regionalism in the Himalayas. Changes in the flow of the Kabul River, which is not managed through any regional treaty, might lead to a restructuring of relationships in that river basin linking northern Pakistan to eastern Afghanistan. It might also be useful to look at the regional dynamics that are emerging around centers of rapid urban growth, because cities must import vast quantities of energy and food from somewhere in order to survive and flourish. How will the United States recognize the emergence of new regions, and how can it promote security, development, and cooperation in them? Creating a task force around this issue would be a good starting point.

Step up regional diplomacy. Climate change impacts are more likely to be managed by societies that are stable and resilient. The United States, which has moral and prudential reasons for promoting stability and resilience, should carefully assess where it might be able to assist China, India, and others in addressing the numerous flashpoints in Asia. The obvious priorities are Pakistan, in terms of nuclear proliferation; Afghanistan and Pakistan, in terms of governance capacity, poverty, and conflict potential; Bangladesh, in terms of climate effects; and India, Nepal, Sri Lanka, and Thailand, in terms of festering conflict that could have broader impacts. Climate change mitigation and adaptation, and sustainable development and conservation more generally, may offer very productive ways to deepen and extend engagement in various regions of Asia. To succeed here the United States must come to some resolution on two foreign policy issues. First, what is the diacritical feature of the U.S. relationship with China: is Beijing a partner, a competitor, or an adversary? Second, what is the mix of investment in diplomacy, development, and defense that the United States wants to make in different regions of Asia? As was argued above, creating a task force to expand debate on this issue beyond Washington and include a more substantial knowledge base from the conservation and business communities would be a good beginning.

Help create a global humanitarian response capability. The cost of humanitarian response is very high, and the demand is growing. The United States tends to send extremely expensive resources such as Marine Corp units, because they are ready to go and able to provide a wide range of

---

[67] This has happened in parts of Africa, such as the Great Lakes region, due to chronic conflict.

services in any operating environment. This, however, is not a sustainable approach to a problem that is worsening. Instead, the United States should assist in the creation of a global emergency response plan that cultivates local capacity, supplements that capacity when needed, and provides a reliable and transparent coordinating service to ensure that assistance is not wasted but is streamed in the most efficient and enduring manner possible.

EXECUTIVE SUMMARY

This chapter examines the prospective impact of demographic changes on the strategic balance in Asia.

MAIN ARGUMENT:
Over the coming decades, the demographic profiles of the major powers of the Asia-Pacific region—China, India, Japan, Russia, and the U.S.—stand to be transformed significantly. Impending changes will directly affect the ability of these states to augment power and extend influence internationally. The strategic balance will be affected not just by changes in human numbers but by changes in human resource profiles (health and educational patterns) that bear on economic productivity and thus on military potential.

POLICY IMPLICATIONS:
• As the trend lines vary widely across the Asia-Pacific's major powers, important shifts in relative potential may be in store for these states in the coming generation. Demographic trends portend serious relative economic decline in Russia, severe complications for the prospect of "China's rise," relative economic decline for Japan, a relatively positive outlook for India, and, comparatively speaking, the most auspicious fundamentals for the U.S.

• Moscow and Beijing, in particular, do not yet seem to appreciate the extent to which demographic constraints conflict with their current international strategies—a disjuncture that could lead to unpredictable changes in their external behavior.

• For the U.S., the main strategic demographic challenges appear to be contending with questions of domestic human resources, including education and health, and dealing with the impending demographic decline of strategic allies. Unfolding demographic trends underscore the importance of extending the U.S. alliance structure to new states that share U.S. interests and affinities.

Asia-Pacific Demographics in 2010–2040: Implications for Strategic Balance

Nicholas Eberstadt

Demographic trends gradually but relentlessly alter the realm of the possible, not only for individual human beings but also for the societies they constitute and the states that represent them. The impact of population trends on state capabilities—on the capacity of governments to augment power and exercise influence internationally—is manifest not only through alterations in raw demographic totals (changes to overall population structure through patterns of births, deaths, and migration) but also through the changing characteristics and socio-economic profiles of the children, men, and women who compose the national populations in question. This chapter will examine the prospective role that demographic trends may play in Asia and the Pacific in shaping new constraints on, and opportunities for, the major powers of the region in the decades ahead.[1]

The horizon for this analysis will extend out three decades to the year 2040. The reason that this chapter may dare offer demographic projections over such an extended horizon is simply this: the overwhelming majority of people that will be living in the major states of the Asia-Pacific region 30

Nicholas Eberstadt holds the Henry Wendt Chair in Political Economy at the American Enterprise Institute. He can be reached at <eberstadt@aei.org>.

The author would like to express his thanks to Apoorva Shah for permission to present some co-authored research here, as well as to Frances Chen for her research assistance.

[1] In a century that effectively commenced with the September 11 terror attacks on New York and Washington, any observer of international affairs must be alert to the role that nonstate actors now play in the international arena. Even so, state actors still dominate the friendly and sometimes unfriendly competition that takes place on the global chessboard, and the primacy of states in establishing the contours of the international security environment is unlikely to be replaced any time soon.

years hence are already alive today and living in those countries now.[2] Such projections obviously do not and cannot make any provision for cataclysmic upheavals or disasters in the years ahead. Further, it is important to recall that more prosaic but nonetheless consequential demographic surprises have occurred with some regularity in the past—both in Asia and elsewhere; though unforeseen at present, more of these surprises no doubt lie in store in the coming decades. The point, however, is that demographic projections today can afford a reasonable approximation of the population profiles of the major countries in the Asia-Pacific region 30 years hence. These prospective demographic profiles can be highly informative about the coming pressures on economic performance as well as on such essential but largely incalculable factors as social cohesion and the perceptions and calculations of national leadership—and thus, by extension, on prospective relative changes in state capacities for competition on the international stage.

The projections outlined in this chapter point to some dramatic prospective changes for the population profiles of the region's major states in the decades immediately ahead. These transformations will be difficult to mitigate in any appreciable measure, will be all but impossible to forestall entirely, and could have a major influence on the relative capabilities of state actors to engage in sustained international strategic competition.

This chapter proceeds through five sections. The first briefly considers the general impact of national population trends on state capacities for augmenting power and extending international influence. The second section provides an overview of key demographic trends for Asian and selected additional countries over the past generation, as well as the outlook for the decades immediately ahead. The third offers a summary review of the demographic trends altering the realm of the possible for five major powers of the Asia-Pacific region: China, India, Japan, the Russian Federation, and the United States. The fourth section compares prospective demographic trends for these five states in three realms that may have special bearing on relative national power: military-age manpower, working-age manpower, and highly trained manpower and "knowledge production." The final section offers an overall assessment of, and some tentative conclusions

---

[2] Given the relatively low birth and death rates currently prevailing throughout the region, current projections suggest that people living in India as of 2010 will still account for roughly three-fifths of the country's total population in the year 2040; for China and the United States, the corresponding fraction will be closer to two-thirds; for Russia, perhaps 70% or more; and in Japan, that fraction could be close to three-fourths. Here, as elsewhere in this study, I rely heavily on the UN Population Division (UNDP), "World Population Prospects: The 2008 Revision," http://esa.un.org/unpp/index.asp; and the U.S. Census Bureau, International Data Base, http://www.census.gov/ipc/www/idb/. The U.S. Census Bureau produces a single projection for the countries it analyzes; unless otherwise indicated, all references to UNDP projections cite medium-variant projections.

about, the manner in which demographic trends may shape the strategic balance in Asia in the decades ahead.

Assessing the Influence of Population on National Power

In long-term geopolitical competition, a country's population surely matters—but just how much? The seeming precision of national population counts and other demographic statistics may convey the illusion that the role of the population factor in international affairs can be correspondingly calculated with regularity and exactitude, but this simply is not so. Though population trends can help us understand some of the complex pressures that bear on the international strategic balance and states' potential for exerting influence abroad, at the end of the day the assessment of the role of population in shaping the strategic environment remains more of an art than a science. Mechanistic or deterministic readings of the population factor in world affairs are unwarranted—and even worse, are likely to mislead.

At the simplest of levels, many observers of geopolitics casually seem to subscribe to the proposition that "there is strength in numbers." It is surely unobjectionable to suggest that in the modern era a relatively large national population seems to be a necessary precondition for attaining great-power status.[3] Additionally, differentials in population growth are commonly (though not always explicitly) believed to affect the balance of power between nations and even entire regions. There are numerous historical examples that would appear to reaffirm this notion: perhaps most famously, the Franco-Prussian rivalry in the nineteenth century. Over that long period, Germany not only out-peopled France but also displaced France as Europe's predominant continental power. Germany's relatively rapid demographic growth may well have counted as an advantage in Berlin's contest against Paris, but population trends were hardly the only quantity that was tilting the balance between these two states over those generations. Indeed, given all the other critical non-demographic factors in play during those years, it is not at all self-evident that demographics were a necessary, much less sufficient, condition for Berlin's ascendency over Paris.[4]

---

[3] This precondition is famously suggested, for example, by Katherine Organski and A.F.K. Organski, *Population and World Power* (New York: Knopf, 1961).

[4] To mention just a few of the most obvious additional factors: the unification of Germany under Prussian governance; the florescence of German higher education, science, and technology; the industrial-chemical revolution that underpinned Germany's burst of industrialization; the transformation of German banking and public finance; and the advent of a world-class cadre of strategists in the Prussian General Staff whose members devised and implemented a nineteenth-century "revolution in military affairs." See Nicholas Eberstadt, "Demography and International Relations," *Washington Quarterly* 21, no. 2 (Spring 1998): 33–52.

In the present day, the simplistic variant of the strength in numbers thesis is confronted by the obvious counterexamples of China and sub-Saharan Africa. China's rise in international influence since 1978 (when Deng Xiaoping's program of reforms was embraced by the Chinese Communist Party) is arguably the single most important change in the geopolitical balance since the end of the postwar era, excepting only the collapse of the Soviet empire. However, China constitutes a smaller fraction of world population, and Asian population, today than in 1978.[5] Conversely, sub-Saharan Africa's share of total world population has increased tremendously in the era since decolonization (from about 7% in 1963 to over 11% today). Yet this demographic surge has not exactly translated into increasing international influence for the sub-Saharan region or its various governments.

As the cases of China and the sub-Sahara should underscore, the role of human numbers per se in the strategic competition between states depends crucially, at the very least, both on the economic potential of the human beings in question and on government capabilities for translating that potential into international influence. Taking a measure of this human potential must be qualified, more than ever before, by the evident new potentialities for sudden and increasingly rapid improvements in economic potential per capita. The recent economic history of East Asia underscores this point.[6] Such extraordinarily rapid alterations in the average economic potential of a country's citizenry only emphasize how hazardous it is to presume that a state's economic, diplomatic, or military fortunes depend mainly—or even largely—on raw human numbers alone.

For a more informative and reliable evaluation of the role that population may play in recasting the strategic environment in the years ahead, one clearly needs to look beyond the basics arithmetic of births, deaths, migration, and overall population structure by age and sex. Both today and in the years ahead, the economic and military potential of societies in the Asia-Pacific region—and by extension, the capabilities of the governments representing these populations—will be profoundly affected by the human resources in the countries under consideration. By paying some attention to "human capital"—as proxied, however imperfectly, by

---

[5] Between 1978 and 2008, China's estimated share of global population dropped from 22% to 20%; its share of Asia's population (with Asia defined to include Iran and all countries east of it) fell from 39% to 33%. U.S. Census Bureau, International Data Base.

[6] According to estimates by the eminent economic historian Angus Maddison, per capita GDP in the postwar era leapt nearly seven-fold in just 30 years in both China (1978–2008) and Japan (1950–80) and over seven-fold in Taiwan (1960–90) and Singapore (1965–85), while in the Republic of Korea (ROK, or South Korea) per capita GDP soared eight-fold over a thirty-year period (1965–85). See Angus Maddison, "Statistics on World Population, GDP and Per Capita GDP, 1–2008AD," March 2010, available at http://www.ggdc.net/maddison/.

national health and educational profiles—we can move toward a greater appreciation of the prospective role of human resources in the strategic balance of the Asia-Pacific. This chapter will offer a preliminary exposition of some of these prospective trends and their potential bearing on the future capabilities of the major powers in the Asia-Pacific region.

Overview of the Basic Demography of the Asia-Pacific Region

In an earlier volume in the *Strategic Asia* series, I outlined the basic demographic contours of the Asia-Pacific region (defined to include Asia east of Iran) and the demographic forces driving population change in this diverse amalgam of countries.[7] There is no need to repeat those findings in detail, but given intervening demographic changes, some updates are necessary.

Table 1 provides a summary overview of the basic demographic situation today in Eastern Asia, Southeastern Asia, and South-Central Asia (as these territories and countries are grouped by the current conventional United Nations classification) plus several other countries intimately involved in Asian affairs: namely, Australia, the Russian Federation, and the United States.

The inhabitants of the regions and countries included in this table account for a projected total of about 4.4 billion persons in 2010: nearly1.6 billion in East Asia, 600 million in Southeast Asia, 1.8 billion in South-Central Asia, and half a billion in Australia, Russia, and the United States. Taken together, these territories encompass nearly two-thirds (64%) of the planet's current population, a roughly similar share of total global output and likely an even larger share of global military potential.

For all the diversity on display in Table 1, the countries and territories of the Asia-Pacific region have been profoundly impressed by some important and common demographic trends over the past generation: among them, continuing but highly uneven improvements in life expectancy and health and generally low rates of inter-country migration (with a few exceptions duly noted). Demographic profiles today have also been affected by some unexpected surprises from the past generation, including the unnatural increase in sex ratios at birth throughout most of East Asia and parts of Southeast and South-Central Asia and the ongoing health crisis in the Russian Federation. The overarching trend that has

---

[7] Nicholas Eberstadt, "Strategic Implications of Asian Demographic Trends," in *Strategic Asia 2003–04: Fragility and Crisis*, eds. Richard J. Ellings, Aaron L. Friedberg, and Michael Wills (Seattle: National Bureau of Asian Research, 2003).

while India's overall fertility levels are still above replacement, large parts of the country—including most urban agglomerations and much of the rural south—are now sub-replacement settings.

Low fertility and even sub-replacement fertility are now being achieved voluntarily, even in locales where incomes are very low, educational access is distinctly limited, and agricultural lifestyles remain the norm. And though we cannot know where (or whether) further fertility decline will occur in the Asia-Pacific in the decades ahead, one new emerging trend suggests increasing downward pressure on birth rates for a growing number of countries within the region—what Gavin W. Jones has called "the flight from marriage in South-East and East Asia."[14] In contrast with the recent past, when universal female marriage at younger ages was the notional norm (if not always the practicable reality), women in East and Southeast Asia are increasingly choosing to postpone marriage to ever later ages or not to marry at all (see **Table 2**).

To date, no appreciable "flight from marriage" is evident in Asia's demographic giants, China and India, but it is by no means obvious that these countries will be impervious to the spread of such social norms and customs in the decades ahead. This wild card could have big implications for Asian childbearing patterns over the next generation.

Fertility trends are typically the main determinant of future changes in population size and structure for settled societies. Fertility patterns in the Asia-Pacific have several implications for pending transformations within this region over the coming decades. First, due mainly to current differentials in fertility, big differentials in population growth between certain countries are a fact of life today, and appreciable shifts in relative population size between countries in the region can be expected in the years ahead.[15] Second, given the dramatic fertility decline throughout the Asia-Pacific region over the past generation, and pervasive low or sub-replacement fertility in so much of the region today, the age of the Asian

---

[14] See Gavin W. Jones, "The 'Flight from Marriage' in South-East and East Asia," Asia Metacentre, Research Paper Series, no. 11, June 2003, http://www.populationasia.org/Publications/ ResearchPaper/AMCRP11.pdf.

[15] This will hold true even if fertility falls rapidly in some countries that are currently experiencing rapid population growth, owing to the phenomenon of "demographic momentum." For example, even if Afghanistan immediately shifted to net replacement fertility, a much larger cohort of young girls would be replacing today's women of childbearing age. The population thus would continue to grow vigorously for at least one more generation.

TABLE 2   Asia's "flight from marriage": Women never married at ages 35–39 (%)

	1970	1980	1990	2000	2005
Hong Kong	3.0	4.5	10.2	17.5	20.3
Burma	7.0	8.9	13.8	18.6	–
Japan	5.8	5.5	7.5	13.8	18.4
Taiwan	1.2	2.1	6.0	11.1	15.9
Singapore	5.1	8.5	14.8	15.1	15.0
Thailand	5.2	7.3	9.6	11.6	–
Peninsular Malaysia - Chinese	5.7	7.6	9.1	10.5	–
Philippines	8.0	8.0	8.7	9.5	–
Vietnam	–	–	8.9	8.7	–
South Korea	0.4	1.0	2.4	4.3	7.6
India	0.5	0.6	0.9	1.3	–
China	–	0.3	0.3	0.5	0.7

SOURCE: Gavin W. Jones, "The 'Flight from Marriage' in South-East and East Asia," Asia Metacentre, Research Paper Series, no. 11, June 2003, http://www.populationasia.org/Publications/ResearchPaper/AMCRP11.pdf.

population explosion is effectively over.[16] Not everywhere, to be sure (e.g., Afghanistan, Pakistan), but overall the Asia-Pacific region and each of its major sub-groupings have already seen the peaking of growth rates for both total population and working-age manpower (conventionally defined as ages 15–64) and can expect further slowdowns—or in some cases, absolute declines—in the generation ahead. Finally, and not least important, due to low or sub-replacement fertility the Asia-Pacific region stands to be swept by a wave of population aging never before witnessed on a national scale. By 2040, Japan's median population is projected to be approaching 55 years. Projections for other countries are less extreme, yet

---

[16] Many analysts nevertheless worry about the implications of rising human population totals for food security, resource use, and environmental degradation. These issues are incontestably important and could have far-reaching reverberations on the strategic horizon, but they are not addressed in this chapter. For a cautiously optimistic assessment of the prospective impact of future population growth on the planetary food and resource situation, see Nicholas Eberstadt, "Too Many People?" International Policy Network and the Sustainable Development Network, July 2007, http://www.policynetwork.net/sites/default/files/Too_Many_People.pdf.

hardly less dramatic.[17] By 2040, for example, China's projected proportion of senior citizens 65 years and older would be far higher than that of the United States or Europe today—indeed, possibly higher than any level yet recorded for a national population. A number of lower-income Asian societies, including Sri Lanka and Vietnam, would also have ratios of senior citizens to total population that match or exceed Europe's current levels.

This summary overview of prospective demographic trends for the greater Asia-Pacific region underscores a number of important but often overlooked points. First, a coming "old-age tsunami" stands to saddle many countries in the region with a much greater old-age burden (as conventionally measured by demographers) than most of today's affluent countries have faced—even though many of the Asian states now facing this impending wave are far poorer at present than the Organisation for Economic Co-operation and Development (OECD) countries. Second, the confluence of the rising old-age burden, aging workforces, and slowing growth (or actual absolute declines) in available manpower pools could put increasing pressure on existing arrangements for eliciting economic growth in many Asian countries. Without significant overhauls of institutions, governance, economic and social policies, arrangements for technological innovation, and the like, these demographic pressures may augur more sluggish economic performance over the long-run in a number of the countries under consideration than was enjoyed in recent decades.[18] Third, and not least important, the demographic pressures outlined, as well as additional demographic trends not yet discussed, will have a differential impact across the region, affecting some societies (and the governments representing them) more intensely than others. For this reason, the demographic factor promises to have an independent impact on the strategic balance in the Asia-Pacific region in the decades ahead. Some of the prospective implications for the major regional powers will be examined in the next few pages.

---

[17] A number of today's lower-income societies—Bangladesh, Myanmar, and Vietnam, among them—would have median ages above 35 years—equal to or higher than the United States' median age in 2000. Indonesia and India, major population centers with current per capita GDP levels estimated at one-seventh and one-tenth respectively of U.S. levels, are projected by 2040 to have median ages nearly as high as the that of the United States today.

[18] At the same time, smaller youth populations will have a tendency to reduce overall dependency ratios and increase possibilities for human capital investments in the rising youth generation—a potentially mitigating and compensating factor for the economic outlook in rapidly aging, low fertility societies. This point is made in Andrew Mason, Sang-hyop Lee, and Ronald Lee, "Will Demographic Change Undermine Asia's Growth Prospects?" in *Asia's Regionalism in the World Economy*, ed. Jong-Wha Lee, Masahiro Kawai, and Peter Petri (Manila: Asian Development Bank, forthcoming).

A Survey of Impending Demographics Changes for the Region's Major Powers and Their Strategic Implications

For the time being, five states in the Asia-Pacific region qualify as "major powers": China, India, Japan, the Russian Federation, and the United States. This collectivity of powers is distinguished from other states and would-be powers by characteristics that are both quantitative and qualitative, including economic potential, military potential, and the international ambit of state leadership.[19] This section identifies some of the unfolding demographic changes that promise to enhance or compromise the capacities of these states to augment power and extend influence internationally. At the outset, it is important to underscore the fact that changing capacities are just one factor affecting the international and strategic behavior of states; the decisions and behavior of state actors in the face of constraints and opportunities—including their mistakes and miscalculations—are hardly less crucial in shaping the international strategic environment.

China: Looming Demographic Constraints on Long-Term "Peaceful Rise"

China's current (2010) and prospective (2040) population structures, as estimated and projected by the UNPD, are contrasted in **Figure 1**.

The main engine driving this demographic evolution is sub-replacement fertility. While there is some uncertainty about China's current fertility levels, there is no doubt that they are well below the replacement level for the country as a whole. In urban China, fertility today is extraordinarily low, with TFRs averaging perhaps 1.2 and TFRs of barely 1.0 in the largest metropolitan areas such as Beijing, Shanghai, and Tianjin.

Just how much Beijing's coercive "one-child policy" is actually responsible for modern China's childbearing patterns remains a matter of some dispute. In any case, China's new childbearing patterns have conjured up a host of new and unfamiliar demographic problems for the country—all of which will descend simultaneously and inexorably in the generation immediately ahead. Four of these problems deserve special mention.

The end of manpower growth. China's explosion of economic growth over the three decades between 1979 and 2008 was powered in part by a surge of labor force growth and a sharp rise in the share of working-age (15–64) groups within the total population. Over the next three

---

[19] The delineation between the major powers and other states, of course, is not always clear cut. In the next section, Indonesia and Pakistan will also be included in the discussion, given their demographic potential for emerging as major powers in the decades ahead. For better or worse, other places with arguably significant future potential for influencing international affairs, such as Thailand, Vietnam, and a hypothetically reunited Korean Peninsula, are not examined in any detail here.

FIGURE 1   China's estimated and projected population by age and sex, 2010 vs. 2040

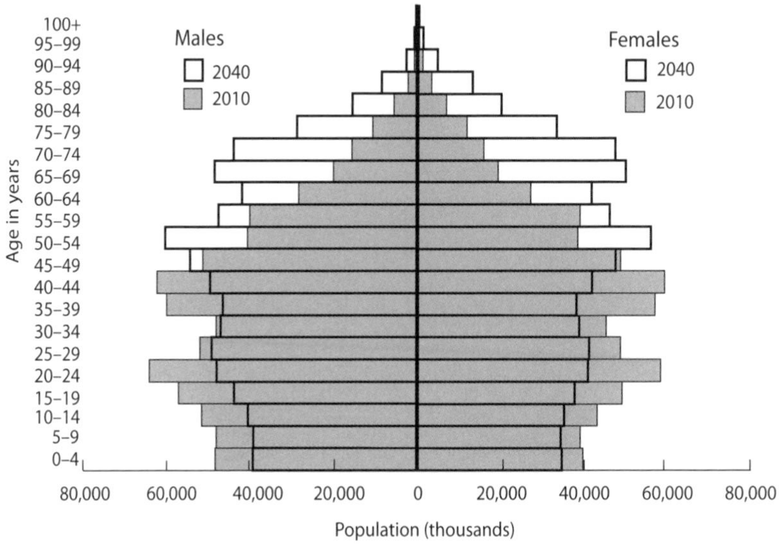

Population (thousands)

SOURCE: UNPD, "World Population Prospects: The 2008 Revision."

decades, China's prospective manpower growth rate is negative, with the total working-age population commencing an indefinite decline around 2015, and possibly earlier. The share of men and women of working age within China's total population, furthermore, is set to fall steadily and significantly in the decades ahead. Moreover, an unfavorable shift in the composition of China's working-age population is also underway: youthful, relatively well-educated manpower will make up a smaller share of China's labor force, while the older, less healthy, and less-educated 50–64 year-old group will account for a progressively larger fraction of the county's manpower.

A coming senior tsunami. By any yardstick one cares to select, Chinese society overall will be graying at a tremendously rapid, and indeed almost historically unprecedented, pace over the next generation. According to UNPD projections, between 2010 and 2040 China's population aged 65 and older is set to grow at almost 3.6% per annum, and by 2040 over one in five Chinese (22%) would be 65 or older. The situation is likely to be even more acute in the countryside, due to the ongoing migration of younger rural-born workers to towns and cities. According to research by Zeng Yi of Peking University and his colleagues, China's rural areas are already grayer than the cities. By 2040, Zeng's team projects that over 30% of the country's rural residents would be 65 or older.[20]

China may find it much more difficult to cope with the impending old-age support problem than the graying societies of the West for several reasons. First, income levels for China are much lower than they were in developed countries at comparable stages of population aging. Second, China still lacks a national public pension system. Third, sub-replacement fertility means that China's future presumptive retirees will have fewer sons and daughters on which to rely.

The rise of the unmarriageable male. Since the advent of the one-child policy, the country's sex ratio at birth (SRB) has veered sharply upward from the traditional, biological norm of about 105 boys born for every 100 girls. By the 2005 "mini-census," China's reported SRB was 119; and the official sex ratio for children 1–4 years of age was 123. Today's surplus baby boys will be tomorrow's would-be bridegrooms; thus, a "marriage squeeze" of monumental proportions is in the works for China. Calculations by Zeng and his colleagues point to the prospective magnitude of the coming problem. Today, roughly 5% of Chinese men in their late 30s have never been married. Largely as a consequence of the "marriage squeeze," that fraction could exceed 15% by 2020 and could reach 25% by 2040.[21]

This percentage is a countrywide average, but the situation could be even more extreme in the countryside, given that rural men may be more likely to lose out to more affluent and educated urban suitors in the national marriage race. Chinese culture upholds a norm of universal marriage; however, this is an arithmetic impossibility for China's coming generation. The social consequences of the coming marriage squeeze are unpredictable at present but could be significant.

Radical changes in family structures. China's new fertility patterns may presage the demise of the extended family network and the rise of a peculiar new family type altogether unfamiliar in China's historical experience. With the advent of steep sub-replacement fertility in many parts of China, single-child families are becoming increasingly common. Continued into the future, steep sub-replacement fertility portends the emergence of a new family type: only children begotten by only children. In such families, children would have no siblings, no uncles and aunts, and no cousins—their

---

[20] See Zeng Yi, Zhenglian Wang, Jiang Leiwen, and Danan Gu, "Projection of Family Households and Elderly Living Arrangement in the Context of Rapid Population Aging in China—A Demographic Window of Opportunity until 2030 and Serious Challenges Thereafter," *Genus* LXIV, no. 1–2 (2008): 9–36.

[21] Calculated from the baseline data and the PROFAMY software described in Yi, Wang, Leiwen, and Gu, "Projection of Family Households." Thanks go to Professor Zeng and his colleagues for generously sharing the background information that made these calculations possible.

only blood relatives would be ancestors and descendants. Research by Guo Zhigang of Peking University and his colleagues suggests that by 2020 roughly 42% of urban China's prospective parents would be only children, and that by 2030 only children would account for the clear majority (58%) of adults in this group.[22]

By such a reckoning, this new family type could be prevalent, if not predominant, in China's cities within a generation. The emergence of what might be termed the "kin-less family" can only be expected to pose extraordinary cultural and social—as well as economic—challenges for China in the decades immediately ahead.

Russia: Demographic Decline in the Midst of a Health Crisis

The Russian Federation's current (2010) population structure is contraposed against the UNDP's projections for 2040 in **Figure 2.**

FIGURE 2 The Russian Federation's estimated and projected population by age and sex, 2010 vs. 2040

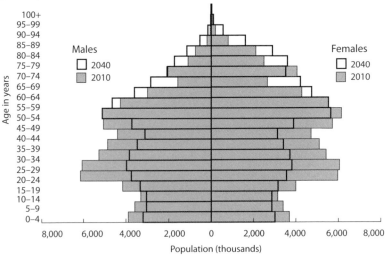

SOURCE: UNDP, "World Population Prospects: The 2008 Revision."

---

[22] Guo Zhigang, Liu Jintang, and Song Jian, "Birth Policy and Family Structure in the Future," *Chinese Journal of Population Science* 1 (2002): 1–11.

These projections, and virtually all others, envision a much smaller population for Russia 30 years from now than exists there today. But Russia's population is already in decline, falling by roughly seven million people since 1992.[23] In absolute terms, Russia has experienced the modern world's steepest drop in total population since the catastrophic consequences of Maoist China's Great Leap Forward. Arithmetically, the country's current depopulation has been driven by two separate but interrelated factors: a steep drop in births and an upsurge in deaths. Since the end of Communism, Russia has tallied nearly thirteen million more deaths than births: that is to say, nearly three deaths for every two births. Although net immigration has partially compensated for the gap between deaths and births, it has not been sufficient to prevent an overall depopulation. Over the coming decades, Russia's demographic trends are set to constrain the country's economic potential in the following key respects.

Sub-replacement fertility. With the collapse of the Soviet state, the country's TFR fell below 2.0 and has not returned to that level since. Over the past decade, that rate has crept up (to 1.5 as of 2008), but that is still over 30% below the Gorbachev-era peak and almost 30% below the replacement level.[24] Over the past several generations, Russia's fertility levels have been among Europe's lowest—and there are few indications that this now historical pattern is set to change anytime soon. Russia's baby bust presages, among other things, a dramatic drop-off in the working-age population over the decades immediately ahead. By UNPD and U.S. Census Bureau projections, Russia's working-age population (aged 15–64) stands to fall by well over 20%, and the working-age group as a proportion of national population also stands to drop appreciably.

Russia's health and mortality calamity. Russia also faces the tremendous problems of declining health standards and severe excess mortality. Impossible as it may seem, overall life expectancy at birth in Russia is no higher today than it was in the early 1960s, almost half a century ago. Indeed, life expectancy for men is actually lower today than it was in the late 1950s.[25] The Russian health failure, it appears, has been concentrated among persons who would normally be considered to be in their prime of life. As of 2005, death rates for men between the ages of 30 and 50 were typically 100% higher than they were for their counterparts 40 years earlier;

---

[23] For a fuller exposition, see Nicholas Eberstadt, "Russia's Peacetime Demographic Crisis: Dimensions, Causes, Implications," National Bureau of Asian Research, Project Report, May 2010.

[24] See Russian Federal Service of State Statistics (Rosstat), "Demographic Yearbook of Russia 2009," 2009, available at http://www.infostat.ru/eng/catalog.html?id=309&page=info.

[25] For estimates of Russian postwar life expectancy trends, see UNPD, "World Population Prospects: The 2008 Revision."

no less remarkably, death rates for Russian women in their 30s, 40s, and early 50s were typically 50% higher than four decades before.[26] Unhealthy and debilitated labor forces are poorly disposed to elicit major increases in economic productivity, and the outlook for health improvements in Russia at present is not encouraging. UNPD projections, for example, currently posit Russian male life expectancy at levels lower than the average for the less-developed regions through the year 2050.

Unhealthy population aging. Thanks to the country's steep sub-replacement birth rates, Russia can expect to be an aged society in the coming decades. By 2040, in UNPD projections, every fifth Russian would be over 65 years of age. Given Russia's adverse health patterns, however, its seniors in the years ahead may be unusually frail, as may be the working-age population that will be needed to support them. Russia's old-age burden may thus be even heavier than population structure alone would suggest. Russia has a national pension system, but this system affords at best a penurious existence (being currently pegged close to the country's own extremely stringent definition of poverty). Moreover, although Russia has benefited from oil and energy export windfalls in recent years, projections suggest that the government's energy funds could be completely depleted by pension fund deficits before the year 2030.[27]

Migration uncertainties. While net in-migration has helped cushion Russia's depopulation over the past two decades, the influx of newcomers from Russia's near abroad—many from traditional regions of Islamic heritage—raises the question of assimilation for Russia's social fabric in the years ahead. This issue will become more pressing insofar as the standards for Russian-language training in the Central Asian Republics and the Caucasus appear to be distinctly lower today than in the Soviet era. Further, the country is experiencing significant out-migration from the Russian Far East. Over the past two decades, the population of that region has plunged by about 25%.[28] If emigration from the Russian Far East continues, the viability of Russian sovereignty over this largely empty expanse sharing a long land border with China may not be taken for granted indefinitely.

---

[26] See the Human Mortality database, available at http://www.mortality.org.

[27] See Nicholas Eberstadt and Hans Groth, "The Russian Federation: Confronting the Special Challenges of Aging and Social Security Policy in an Era of Demographic Crisis," *International Social Security Review* (forthcoming).

[28] "Medvedev Concerned Over Demographic Situation in Russian Far East," Itar-Tass, July 3, 2010.

India: A Rising Power Beset by Regional Disparities in Human Resources

India's current population structure is contrasted with UNPD projections for 2040 in **Figure 3**.

India would appear to be on the verge of becoming an almost ideal exemplar of a society ready to benefit from a phenomenon that has been called the "demographic dividend." In the three decades immediately ahead, India's pool of working-age manpower is projected to grow by nearly 40% (an average of over 1% a year), and the proportion of working-age to total population to rise steadily. At the same time, by these projections India would still remain a relatively youthful country in 2040, with a median age of 35, a 65 years and older cohort accounting for less than 11% of the total population, and a ratio of working-age to 65 years and older of over six to one (a level last witnessed in some of today's more developed countries in the early postwar era). A number of demographic economists have argued that this sort of population structure encourages rising savings rates, rising investment ratios, and accelerating economic growth.[29]

FIGURE 3   India's estimated and projected population by age and sex, 2010 vs. 2040

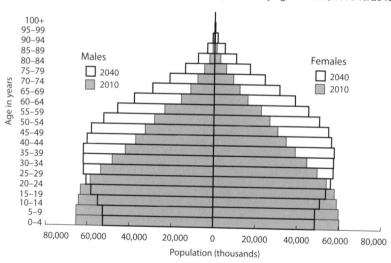

SOURCE: UNPD, "World Population Prospects: The 2008 Revision."

---

[29] See, for example, David E. Bloom and Jeffrey G. Williamson, "Demographic Transitions and Economic Miracles in Emerging Asia," *World Bank Economic Observer* 12, no. 3 (1998): 419–55; and David E. Bloom, David Canning, and Jaypee Sevilla, *The Demographic Dividend: A New Perspective on the Economic Consequences of Population Change* (Santa Monica: RAND, 2003).

Yet national population aggregates by themselves can be misleading. Closer examination, indeed, reveals that such aggregates for vast India often only offer an arithmetic average for what constitute diverse and disparate regional populations. India's coming demographic challenges in augmenting national economic potential, and thus in extending international influence, may be considerably more complex than the national population numbers might of themselves suggest.

Regional demographic disparities. Although fertility rates for the country as a whole have fallen by over 40% in the past three decades, fertility levels across India vary dramatically today.[30] India has many high fertility districts (local administrative areas) with TFRs of 4.5 or more but also many low fertility districts where sub-replacement fertility prevails. Most of the former areas are in India's north, while many of the latter are in the south of the country. Consequently, two distinctly different future regional population profiles are emerging within India: one in the north that is characterized by relatively rapid population growth and a more traditional "developing society" population structure, and another in the south that is characterized by demographic stagnation and more pronounced population aging.

Regional health disparities. While all countries record differences in health profiles from one region to another, India's are unusually dramatic. According to official estimates for the years 2002–06, India's healthiest state, Kerala, and its least-healthy state, Madhya Pradesh, were separated by a seventeen-year gap in life expectancy.[31] India's big regional health disparities help explain why the country's overall life expectancy is currently estimated to be nearly a decade lower than China's. Health levels tend to be poorest in India's high fertility areas, which will account for the bulk of India's labor force growth over the next three decades.

Educational shortfalls. Regional health disparities correspond with and are reinforced by regional educational disparities. Over the coming decades, these regional educational disparities will remain glaring and India's overall levels of educational attainment will remain surprisingly low. In Kerala (India's most-educated state) in 2026, almost everyone of working age (15–64) is projected to have some schooling, and the majority of the economically active manpower would have a high school diploma or better. In Bihar (India's least-schooled state), on the other hand, less than

[30] See, among other things, Christophe Z. Guilmoto, "Fertility Decline in India: Maps, Models and Hypotheses," in *Fertility Transition in South India*, ed. Christophe Z. Guilmoto and Irudaya Rajan (Thousand Oaks: Sage Publications, 2005), 385–435.

[31] Government of India, *Economic Survey of India 2009–2010* (New Delhi: Oxford University Press, 2010), Table 9.1, available at http://indiabudget.nic.in/es2009-10/chapt2010/tab91.pdf. It should be noted that these official life expectancy estimates cover just the 15 most populous of India's 35 states and regions, territories that accounted for over 90% of the country's population as of the 2001 census.

one-third of the economically active population (aged 15–64) in 2026 is projected to have even completed grade school, and well over two-fifths of the economically active population would be illiterate, with no schooling whatsoever.[32] By these same projections, in 2026 nearly one-third (32%) of Indians 25 years of age or older would be illiterate, with no formal schooling. Thus, India's rate of adult illiteracy in 2026 for those 25 years and older would be roughly comparable to the levels in Latin America and the Caribbean around 1970 (36%) or East Asia around 1980 (30%)—that is to say, about two generations earlier.[33]

For rapid growth to be sustained in India, the national economy will require not just a growing pool of manpower but a growing pool of skilled manpower. India's regional demographic disparities complicate this objective. Economic growth in India has been spurred by the success of coastal cities and parts of the Indian south (including such locales as the state of Kerala and the city of Bangalore); however, these places are part of what may soon be known as "old India." In such places, the labor force is relatively skilled but is also older. With low or sub-replacement fertility, and absolute supplies of local manpower, the labor force will soon peak and begin to shrink. Other parts of India, by contrast, will have abundant and growing supplies of labor, yet a disproportionate share of that manpower will be either entirely unschooled or only barely literate. Human resource challenges may thus pose a greater challenge for India's prospective economic development in the decades immediately ahead than is commonly appreciated today.

Japan: A Prosperous, Healthy Depopulation

Japan is on the cusp of a sustained, unremitting, and accelerating depopulation; the only real question is how fast and how far the population will shrink in the next 30 years. By UNPD projections, Japan's total population would drop from 127 million to 110 million over these three decades—a decline of about 17 million, or over 13%. Official Japanese projections currently anticipate an even greater drop to just under 106 million by 2040—a fall of over 21 million, or almost 17%. In all projections, Japan's depopulation gradually gathers speed over time, and by 2040 official

---

[32] Anne Goujon and Kirsty McNay, "Projecting the Educational Composition of the Population of India: Selected State-Level Perspectives," *Applied Population and Policy* 1, no. 1(2003): 25–35.

[33] These estimates come from the Barro-Lee educational database. For more details, see the World Bank, "Education Attainment in the Adult Population (Barro-Lee Data Set)," available at http://web.worldbank.org/WBSITE/EXTERNAL/TOPICS/EXTEDUCATION/EXTDATASTATISTICS/~EXTEDSTATS/0,,contentMDK:21218180~menuPK:4324130~pagePK:64168445~piPK:64168309~theSitePK:3232764~isCURL:Y,00.html.

Japanese projections depict the country's population spiraling downward by over one million persons a year, almost 1% per annum.[34]

Figure 4 compares UNPD projections of Japan's population structure in 2010 and 2040. Japan's present population profile and future population outlook are shaped by three overarching long-term trends: sharply declining and by now extreme sub-replacement fertility, near-zero net immigration, and a remarkable record of continuing health progress that has made the Japanese the longest-living people in the world today.[35]

Given these dynamics, Japan is set to undergo a radical shift in population composition over the next 30 years. Between 2010 and 2040, the UNPD projects a decline of more than 40% in the number of children under the age of 15, and a drop of 30% in the working-age population (aged 15–64). Japan's cohort of senior citizens, however, is projected to grow by roughly one-third between 2010 and 2040, and the ranks of the oldest Japanese would increase even more rapidly, both absolutely and relatively.

FIGURE 4   Japan's estimated and projected population by age and sex, 2010 vs. 2040

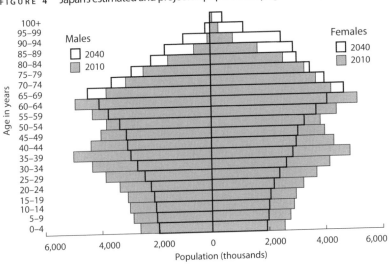

SOURCE: UNPD, "World Population Prospects: The 2008 Revision."

---

[34] "Table 2-2: Future Population Projections," *Japan Statistical Yearbook 2010* (Tokyo: Statistics Bureau of the Ministry of Internal Affairs and Communications, 2010), available at http://www.stat.go.jp/english/data/nenkan/1431-02.htm.

[35] See the Human Mortality database, http://www.mortality.org.

By UNPD projections, a remarkable 14% of all Japanese in 2040 would be 80 or older—nearly one in seven. Japan is already the world's grayest society, and, as noted earlier, the country is on course to become far more elderly over the coming decades.

Depopulation with Japanese characteristics constrains Japan's prospective ability to augment economic potential and extend influence abroad in a number of important respects.

Pressures for relative international economic decline. Thirty years ago, Japan's population of working age accounted for almost 3% of global working-age manpower. In 2010 the corresponding figure is under 2%, and by 2040, according to UNPD projections, this percentage would be just 1%. Under such circumstances, it will be very difficult to keep Japan's share of global GDP from shrinking.

Pressures on per capita economic performance. Japan's looming old-age burden could weigh heavily on the national economy. Pronounced population aging would be expected to affect national savings rates adversely and could have corresponding implications for investment rates and the growth outlook. The health and pension claims of Japan's burgeoning elderly population on the nation's public treasury are set to skyrocket over the next three decades (even though Japanese senior citizens may be the world's healthiest). Japan's household savings rates have dropped below 4% in recent years, and due to heavy and continuing deficit spending, Japan's ratio of gross public debt to GDP is now the OECD's highest (over 200%)—background details that will make dealing with the macroeconomic impact of population aging all the more challenging.

Mounting physical and mental disabilities. No society has ever had to cope with the needs of a population as aged as Japan's will be in 2040. Of particular concern here are not only needs arising from physical frailty but also those arising from mental disability. The prevalence of dementia, including Alzheimer's disease, seems to rise progressively in populations over the course of older age. Absent radical medical breakthroughs, in the year 2040 Japan faces the prospect of being a society where millions of people will suffer from Alzheimer's disease—by very rough calculations, perhaps as many as 1 person in 25.[36] No modern country has ever before faced such a prospective social and economic burden.

Yet the outlook for Japan, given its demographic fundamentals, is by no means altogether bleak. Unlike Russia, Japan's health prospects look

---

[36] See, for example, "Dementia in the Asia Pacific Region: The Epidemic Is Here," Access Economics PTY Limited, September 21, 2006, available electronically at http://www.alz.co.uk/research/files/apreport.pdf. The estimates and projections in this study imply that the prevalence of Alzheimer's disease in Japan will rise from 1.5% of total population in 2005 to 4.8% of total population by 2050.

very good. Japan's older population, furthermore, tends to stay in the workforce longer than counterparts in Europe or even the United States. No less important, Japanese science and technology, including engineering and health sciences, are at the very front ranks in the world today. And, lest it go unsaid, Japan happens to be a very wealthy society, two decades of slow post-bubble growth notwithstanding. The plain fact is that such wealth affords vast potentialities for underwriting both national policies and international strategic efforts if the Japanese public is willing to use it for such purposes.

The United States: "American Demographic Exceptionalism"

From a purely demographic standpoint, the prospective trends for the United States over the coming three decades appear to be relatively favorable—indeed, arguably more favorable than those of the other major powers in the Asia-Pacific. The overall outlook for the United States can be seen by comparing the country's population structure today with its projected structure for 2040 (see **Figure 5**).

FIGURE 5 The United States' estimated and projected population by age and sex, 2010 vs. 2040

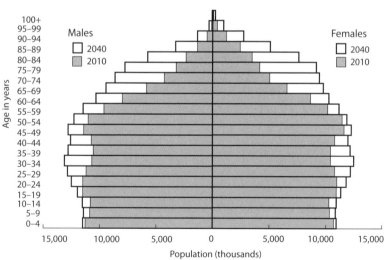

SOURCE: UNPD, "World Population Prospects: The 2008 Revision."

By UNPD projections, over the next 30 years the total U.S. population would rise from around 315 million to just under 400 million, or by roughly 22%.[37] The United States would remain the world's third-most populous country three decades hence (while Russia would slip from ninth to fourteenth in global rankings, and Japan from tenth to sixteenth). Additionally, in 2040 the U.S. population is projected to still be growing, unlike China's, Russia's, or Japan's—at an envisioned tempo of just under 0.5% per annum, approximately the same as India's. The composition of prospective U.S. population growth likewise appears to be relatively favorable. Between 2010 and 2040, the conventionally defined working-age population (ages 15–64) is expected to increase rather than decline,[38] and to still be increasing three decades hence (unlike Russia's, Japan's, or China's). Although the United States will, of course, be an aging society, the projected trajectory of population aging between 2010 and 2040 is more moderate than for any of the other major powers of the Asia-Pacific region. The median age is seen as rising by far less in the United States than in any of the other major regional powers. By 2040, the U.S. median age, in UNPD projections, would be thirteen years lower than in Japan, nearly five years lower than in Russia, and three years lower than China's. Likewise, the 65 and older cohort would constitute a much smaller share of total population than in Japan and a somewhat lower share than in China.[39]

The United States' relatively robust prospective demographic growth and relatively slow prospective pace of population aging are consequences of anticipated trends for fertility and immigration. Those trends are highly distinctive, and indeed can even be described as "American demographic exceptionalism."[40] The current total fertility rate in the United States is the highest for any affluent OECD country—nearly 30% higher than for the EU-15 and over 50% higher than in Japan or South Korea (see **Figure 6**).

Moreover, fertility levels in the United States have actually risen since the 1970s, averaging just over two births per woman per lifetime for the past

---

[37] The U.S. Census Bureau projects somewhat greater growth for the United States—with the U.S. population reaching 405 million in 2040, implying an increase of 31% between 2010 and 2040.

[38] This increase will be roughly 13% in UNPD projections and about 19% in U.S. Census Bureau projections.

[39] India's 65+ fraction would still be much lower than the United States'—11% vs. 21%—and Russia's would be fractionally lower than the United States' as well, thanks only to the exceptionally poor survival prospects for Russian seniors.

[40] For background, see Nicholas Eberstadt, "'Demographic Exceptionalism' in the United States: Tendencies and Implications," *Agir*, no. 29 (January 2007): 125–36. Not all demographers concur with this assessment, however; see, for example, Ron J. Lesthaeghe and Lisa Neidert, "The Second Demographic Transition in the United States: Exception or Textbook Example?" *Population and Development Review* 32, no. 4 (December 2006): 669–98.

FIGURE 6   Total fertility rates for Japan, South Korea, the United States, Germany, and the EU-15, 1970–2006

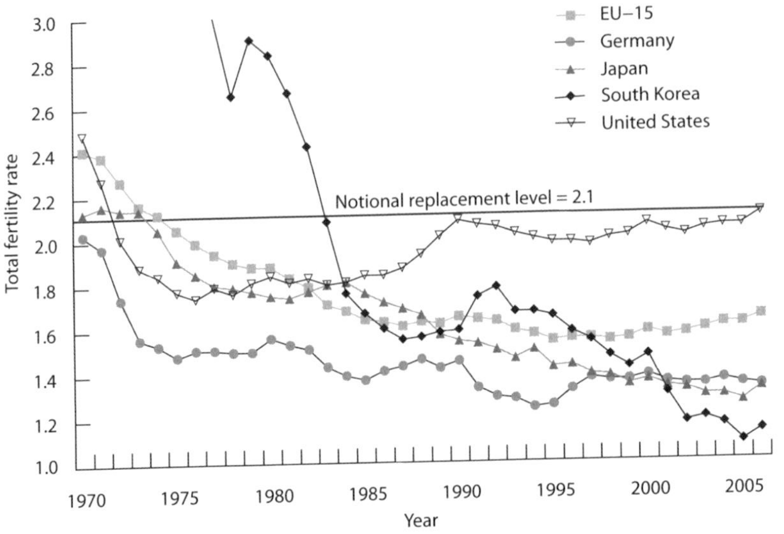

SOURCE: OECD, *Society at a Glance 2009—OECD Social Indicators* (Paris: OECD, 2009), http://www.oecd.org/els/social/indicators/SAG.

25 years[41]—very close to the level required for net population replacement.[42] As for immigration, the United States has been absorbing a net influx of roughly one million newcomers a year over the past two decades (a significant fraction of these being illegal or undocumented immigrants). In absolute terms, the United States accepts far more immigrants annually than any other contemporary society; in relative terms, net immigration rates for the United States are also much higher than for any other large country. UNPD and U.S. Census Bureau projections assume that U.S. fertility and net immigration rates will remain relatively high between now and 2040.

[41] The United States is a multi-ethnic society, of course, and fertility levels differ by ethnicity, with the highest levels currently being reported by Latinos/Hispanics in general and Mexican-Americans in particular (with a calculated TFR of about 3.0). However, fertility levels are also relatively high, in comparison to other affluent countries, for all other U.S. ethnicities, including Anglos (i.e., non-Hispanic whites), whose TFRs have averaged 1.8–1.9 over the past generation. This level is slightly below the replacement level but is nonetheless higher than the corresponding levels in the rest of the West, Russia, and China.

[42] Technically, these TFRs estimates are for "period" rates rather than "cohort" rates—synthetic estimates indicating what the national fertility level would be at any given point in time if a woman were to pass her entire childbearing years through the birth probabilities then prevailing, as opposed to tracking total childbearing over the life course for women born in a given year.

All other things being equal, these overall demographic trends would seem to confer a relative advantage on the United States. But the more detailed particulars of the U.S. population profile will also matter greatly to the country's future economic potential, and a number of clouds can already be seen on this horizon. To mention just the most important of these issues:

- *Immigration*: The question of assimilation bears directly on both economic performance and social cohesion.

- *Education*: The United States' public K-12 system produces notoriously mediocre results, and high school graduation rates are decelerating, heading toward stagnation.

- *Family structure*: An increasing proportion of American children are born outside of marriage or are being raised in single parent homes—a circumstance that cannot be socially and economically advantageous.

- *Health*: The U.S. ranking among developed countries has gradually been falling over the past two generations. U.S. life expectancy is now slightly lower than that of East Germany, limiting not only social well-being but also quite possibly economic productivity in the United States.

- *Ballooning health care costs*: Unfunded future liabilities and commitments related to health care are staggering and have implications both for overall U.S. economic performance and for the country's budgetary ability to maintain an adequate defense.

Toward a "Net Assessment" of Demographic Impacts on the Major Powers of the Asia-Pacific

The previous section of this chapter outlined the demographic challenges facing the major powers of the Asia-Pacific region in broad, descriptive terms. Is it possible to arrive at a summary net assessment of the prospective impact of demographic change on the strategic environment in the Asia-Pacific region or on the prospective strategic balance between the region's major powers?

A single summary statistic to assess these changes is not within reach today—nor is it likely to be in the future, owing to the complex and often qualitative factors that relate demographic change to overall strategic competition. There are three meaningful and measurable areas, however, in which the influence of prospective population trends and profiles on national economic capabilities (and thus on the potential for exerting influence internationally) are susceptible to some measure of quantification and evaluation. These are, first, projected trends for military-age manpower; second, projected trends for working-age manpower; and third, national capabilities in scientific-technical "knowledge production" and prospective trends for highly educated manpower.

Recent and Prospective Trends in Military-Age Manpower

The prospective pool of military-age manpower—and more specifically in an era of increasingly complex weaponry and information-intensive military systems, the pool of relatively educated military manpower—has an obvious bearing on strategic capabilities and defense potential for major powers and would-be powers. The male population between 15–24 years of age serves as an approximation of prospective military manpower, given that conventional demographic projections typically disaggregate populations into five-year groupings. This chapter relies on UNPD 2008 projections for tracing trends for total military-age manpower and on projections produced in recent years by a team of researchers at the International Institute of Applied Systems Analysis (IIASA) and the Vienna Institute of Demography (VID) for tracing trends in military-age manpower with higher educational attainment (secondary or tertiary education).[43] There are some inconsistencies between these two sets of projections, but for the most part these inconsistencies are small and need not be of concern here.[44]

Figure 7 presents UNPD estimates and projections for the total 15–24 year-old male population for the major Asia-Pacific powers over the past 30 years (1980–2010) and the next 30 years (2010–40).

China and India of course dwarf all other countries; however, India's young male manpower exceeds China's around the year 2010, at which point China's totals head into long-term decline. In 30 years (by 2040), India's 15–24 year-old male population is projected to be over 20% larger than China's. By contrast, China's 15–24 male pool was about 40% larger than India's in 1980, 30 years ago.

---

[43] W. Lutz, A. Goujon, Samir K.C., and W. Sanderson, "Reconstruction of Population by Age, Sex and Level of Educational Attainment of 120 Countries for 2000–2030," *Vienna Yearbook of Population Research 2007* (Vienna: Vienna Institute of Demography, 2008), 193–235; and Samir K.C. et al., "Projection of Populations by Educational Attainment, Age, and Sex for 120 countries for 2005–2050," *Demographic Research* 22, article 15 (March 16, 2010): 383–472, available at http://www.iiasa.ac.at/Research/POP/Edu07FP/KC_etal_projection%20of%20population_2010.pdf.

[44] The only inconsistency worth noting is that IIASA-VID's projections for China anticipate a somewhat earlier peaking of working-age population and total population than the UNPD projections. Whereas, for example, UNPD projections envision a decline in China's working-age population of 0.2% per year for 2010–40, the IIASA projections posit a decline averaging 0.5% per year.

FIGURE 7   Estimated and projected male population ages 15–24, 1980–2040

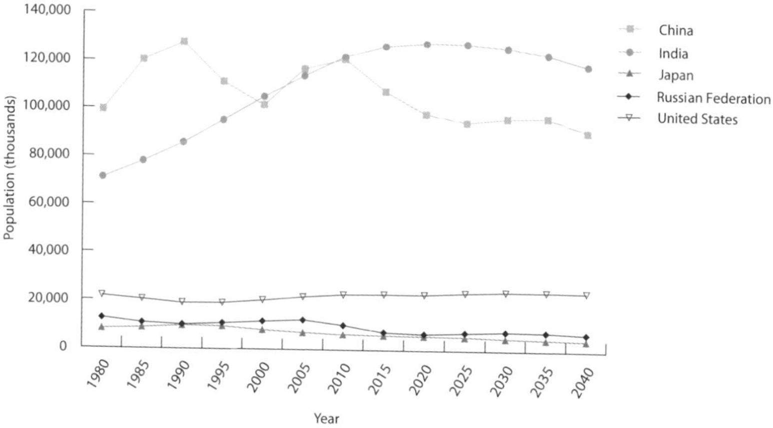

SOURCE: UNPD, "World Population Prospects: The 2008 Revision."

Russia and Japan, for their part, are projected to witness substantial declines in their prospective male populations 15–24 years of age over the next 30 years. By UNPD projections, the pool of young males in both Russia and Japan would be roughly one-third smaller in 2040 than today. In the United States, on the other hand, the pool of young manpower would gradually continue to increase. By 2040, UNPD projections anticipate that there would be roughly 3.5 American men between the ages of 15 and 24 for each counterpart in the Russian Federation and nearly 5.5 for every young man in Japan.

Prospective trends for young men with secondary or tertiary education present a somewhat different picture (see **Figure 8**). The most important differences concern China and India. In these projections, India still overtakes China in relatively educated young manpower, though not until around 2020. The long-term shift between China and India in relative totals of educated young men, however, is much more striking than the relative shift in total young male manpower. Only 30 years ago, China had nearly three times as many military-age men that possessed a secondary or tertiary education as India; 30 years hence, in these IIASA-VID projections, India's pool of such young men could be 40% larger than China's.

In the IIASA-VID projections, the pool of relatively educated young male manpower falls steadily in both Japan and Russia over the coming three decades, while growing steadily (albeit slowly) in the United States. Adding

FIGURE 8 Estimated and projected male population ages 15–24 with secondary or tertiary education, 1980–2040

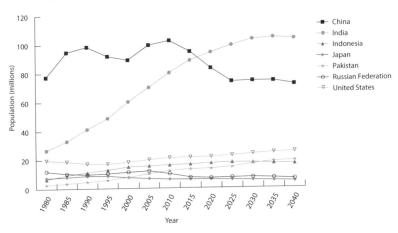

SOURCE: Lutz et al., "Reconstruction of Population by Age, Sex and Level of Educational Attainment"; and K.C. et al., "Projection of Populations by Educational Attainment, Age, and Sex."

Indonesia and Pakistan—two countries with considerable demographic potential—to the mix only emphasizes the relative decline of Japan and Russia. In 2010 the pool of relatively educated men of military age is already larger in both Pakistan and Indonesia than in either Japan or Russia. By 2040, Pakistan is projected to have over three times as many men of military age with relatively high educational attainment (secondary education or higher) as Russia. Likewise, Indonesia is projected to have nearly four times as many such men as Japan. Though the IIASA-VID projections cannot speak to the quality of education for matriculates in any of these countries, the relative shifts indicated in Figure 8 are nonetheless suggestive of some major changes in relative defense potential.

Recent and Prospective Trends in Working-Age Manpower

Trends for working-age manpower (ages 15–64) afford a glimpse of comparative economic potential for the major Asia-Pacific powers over the coming decades.[45] Basic manpower projections are available from the UNPD. To help assess prospects for the productivity of working-age manpower, this section examines projected trends in urbanization (also prepared by the UNPD) along with the IIASA projections on educational attainment by country.

Overall prospects for change in conventionally defined working-age populations for the five major powers have been discussed earlier in this study. As will be recalled, UNPD projections suggest that both Japan and Russia are set to experience a significant (greater than 20%) decline in their working-age populations over the coming three decades, while the U.S. working-age population is projected to grow slowly but steadily. (By 2040, the projected U.S. working-age population would be almost three times as large as Russia's and roughly four times as large as Japan's.) Perhaps the most intriguing trends, however, concern India and China. In 1980, 30 years ago, China's working-age population was almost 50% larger than India's. Today, China's is only about 25% larger. Further, by UNPD projections, 30 years from now India's pool of working-age manpower would be distinctly larger than China's.

These raw numbers, of course, convey little information about the potential productivity of the populations in question. One hint as to prospective labor productivity comes from urbanization patterns, since per capita output of urban populations is almost always higher than for rural groups and the urban-rural productivity gap is often substantial in the earlier stages of modernization.[46] The UNDP's latest projections for urbanization prospects for the region's major powers are presented in **Figure 9**.

For all five major powers, a deceleration in total urban population growth looks to be in store. Yet there are also notable differentials between these countries. Russia's total urban population is envisioned as falling in absolute terms over the coming three decades—a harbinger of the growing constraints on Russian economic performance and, indeed, relative economic decline. Japan's urban numbers are seen as stagnating— an inauspicious sign for future economic growth. For the United States, by contrast, total urban numbers are projected to grow at an average of about 1% per year.

---

[45] It should of course be recognized that only a fraction of the people in this grouping are actually in the labor force, while some workers engaged in the labor force fall outside this age bracket; thus, the 15–64 population grouping only approximates an actual economically active manpower profile for any given country. This imperfect approximation of labor availability nonetheless offers useful information regarding comparative economic potential.

[46] For greater detail, see C. Peter Timmer, *A World without Agriculture: The Structural Transformation in Historical Perspective* (Washington, D.C.: American Enterprise Institute Press, 2009).

FIGURE 9   Estimated and projected average annual growth of urban population

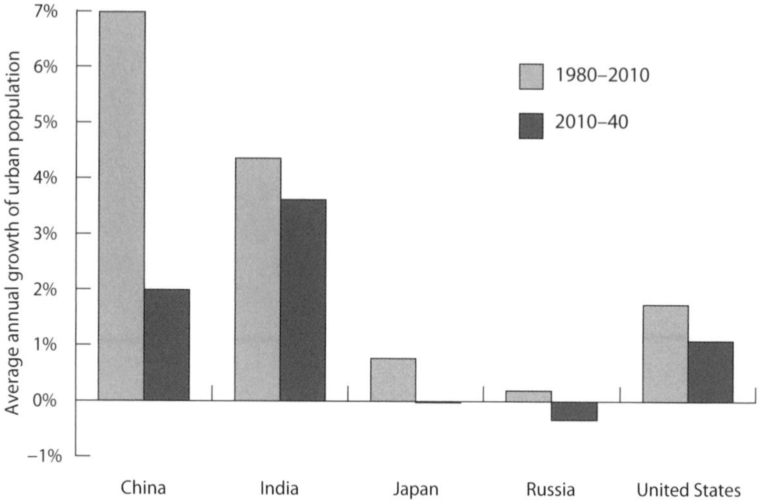

SOURCE: UNPD, "World Population Prospects: The 2006 Revision," http://esa.un.org/unpp/index.asp; and UNPD, "World Urbanization Prospects: The 2007 Revision," http://esa.un.org/unpp/index.asp.

NOTE: These numbers represent total urban population, not just working-age population.

As for China, a radical slowdown in urban population growth looks to be in the works for the years immediately ahead: from 7% per annum in the three past decades to 2% per year for the three coming decades. Absent other compensating changes in economic arrangements, this would seem to portend a much slower tempo of economic growth in China than in the immediate past. India's projected urban growth rate, however, is projected to slow only slightly in the period ahead. For 2010–40, India's projected tempo of urban growth is projected to be 3.6% per year, a rate far higher than for any of the other major powers of the region. Rapidly growing urban populations, to be sure, can raise the specter of social tensions and even political challenges. But over the next 30 years, India's urban population may be growing almost twice as rapidly as China's—a factor that might well bear on the relative economic balance between these two demographic giants.

More educated workers tend to be more productive workers; consequently, the educational profiles of the working-age populations of the major powers of the Asia-Pacific are a matter of considerable import. **Figure 10** depicts the projected trends for working-age populations with

FIGURE 10   Estimated and projected population of working age (15–64) with secondary or tertiary education, 1980–2040

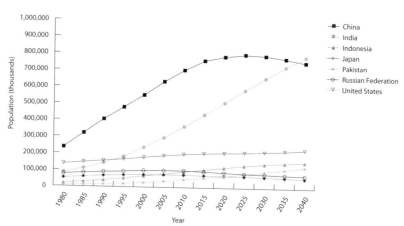

SOURCE: Lutz et al., "Reconstruction of Population by Age, Sex and Level of Educational Attainment"; and K.C. et al., "Projection of Populations by Educational Attainment, Age, and Sex."

secondary education or higher for the major powers plus Indonesia and Pakistan through 2040.

For Russia and Japan, the projected absolute size of this pool of relatively educated manpower declines progressively over the next three decades, while it grows progressively in the United States. Note that Indonesia's pool of relatively educated manpower is projected to surpass both Russia's and Japan's by 2015, and that Pakistan overtakes Japan after 2020 and Russia by 2030.

Once again, the contrast between China and India is highly instructive. In 1980, China was estimated to have nearly three times as many relatively educated people of working-age as did India. Today, China has almost twice as many. By 2040, however, India's pool of relatively educated manpower is projected to exceed China's. Even so, the educational attainment of the Indian workforce (as measured by years of schooling) is set to lag far behind that of China for decades to come. This may be seen in **Figure 11** and **Figure 12**.

Today, almost all of China's men and women in their twenties and thirties have had at least some schooling. In India, by contrast, almost a quarter of the country's young manpower has never been to school. That share is projected to diminish gradually over the coming decades, but by

FIGURE 11   Population in China, ages 20–39, by education level as a percentage of the total population, 1970–2050

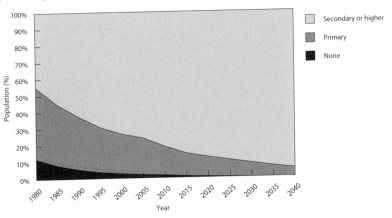

SOURCE: Lutz et al., "Reconstruction of Population by Age, Sex and Level of Educational Attainment"; and K.C. et al., "Projection of Populations by Educational Attainment, Age, and Sex."

FIGURE 12   Population in India, ages 20–39, by education level as a percentage of the total population, 1970–2050

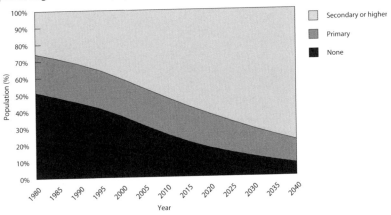

SOURCE: Lutz et al., "Reconstruction of Population by Age, Sex and Level of Educational Attainment"; and K.C. et al., "Projection of Populations by Educational Attainment, Age, and Sex."

2040 roughly a tenth of India's men and women in their twenties and thirties would still be totally unschooled. If lack of schooling stands as a measure of illiteracy, India would appear to be approximately half a century behind China in the quest to achieve universal literacy. This enormous discrepancy in human resource profiles weighs heavily against India in its long-term economic race against China, favorable though many other demographic factors in this competition may be.

"Knowledge Production" and Prospects for Highly Trained Manpower

A third potentially important contribution of human resources to national capabilities that bear on the international strategic balance comes from what might be called "knowledge production": the inventions, discoveries, and technological innovations generated by a country's cadre of highly skilled scientists, engineers, technicians, and researchers. Such knowledge production can enhance a country's overall economic productivity and may also have implications for defense potential.

Current international performance in "knowledge production" can be proxied through two separate but related measures: total patent awards (as issued by the U.S. Patent and Trade Office, or PTO) and out-of-country patent applications (as tracked by the UN World International Property Organization, or WIPO).[47] **Figure 13** shows the number of PTO patents awarded over the years 1995–2008 on a per capita basis for various Asian countries plus the United States and Russia.

---

[47] Data on PTO awards from "Patents By Country, State, and Year - All Patent Types," U.S. Patent and Trade Office, December 2008, http://www.uspto.gov/go/stats/cst_all.htm; and data on World Intellectual Property Organization (WIPO) out-of-country patent applications from "World Intellectual Property Indicators 2009," WIPO, September 2009, http://www.wipo.int/ipstats/en/statistics/patents/. There are a number of objections that can be raised to using such measures for estimating national performance in knowledge production. For one thing, modern commercial competition may result in the generation or trivial, redundant, and or "defensive" patents of immediate proprietary commercial interest to the entities concerned but of little overall impact on knowledge promotion or productivity. For another, it is possible that some important advances in knowledge and research, especially in the defense area, may be deliberately excluded from patent consideration to protect such innovations from international commercial attention. Reliance on the PTO as an arbiter of international patent awards, furthermore, may bias in international rankings, making for an unwarranted U.S.-centric slant in ratings. And of course the global patent market is, in a fundamental sense, international—meaning that, at least in theory, all countries can avail themselves of the potential productivity enhancements these patents may afford even if they were generated in other countries. These and other objectives notwithstanding, national patent performance may nonetheless offer a tolerably good first approximation of national knowledge generation capabilities today, and thus national possibilities for enhancing economic productivity and defense potential in the years immediately ahead.

FIGURE 13   PTO awarded patents in 1995–2008 per 100 million people in 2008 (out of 102 ranked countries)

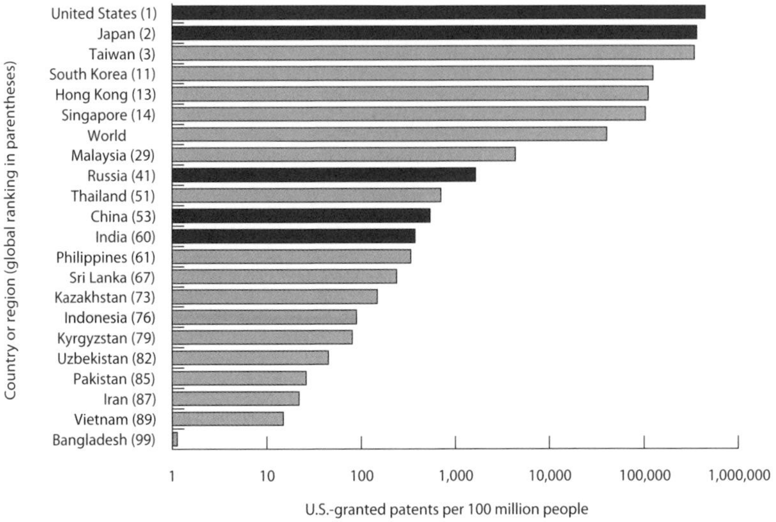

SOURCE: "Patents By Country, State, and Year – All Patent Types"; and "World Development Indicators," World Bank, 2008, CD-ROM.

By the yardstick of PTO patent awards, on a per capita basis the United States ranks first out of the 102 countries covered,[48] with about 440,000 patent issues per 100 million in population. Japan comes in second, with about 360,000 per 100 million people. The three other major Asia-Pacific powers fall far below these rankings; in fact, each of them falls below the world average for PTO awards per capita. Russia ranks 41st in per capita patent awards—an astonishingly poor showing, considering the putative technological prowess of the Russian Federation's predecessor state, the Soviet Union. Though the Russian Federation in 2008 accounted for over 2% of the world's population and about 6% of the world's population of college graduates, the country was awarded only 0.1% of overall PTO awards for 1995–2008. China, ranking 53rd, and India, ranking 60th, generated even fewer PTO patents on a per capita basis. During the years in question, Japan generated over 600 times as many PTO patent awards as China, and the

---

[48] Note that some countries were awarded no patents at all over the years in question. In addition, by PTO and WIPO methodology, foreign nationals working or residing abroad have their patents tallied for the country of residence, not their countries of birth or origin.

United States generated over 1,000 times as many as India.[49] Indonesia and Pakistan, incidentally, lag far behind Russia, China, and India. On a per capita basis, China generated six times as many patents as Indonesia, and India over 13 times as many as Pakistan during the period in question.

Knowledge generation, of course, depends in part on a country's levels of socio-economic development. Perhaps most importantly, it is in large part a function of a country's pool of university graduates and per capita income level. By making adjustments to take these factors into account, a better sense is possible of just how well a country is faring in knowledge production in relation to "where it should be." Attempting these corrections provides a clearer impression of "winners" and "losers" in global knowledge production—that is to say, whether countries are performing better or worse than would be predicted internationally on the basis of their income levels and their pool of highly trained labor. Patent awards per million university-trained adults track quite closely around the world with a country's income level, and the relationship is strongly positive; a doubling of per capita income generally corresponds with a quadrupling of patents and patent applications per million college graduates.[50] Even so, there are clear signs that some countries overperform and others underperform in an international perspective.

With respect to PTO awards, the United States and Japan are tremendous overperformers: each of these nations generates substantially more PTO patent awards than its high income levels would have predicted. China is also an overperformer when its much lower income level is taken into account, as is India, which generates nearly twice as many patents per million college graduates as would have been predicted for a country at its income level. By this metric, all of these countries appear to have significantly stronger national knowledge production capabilities than their incomes alone would suggest. On the other hand, the Russian Federation still stands out as a serious underperformer in knowledge production. A

---

[49] A slightly different take is offered by WIPO rankings of out-of-country patent applications. The most important difference concerns the rankings of Japan and the United States. Japan ranks as number one internationally in the WIPO rankings, while the United States comes in at number twelve (not only behind Japan but also behind South Korea and a number of Western European countries). Though the United States still generated over five times as many out-of-country patent applications as the global average, it produced fewer than half as many as Japan. This metric should challenge any comfortable notions concerning the enduring primacy of a U.S. scientific-technological edge. With the WIPO data, however, per capita performance rankings for Russia (42nd), China (57th), and India (58th) remain essentially unchanged, with all of these countries far below the world average.

[50] This may be a meaningful form of the sort of "increasing returns" described and theorized by the contemporary economic literature's "new growth theory." See, for example, Paul M. Romer, "Increasing Returns and Long-Run Growth," *Journal of Political Economy* 95, no. 5 (October 1986): 1,002–37.

doctrine to a new and more assertive international approach, utilizing the country's still considerable international potential in a much more focused effort to protect and promote the Japanese national interest? Divergent as they may be, neither possibility can be ruled out at the moment.

For India, national demographic prospects appear at first glance to be strongly favorable for the decades immediately ahead. To go by aggregate population projections, the country is set to benefit from a demographic dividend of mild population aging, moderate labor force growth, and an increasing ratio of working-age to total population. A closer view, however, suggests that the picture is not quite as favorable as this overview would suggest. India is marked by deep regional disparities: this national snapshot is an average of sharply disparate subnational trends. Human resource profiles vary widely across India by state, and, on average, both health levels and educational attainment in India are distinctly lower than in China today. India can expect gradual improvements in both health and educational levels, barring unforeseen circumstances. Improvements in "human capital," in conjunction with overall trends for labor and population, suggest that India may well be a rising economic power over the coming generation— perhaps even a country that can hope to rival China in economic potential and international influence. But the weaknesses in India's human resource base suggest that the outcome of any prospective race against China for economic potential may be a longer and tougher slog for India than many observers might otherwise expect.

This leaves the United States. There has been much discussion, both abroad and at home (even in official government circles[52]), of the United States' impending decline. Many non-demographic factors inform those assessments, of course. Yet to judge by the demographic factors reviewed in the preceding pages, talk of an impending U.S. strategic decline may be greatly exaggerated. Demographic exceptionalism in the United States has set the country on a course for moderate population growth, moderate labor force growth, and relatively slow population aging. By both UNDP and U.S. Census Bureau projections, the United States would still be the third most populous country in the world in 2040—and unlike Japan, Russia, or the rest of Europe, the U.S. share of total world population is envisioned to be about the same in 2040 as it is today. Immigration, education, health, and health care costs all pose potentially serious challenges (some of these more immediate than others) to the effectiveness of the United States in nurturing its human resource base and augmenting the productivity of

---

[52] See, for example, U.S. National Intelligence Council, *Global Trends 2025: A World Transformed* (Washington: Government Printing Office, 2008), http://www.dni.gov/nic/PDF_2025/2025_ Global_Trends_Final_Report.pdf.

the country's human capital. For now, the American public and its elected representative seem to regard these long-term issues with a somewhat curious complacency. Nonetheless, these are all challenges that can be addressed through deliberate and well-considered policies, and by no means presage irremediable crisis in and of themselves.

Given the nature of the U.S. political system and the outlook for demographic influences on the U.S. strategic situation, big shifts in international behavior due to demographic surprises or other factors look much less likely for the United States than for China or Russia—and may in fact be less likely than for any of the other major Asia-Pacific powers. Yet given the presumptive relative regularity and predictability of the United States as an actor in the Asia-Pacific, demographic projections over the coming generation place emphasis on one special aspect of the U.S. international position: namely, the country's system of alliances.

The United States' current military allies—in both Europe and Northeast Asia—are set for relative demographic decline in the decades ahead, and in more than a few instances look to be on course for absolute demographic decline. Under such circumstances, these states may require more from their relationships with the United States and may be able to provide less in return. Moreover, given the slow but steady demographic divergence that is separating the U.S. population profile from those of its European and Northeast Asian treaty allies, there is the question of whether basic affinities between these allied societies may also be diverging—a possibility that could only complicate security cooperation and defense policy interactions. The changing demographic prospects for Asia and the world only highlight the importance of the strategic search for new and additional U.S. alliance partners in the years ahead: countries with which the United States shares values and interests, and with whom it can cultivate new and deepening affinities, relationships, and security bonds. Such a quest is never easy—it requires foresight, great patience, and often some measure of luck. As the British experience in the nineteenth century attests, however, such an approach can also generate appreciable long-term dividends of an entirely non-demographic variety.

capitalism) and political Islam—have important negative consequences for U.S. interests. At the same time, U.S. strategic interests in the Asia-Pacific are threatened less by the stalling of democratization than by the changing power dynamics, notably the rise of China.

The chapter comprises five sections. The first section provides an overview of democracy and the authoritarian challenge in Asia. The second section discusses the different democratic paths taken by Asia's established democracies, notably Japan and India. The third section focuses on the authoritarian developmental model followed by many states across Asia, primarily China and Russia. Section four discusses the challenges posed by political Islam to regimes ranging from Pakistan to Malaysia. The concluding section discusses the implications of these changes taking place across Asia for U.S. policy.

Democracy Stalled

The prospects for the march of liberal democracy in Asia remain fraught. The states that have successfully managed to consolidate democracy will maintain their structural features in the years ahead. Indeed, the world's largest democracy, India, will likely become even more representative, however unpredictable in terms of electoral outcomes. There is also little reason to believe that democracy in Japan is at risk, despite the dramatic defeat in 2009 of the well-entrenched Liberal Democratic Party (LDP). If anything, the LDP's defeat may even presage a greater level of openness and transparency in Japanese politics. Already the nascent Democratic Party of Japan (DPJ) government, which until recently was led by Prime Minister Yukio Hatoyama, has stirred up considerable controversy through revelations of the LDP's various secret military pacts with the United States during the Cold War era. In most other states in Asia, however, the global wave of democratization has seemingly stalled (see **Table 1**). This is true not only with respect to the transformation of authoritarian regimes into electoral democracies but also with respect to the transformation of electoral democracies into "well-functioning liberal democracies."[2]

Having been among the first countries in the "third wave" of democratization in East Asia, Taiwan and South Korea possess robust structural attributes of democracy. The likelihood of military takeover in either of these countries, both of which have long histories of martial law, remains remote. These states hold free and fair elections and their citizens

---

[2] See Doh Chull Shin and Rollin F. Tusalem, "East Asia," in *Democratization*, ed. Christian W. Haerpfer, Patrick Bernhagen, Ronald F. Inglehart, and Christian Welzel (New York: Oxford University Press, 2009), 356.

TABLE 1   Freedom House rankings of the status of freedom in Asia

	Free	Partly free	Not free
East Asia	Japan, South Korea, Taiwan, Mongolia, and Indonesia	Hong Kong, Thailand, Malaysia, Singapore, the Philippines, and East Timor	China, North Korea, Myanmar, Laos, Cambodia, Vietnam, and Brunei
South Asia	India	Pakistan, Nepal, Bhutan, Bangladesh, Sri Lanka, and the Maldives	Afghanistan
Russia and Central Asia	–	–	Russia, Kazakhstan, Kyrgyzstan, Turkmenistan, Tajikistan, and Uzbekistan

SOURCE "Freedom in the World 2010: Erosion of Freedom Intensifies," Freedom House, January 12, 2010, http://www.freedomhouse.org/template.cfm?page=505.

NOTE The term East Asia as used in this chapter refers to Northeast as well as Southeast Asia.

enjoy the benefits of a free press and other civil liberties. More quotidian problems, however, such as rampant corruption in high places, will continue to hobble the quality of these democracies. For example, Taiwan's former president Chen Shui-bian and his wife were both sentenced to life imprisonment in September 2009 after being found guilty of corruption and money laundering. While there was little doubt of their guilt, the manner in which the trials were conducted drew massive criticism, leading one analyst to conclude that "Taiwan's legal system was as much on trial as the defendants themselves."[3] Likewise, in South Korea, corruption in high offices and political infighting resulted in the suicide of former president Roh Moo-hyun in May 2009.

Asia's other third-wave democracies—Mongolia and Indonesia—have maintained their robust democratic structures even as some challenges remain. Mongolia faces difficulties not only due to poverty and corruption but also as a consequence of constitutional amendments that have undermined horizontal accountability. The emergence of democracy in Indonesia—the state with the largest Muslim population in the world—is a welcome development. With the re-election of President Susilo Yudhoyono

---

[3] Thomas B. Gold, "Taiwan in 2009: Eroding Landslide," *Asian Survey* 50, no. 1 (January/February 2010): 73.

in 2009, Indonesia has emerged as a surprisingly successful democracy. The future of democracy in that country, however, depends on the role of the military as well as of political Islam in Indonesian society and politics.

All other third-wave democracies in East Asia, such as Thailand and the Philippines, have reverted to authoritarian or semi-authoritarian rule. Similarly, though many countries in South Asia are undergoing democratization, their democratic future is far from assured. In Nepal, the integration of Maoist combatants into the government has led to political instability, whereas terrorism and the presence of the Taliban and al Qaeda are impeding the democratic process in Afghanistan. Likewise, the nascent movement toward a democratically elected government in Bangladesh was marred by the massacre of the country's military officers by the Bangladesh Rifles, a paramilitary unit, in early 2009. In Sri Lanka, the country's first elections in 2010, coming at the end of a 25-year civil war between the majority Sinhalese and the minority Tamils, led to the victory of President Mahinda Rajapaksa. However, the arrest of his former military chief and political opponent, General Sarath Fonseka, soon after the elections does not bode well for democracy in that country.

Most other states in Asia will remain extremely fragile democracies or merely electoral democracies for a host of reasons, including corrupt and incompetent civilian regimes, interventionist militaries, flagging economies, and the rise of radical Islam. In Pakistan, a vast and disturbing array of homegrown Islamist terrorist networks threaten the long-term stability and security of the state. In Malaysia, which has a long tradition of "soft authoritarianism," democratic rights and civil liberties, especially for minorities, appear to be at growing risk. Over the past year, violence against religious and ethnic minorities has been on the rise. Malaysian leaders are also using the Internal Security Act to target their political opponents, thus casting further doubt on the prospects for democracy in this multi-religious, multi-racial state.[4]

The political situation in Thailand has been particularly precarious since the 2006 military coup that deposed Prime Minister Thaksin Shinawatra. The People's Power Party (PPP), the successor party to Thaksin's Thai Rak Thai (TRT), emerged victorious in the December 2007 elections. Despite living in exile in various countries across Asia and the Middle East, Thaksin continues to remain an important figure in Thai politics. In December 2008, Abhisit Vejjajiva of the Democrat Party became the prime minister after winning a special vote in parliament from PPP defectors. Yet the political

---

[4] Siaan Ansori and Greg Lopez, "The Internal Security Act in Malaysia: Abolish, Not Reform It," East Asia Forum, August 27, 2009, http://www.eastasiaforum.org/2009/08/27/the-internal-security-act-in-malaysia-abolish-not-reform-it/.

situation in Thailand continues to remain extremely volatile because of large-scale street protests, especially in Bangkok. There are two major protest groups—the "red shirts," who are Thaksin loyalists, and the "yellow shirts," who are close to the military establishment and the royal family of Thailand. Although elections do not need to be held until 2011, the massive civil unrest and violence, as well as the country's flagging economy, do not bode well for the future of democracy in Thailand.

So what is the future of democracy in Asia? Recent Asian Barometer surveys show that democracy is not "the only game in town" in that region.[5] Rather, as Yun-han Chu argues, "authoritarianism remains a fierce competitor of democracy in East Asia,"[6] and judging by the trends noted above, the same argument can be made for South and Central Asia. Although a comprehensive analysis of the future of democracy in Asia is beyond the scope of this chapter, one important reason why democratization has stalled is that established Asian democracies have followed paths to democratization that may not be replicable elsewhere in the region.

Democratic Paths in Asia

The U.S. military occupation of Japan between 1945 and 1952 resulted in Japan's democratization and the adoption of the so-called Peace Constitution. The new constitution, adopted by the Japanese Diet in 1946, was directly based on a constitution prepared by the occupying forces. Under this constitution, Japan was to be a constitutional monarchy and a parliamentary democracy. Japan renounced war as well as using the threat of force in international affairs and instead focused on economic development in the subsequent decades in a close alliance with the United States. Over the next several decades Japan emerged as a successful democracy and a formidable economic power.

India's democratic trajectory was very different from that of Japan. The historical origins of democracy in India are a product of the Indian nationalist movement, which successfully appropriated liberal-democratic principles from Britain and applied them to India. Indian nationalists can justifiably claim that each step toward self-rule and democratic governance

---

[5] See Juan J. Linz and Alfred Stepan, *Problems of Democratic Transition and Consolidation: Southern Europe, South America, and Post-Communist Europe* (Baltimore: Johns Hopkins University Press, 1996), 5. Linz and Stepan credit Guiseppe di Palma with this telling expression. See also Yun-han Chu, Larry Diamond, Andrew J. Nathan, and Doh Chull Shin, *How East Asians View Democracy* (New York: Columbia University Press, 2008). For details on the surveys, see Asian Barometer, http://www.asianbarometer.org/.

[6] Yun-han Chu, "Third Wave Democratization in East Asia: Challenges and Prospect," *Asien 100* (July 2006): 13.

was the result of sustained and unrelenting political agitation by Indians against authoritarian colonial rule. India's transition to and sustenance of democracy have been the fruits of both structure and contingency.[7] The former includes India's democratic constitution that was adopted in 1950 and sought to represent the interests of the country's diverse communities, while the latter includes the central role played by nationalist leaders such as Mahatma Gandhi and Jawaharlal Nehru who rejected authoritarian rule. The importance of the Indian nationalist movement for the democratization of India is underscored by the fact that the Indian and Pakistani political and military trajectories diverged significantly after independence and the partition of the subcontinent, even though these states were subject to similar political and military institutions under the Raj.

The third-wave democracies of Asia have followed different trajectories of democratization from either Japan or India. Many scholars have argued that modernization theory explains the democratization of countries such as Taiwan and South Korea.[8] However, it seems empirically true that modernization is insufficient for explaining Asian democracy. Although the exact causes of the democratization of Taiwan and South Korea continue to be debated, both polities democratized under a very specific set of conditions that included several decades of economic development under authoritarian rule, a security alliance with the United States, and an international environment open to free trade and easy access to the vast U.S. market. Likewise, modernization theory cannot explain why Singapore and Malaysia have not yet democratized. In the case of Singapore, Larry Diamond has observed that "no nondemocracy has ever been as rich and as successful."[9] Even in Indonesia, modernization under authoritarian rule was not the trigger for democratization; rather, it was the instability generated by the 1997 Asian financial crisis and the fall of President Suharto that proved crucial for democratization.

The Indian and Japanese paths to democracy are unique in as much as democratization was historically conditioned (in the case of India) and geopolitically shaped (in the case of Japan). As such, they are unlikely to be replicated elsewhere. On the other hand, several Asian countries have resisted democratization simply because they were able to achieve spectacular economic success under authoritarian rule. Of the authoritarian

---

[7] Sumit Ganguly, "Introduction," in *The State of India's Democracy*, ed. Sumit Ganguly, Larry Diamond, and Marc F. Plattner (Baltimore: Johns Hopkins University Press, 2007), ix.

[8] See, for example, David Potter, "Democratization at the Same Time in South Korea and Taiwan," in *Democratization*, ed. David Potter, David Goldblatt, Margaret Kiloh, and Paul Lewis (Cambridge: Polity Press, 1997).

[9] Larry Diamond, *The Spirit of Democracy: The Struggle to Build Free Societies throughout the World* (New York: Times Books, 2008), 208.

states that did democratize, most of them had a close security relationship with the world's leading democracy, the United States. As noted above, survey results indicate that East Asians disproportionately favor economic development over democracy.[10] The tendency toward authoritarianism or semi-authoritarianism in some countries is further reinforced by the dominance of a single party in domestic politics. As Shin and Tusalem have argued, by "placing peace and prosperity of the community above the rights and freedoms of its individual citizens," the leaders of these parties have "equated democracy with soft authoritarian rule" and defended it as a viable alternative to liberal democracy.[11]

Confucianism and "Asian values" are often cited to explain the absence of democratization in some parts of Asia.[12] However, these arguments fall short because three of Asia's successful democracies—Japan, Taiwan, and South Korea—share a common Confucian heritage. Furthermore, as it has been argued elsewhere, "the 'Asian values' discourse was an attempt to justify authoritarianism *after* economic development."[13] Japan's and India's politico-economic model, in which the state plays a key role, offers the region's other regimes a pretext for intervening in their domestic economies to control state power and impede democratization. But unlike other states, as a consequence of their unique democratic trajectories, Japan and India have managed to couple democratic politics with such interventionism.

Japan adopted a version of capitalism guided by the state after adopting its democratic constitution. Though the second-largest economy in the world, Japan entered a decade-long period of economic stagnation starting in 1991. In 2001, under the leadership of Prime Minister Junichiro Koizumi, Japan implemented a number of neoliberal economic reforms in an attempt to end the period of economic stagnation. Consequently, the Japanese economy witnessed a period of sustained growth before the onset of the current global financial crisis. The vast majority of Japanese people, however, did not benefit from this period of economic growth, given that in this once uniformly middle-class society the number of people who earn less than half the median income has grown rapidly.[14] Furthermore, Koizumi's successors lacked both his personal charisma and his sound

---

[10] Yun-han Chu, Larry Diamond, Andrew J. Nathan, and Doh Chull Shin, "Asia's Challenged Democracies," *Washington Quarterly* 32, no. 1 (January 2009): 145.

[11] Shin and Tusalem, "East Asia," 358.

[12] Fareed Zakaria, "A Conversation with Lee Kuan Yew," *Foreign Affairs* 73, no. 2 (March/April 1994): 109–26.

[13] Mark R. Thompson, "Pacific Asia after 'Asian Values': Authoritarianism, Democracy, and 'Good Governance,'" *Third World Quarterly* 25, no. 6 (2004): 1,085. Emphasis is in the original.

[14] Tobias Harris, "How Will the DPJ Change Japan?" *Naval War College Review* 63, no. 1 (Winter 2010): 78.

policy agenda. After becoming prime minister in 2009, Hatoyama rejected the "fundamentalist pursuit of capitalism" because Japan had been badly hit by the current global financial crisis. As a consequence, neoliberal reforms have been arrested and even rolled back in Japan. This is most visible in the discord over the country's postal services reform. Consequently, Japan seems to be moving back toward a version of state-guided capitalism.

Unlike Asia's authoritarian regimes, however, where state intervention in the economies is used for political control and acts as an impediment to democratization, democracy is not in any danger in Japan. In fact, the DPJ's victory has only further strengthened Japan's democratic credentials. One analyst has concluded that the DPJ's victory "ended LDP hegemonic rule for good" and unless the LDP gets its act together "the DPJ may become predominant as the LDP used to be."[15] Yet, it is too early to say if this is indeed the case. The LDP's phenomenal victory in the 2001 elections and the DPJ's landslide victory in 2009 have demonstrated the "phoenix-like nature" of both of Japan's major political parties.[16] Japan may very well be moving toward a two-party system. The DPJ is also making dramatic changes in Japan's policymaking apparatus. The DPJ wants to centralize power in the office of the prime minister at the expense of the bureaucrats. This strategy is most visible in the party's proposals to create a national strategy bureau to oversee the national budget and to set priorities for policy. The significance of this changing process of policymaking in Japan has led one analyst to conclude that "Japan is on the brink of a period of policy experimentation not unlike Japan's 'openings' after the Meiji Restoration and the American occupation."[17]

Asia's other established democracy, India, is similar to Japan to the extent that state intervention in the country's political economy has not come at the expense of democracy. India slowly began to open up its economy to the market at the end of the Cold War after several decades of democratic governance. The end of the Cold War in 1991 coincided with a serious balance-of-payments crisis in India. In the midst of this crisis, the government of Prime Minister Narasimha Rao launched a series of structural reforms in the Indian economy under Finance Minister Manmohan Singh. These reforms introduced a new industrial policy and also led to reforms in India's financial sector. As such, India began to shed its socialist shibboleths and started embracing the market. In the political realm, the Congress Party began to lose the near-hegemony that it had enjoyed in Indian politics since

---

[15] David Arase, "Japan in 2009: A Historic Election Year," *Asian Survey* 50, no. 1 (February 2010): 52.

[16] Bert Edström, "Japan: The Quest for Political Leadership," Institute for Security and Development Policy, Policy Brief, no. 18, February 12, 2010.

[17] Harris, "How Will the DPJ Change Japan?" 94.

the birth of the Indian state in 1947. The 1980s witnessed the rise of Hindu nationalism (which found a political voice in the Bharatiya Janata Party, or BJP) as well as caste-based and regional political parties. India had now entered an era of coalition politics.

Since then, political parties in India from across the political spectrum have assumed power in New Delhi. Yet in the midst of these changing political fortunes, the basic democratic nature of the country's politics has remained intact. These governments have also maintained the trend toward the liberalization of the Indian economy even as the pace of reform has varied over the past two decades. During 1988–2006, the Indian economy grew at an average rate of 6.3% per annum.[18] In 2004 the Congress Party made a phenomenal comeback after defeating the BJP, which had been in power for the previous six years. The Congress Party's victory in the 2009 general elections was even more dramatic; these elections saw the decline of the BJP and the leftist parties, as well as of other caste-based and regional parties. Although the BJP is currently down and faces a leadership crisis, the party remains a powerful force in Indian politics.

The success of the Congress Party's victories in 2004 and 2009 was a result of, among other factors, its focus on poverty—that is, on India's large numbers of rural (and urban) poor who were not benefitting from the country's rapid economic growth. Given that the areas in which India needs to implement the next generation of economic reforms in order to unleash the country's full economic potential—small-scale industries, agriculture, and labor law, among others—will have a direct impact on the poor and result in their possible short-term dislocation, India's popularly elected leaders are reluctant to take bold steps to make these changes. Consequently, though the Indian economy is in the process of embracing the market, the Indian state continues to maintain a large interventionist role.

Even though democracy is firmly rooted in India today, this does not mean that the country's democracy has an unblemished record. Rather, Indian democracy faces numerous challenges such as the rise of Hindu nationalism, ethnic insurgencies, and Hindu-Muslim violence, to name just a few. Two important challenges, however, stand out. First, after Russia, India has the largest number of billionaires in the world per trillion dollars of GDP.[19] While it is true that many businessmen and women generated wealth legitimately in India (unlike the state-corporate model of wealth generation in Russia), it also remains true that the

---

[18] Arvind Panagariya, *India: The Emerging Giant* (New York: Oxford University Press, 2008), 6.

[19] Raghuram Rajan, "Is There a Threat of Oligarchy in India?" (speech to the Bombay Chamber of Commerce, Bombay, September 10, 2008), 7, http://faculty.chicagobooth.edu/raghuram.rajan/research/papers/Is%20there%20a%20threat%20of%20oligarchy%20in%20India.pdf.

predominant sources of wealth in India are land, natural resources, and government contracts—all of which come from the government.[20] It is true that India does not yet face the danger of "oligarchic capitalism," in which a small group of rich and politically influential capitalists controls the levers of the state and the direction of policy. However, unless the inequities generated by rapid economic growth are quickly addressed, India may risk falling into the "middle-income trap" in the future if the system of oligarchic capitalism begins to distort economic policymaking for its own vested interests at the expense of the interests of the vast majority of the country's citizens.[21]

Second, and also related to social and economic inequities, is the threat of left-wing Naxal/Maoist violence, which began in the state of West Bengal in the late 1960s but which now unsettles nearly a quarter of India's total administrative districts in a region that stretches along the north-south corridor from the Indo-Nepalese border southward to Andhra Pradesh.[22] While there are a number of causes behind this violent revolutionary threat challenging the Indian state, poverty and social tensions spurred by development are important factors. Though redressing socio-economic inequalities is important for combating the Maoist rebels, India needs a viable counterinsurgency strategy to control and eliminate the violence provoked by this threat. How India manages to avoid the threat of oligarchic capitalism, on the one hand, and the threat of left-wing Maoist violence, on the other—both of which stem from rapid economic development—will shape the nature of Indian democracy in the years ahead.

While Japan and India have managed to maintain their robust democratic politics with state-guided and interventionist political economies owing to unique circumstances, the state's penetration of domestic political economies is being used as a pretext to usurp political power and promote authoritarianism elsewhere in Asia. China's phenomenal economic rise over the past three decades under authoritarian rule may only reinforce this tendency. In order to understand the sustainability and exportability of this model, the next section examines authoritarian development in Asia.

---

[20] Rajan, "Is There a Threat of Oligarchy in India?" 8.

[21] A middle-income trap occurs when a developing country's median income gets stuck in the middle-income bracket even as its economy is growing. See Homi Kharas, "The Challenge Is to Escape the Middle Income Trap," *Financial Express*, June 24, 2009.

[22] Sumit Ganguly, "Fighting the Maoist Menace," *Wall Street Journal*, April 11, 2010.

An Authoritarian State-Market Economy Model for Asia?

Several Asian states have shown interest in the authoritarian developmental model. Not only has the march of liberal democracy halted across much of Asia, but according to a survey by Asian Barometer, "democracy lost favor to economic development by a wide margin" in the region.[23] Furthermore, many Asian states are impressed that China managed to wade through the current financial crisis far better than its Western counterparts, especially the United States. In large part, China's successful management of the financial crisis was driven by the government's massive fiscal stimulus of $586 Billion. The stimulus program further increased the power of the Chinese state in the country's economy while also increasing the power of the central government vis-à-vis the state governments.

At a philosophical level, the noted political scientist John Mueller has argued that capitalism and democracy can exist independently of one another.[24] According to Mueller, "history no longer suggests...that capitalism is a necessary or sufficient condition for democracy," for, generally speaking, "outside the communist world all democracies have been capitalistic, but so also have just about all nondemocracies."[25] South Korea's and Taiwan's rapid economic development in the 1970s and 1980s under authoritarian regimes additionally seems to empirically support the view that capitalism does not need democracy to flourish. This idea of authoritarian development is often dubbed the "China model" or the "Beijing Consensus" due to China's spectacular economic development over the past three decades. As one observer notes, however, the idea "to offer economic growth, jobs, and limited social freedom in exchange for continued control of the political sphere...is neither new nor profound nor uniquely Chinese."[26]

Nevertheless, the demonstration effect of China's phenomenal economic success in the recent past has made authoritarian development a viable model for emulation. Leaders from countries as diverse as Laos, Madagascar, and Iran are traveling to China to better understand how to loosen the reins on their domestic economies while tightening political control in the process.[27] In an ironic twist of fate, even Vladimir Putin's

---

[23] Chu et al., *How East Asians View Democracy*, 145.

[24] John Mueller, *Capitalism, Democracy, and Ralph's Pretty Good Grocery* (Princeton: Princeton University Press, 2001).

[25] Mueller, *Capitalism, Democracy*, 232, 234.

[26] Afshin Molavi, "Buying Time in Tehran: Iran and the China Model," *Foreign Affairs* 83, no. 6 (2004): 9–16.

[27] Joshua Kurlantzick, *Charm Offensive: How China's Soft Power Is Transforming the World* (New Haven: Yale University Press, 2007), 133–34; Joshua Kurlantzick, "State Inc.," *Boston Globe*, March 16, 2008; and Molavi, "Buying Time in Tehran."

United Russia Party is keen to learn from China's political and economic model how to manage a successful economy while maintaining one-party dominance. As a consequence of China's rapid transformation, Stefan Halper argues that "the market-authoritarian model has leveled a powerful challenge in the realm of ideas against preeminence of the market-democratic model."[28]

Moreover, Chinese officials now argue that "their country's resilience in the face of America's meltdown has vindicated China's 'state capitalist' system."[29] In a similar vein, leaders of other Asian countries have also argued that government intervention and guidance is required for the smooth functioning of the economy.[30] The premise of this state capitalist system is not only to deliver economic growth but also to ensure that the state remains "the leading economic actor and uses markets primarily for political gains,"[31] thereby impeding political pluralization while maintaining domestic political stability. There appears to be some appeal for China's authoritarian state-market economy model across Asia and beyond. Whether or not such a model actually addresses fundamental questions of governance and economic growth, however, is the subject of much debate. Indeed, there is some question over whether authoritarianism, even if of the soft or benign variant, acts as a hindrance to growth and continued economic development.

Some scholars inspired by modernization theory have argued that the economic growth and economic liberalization underway in China since the beginning of economic reforms in 1978 under the leadership of Deng Xiaoping will inevitably lead China down the path toward democratization (or a commensurate growth of political liberties).[32] Yet this long-held belief by many U.S. political analysts and commentators has proven highly questionable. As has already been mentioned, modernization theory does not posit a definitive causal link between economic growth and political liberalization or democratization.

In fact, these geopolitical and economic changes suggest that China has made a transition from totalitarianism to an increasingly stable classic

---

[28] Stefan Halper, *The Beijing Consensus* (New York: Basic Books, 2010), 134.

[29] Ian Bremmer, "China Knows That the Time for Lying Low Has Ended," *Financial Times*, March 28, 2010.

[30] See Tony Tan Keng Yam, "Post Financial Crisis—New Global Paradigm and Asia's Role" (speech delivered at the Commonwealth Economic Forum, Taipei, January 18, 2010), http://www.gic.com.sg/PDF/Speech_by_Dr_Tony_Tan_at_the_Commonwealth_Economic_Forum.pdf.

[31] Ian Bremmer, "State Capitalism Comes of Age," *Foreign Affairs* 88, no. 3 (2009).

[32] For example, see Henry S. Rowen, "When Will the Chinese People Be Free?" *Journal of Democracy* 18, no. 3 (July 2007): 38–52; and Dali L. Yang, "China's Long March to Freedom," *Journal of Democracy* 18, no. 3 (July 2007): 58–64.

authoritarian regime.[33] This is in spite of the fact that "very little progress has been made in the reform of China's core political institutions, which are essentially the same ones that existed" at the start of its economic reforms in 1978.[34] To be sure, Chinese citizens enjoy more personal freedoms today than at any time since the emergence of the People's Republic in 1949. Furthermore, China's policymaking process has definitely become more pluralized with the decentralization of decisionmaking authority as well as the addition of new political actors. However, this decentralization largely holds true only in the realm of economic decisionmaking, and even there the hegemony of the Chinese Communist Party (CCP) is unquestionable. Indeed, the CCP is proactively learning lessons from former Communist states, as well as from non-Communist one-party states, which, as David Shambaugh observes, will help the party "relegitimate itself, strengthen its core capacities, expand its constituencies, and adjust its policies to new conditions" in order to ensure its survival and dominance.[35]

Thus, China has modernized not only its economy but also its authoritarianism—a combination that is likely to survive, at least for a while. First, the CCP is stifling the growth of civil society in China by co-opting the country's emerging elite, including private entrepreneurs, top students, and other members of the intelligentsia. Coupled with media censorship in China, this does not bode well for the emergence of a society espousing plural points of view. Second, while China has made some limited progress in establishing institutions for legal participation, the country is still not a "rule of law" state. Most of the legal changes introduced do not concern citizens' rights and obligations; instead, they deal with the administrative management of an economy embracing the market. There are no real judicial constraints on the exercise of the CCP's power. Third, the CCP has shown considerable willingness to resort to coercion at various levels—ranging from controls on electronic media to the use of military force—to contain the possibility of public demonstrations and protests. At the same time, the CCP uses nationalism to bolster its legitimacy. This, for example, has enabled the CCP to use brute force to repress any political activity or even expression of autonomy in the restive Tibet and Xinjiang regions.

Finally, elite politics in China has become institutionalized to a limited degree, especially in administrative matters, as demonstrated by new

---

[33] Andrew J. Nathan, "Authoritarian Resilience: China's Changing of the Guard," *Journal of Democracy* 14, no. 1 (January 2003): 16.

[34] Andrew G. Walder, "Unruly Stability: Why China's Regime Has Staying Power," *Current History* 108, no. 719 (September 2009): 257.

[35] David Shambaugh, *China's Communist Party: Atrophy and Adaptation* (Washington, D.C.: Woodrow Wilson Center Press, 2008), 103.

procedures such as the age-70 rule for retirement of Politburo-level officials and the two-term limit for the premier.[36] More importantly, leadership succession in China has become less violent, though the process remains opaque. Since the passing of Deng Xiaoping, who handpicked Jiang Zemin and Hu Jintao, no CCP leader has chosen his own successor. Unless the CCP is capable of the systemic transfer of power to a successor with a different set of policy preferences from the incumbent, Chinese elite politics is likely to remain under-institutionalized.

China's national leadership is nonetheless remarkably unified today. This is true even of the so-called fifth-generation leadership that will assume power in China in 2012. To be sure, factional politics has made a remarkable comeback in China, as the emergence of two equally powerful coalitions representing different social and geographical backgrounds demonstrates. The first group—the populist coalition (*tuanpai*)—hails mostly from the inland provinces and is focused on regional development and inclusive growth, whereas the second group—the elitist coalition ("princelings")—includes children of high-ranking CCP officials and is focused on rapid economic growth in the coastal provinces. But in spite of the emergence of this "one party, two coalitions" system in the CCP, there is a remarkable inner-party bipartisanship. The country's ruling elite are united by the desire to maintain the hegemony of the CCP domestically while enhancing China's status as a great power abroad.[37] Importantly, both factions of the fifth-generation leadership are equally represented in the 17th Politburo and Secretariat of the CCP that was elected by the Central Committee of the CCP in 2007.[38] Given their generally conservative outlook on political reform and a highly state-centric version of economic development, the authoritarian nature of the CCP is expected to continue with the next generation of leadership. However, because a large number of fifth-generation leaders were trained in law, politics, or the social sciences in college as opposed to the more technical educational background of the fourth-generation leadership, it is possible that China may evolve into a

---

[36] Frederick C. Teiwes, "Normal Politics with Chinese Characteristics," *China Journal* 45 (January 2001): 74. Given its informal nature, the implementation of the age-70 rule has at times been arbitrary. For example, Jiang Zemin is believed to have introduced this new rule in 1997 to eliminate his rival Qiao Shi. It is further believed that the retirement age was temporarily lowered to 68 in 2002 in order to force Li Ruihuan to step down. See Susan Shirk, *China: Fragile Superpower—How China's Internal Politics Could Derail Its Peaceful Rise* (New York: Oxford University Press, 2007), 45.

[37] Cheng Li, "One Party, Two Coalitions in China's Politics," East Asia Forum, August 16, 2009, http://www.brookings.edu/opinions/2009/0816_china_li.aspx.

[38] Cheng Li, "China's Fifth Generation: Is Diversity a Source of Strength or Weakness?" *Asia Policy*, no. 6 (July 2008): 53–94. This includes Li Keqiang (of the populist faction) and Xi Jinping (of the elitist faction), the two most important leaders of the fifth generation and possible successors to Hu Jintao and Wen Jiabao.

"consultative rule of law regime" to ensure the dominance of the CCP by making its rule more legitimate.[39]

Like China, Russia is keen to create a rapidly growing economy under the leadership of an authoritarian (or semi-authoritarian), hegemonic party. Russia is currently in the process of establishing a classic "hybrid regime."[40] A hybrid regime combines elements of democratic as well as authoritarian politics. The process of political opening that had begun under the Soviet president Mikhail Gorbachev continued in post-Communist Russia with the establishment of an electoral democracy and the introduction of basic political and civil liberties in the early 1990s. However, "shock therapy" reforms in the 1990s to help the ailing Russian economy transition to a market economy resulted in a massive contraction of the Russian economy, with the country's GDP declining at an annual rate of 6.8% from 1992–98.[41] It was under these conditions that former president Boris Yeltsin struck a partnership with Russia's business elite (or oligarchs) and clamped down on the media in order to maintain and consolidate political power. This erosion of democracy has continued under Vladimir Putin and his successor Dmitry Medvedev.

Under Putin, political power became increasingly concentrated in the executive branch, as informal institutions backed by the president, such as the Public Chamber, replaced the parliament in the policymaking process. With no viable opposition party, the dominant political party, United Russia, has simply become an instrument of executive power. At the same time, the opportunities for political participation have been reduced by the narrowing of media freedom. In 2008, 69 journalists were physically attacked and 5 were killed, some under circumstances that indicated government involvement.[42] Likewise, political and military developments in the secessionist Chechen region have resulted not only in restrictions on civil liberties in Russia but also in extrajudicial executions, arrests, and extortion of civilians as well as in a spate of violent terrorist attacks in the country, including the March 2010 attacks in Moscow. These developments have led some analysts to refer to Russia's hybrid regime

---

[39] Pan Wei, "Toward a Consultative Rule of Law Regime in China," in *Debating Political Reform in China: Rule of Law vs. Democratization*, ed. Suisheng Zhao (Armonk: M.E. Sharpe, 2006), 3–40.

[40] Larry Diamond, "Elections without Democracy: Thinking about Hybrid Regimes," *Journal of Democracy* 13, no. 2 (April 2002): 21–35.

[41] Jim Nichol et al., "Russian Political, Economic, and Security Issues and US Interests," Congressional Research Service, CRS Report for Congress, RL33407, January 29, 2010, 12, available at http://www.fas.org/sgp/crs/row/RL33407.pdf.

[42] Ibid., 8.

as an "overmanaged democracy."[43] Although Russia maintains the basic feature of a democracy by holding periodic elections, elections in Russia are neither free nor fair.

Despite Russia's movement away from democracy, the country's emergent hybrid regime enjoys widespread public support.[44] The most important reason for the popularity of this form of governance has been its ability to generate spectacular economic growth over the past decade before the onset of the current global financial crisis. This turn in Russia's economic fortunes, however, is largely due to the country's emergence as an energy superpower. In addition, the Kremlin has used its effective control of the state's media to whip up nationalist passions by promoting national renewal, nostalgia for former glory, and anti-Western xenophobia. Furthermore, corruption remains endemic in the Russian economy as well as in politics. Finally, the legal system in Russia remains extremely weak, and a dual justice system has emerged, in which the courts handle only mundane cases while avoiding issues involving powerful actors in the country.

Politics in Russia have become more complicated after the election of Dmitry Medvedev as president in May 2008. With Putin serving as prime minister, a "diarchy" has emerged in Moscow, and it is quite possible that Putin may try to return as president in 2012. This situation has given rise to a power struggle between Medvedev and his colleagues—the so-called *civiliki*, or people of civil law—and Putin and his colleagues—the so-called *siloviki*, or people of force.[45] Although Medvedev is more reform-minded than Putin in as much as he wants to implement economic reforms to reduce Russia's dependence on the export of energy resources, neither of the two leaders is pushing for the liberalization of the political order. This is primarily because the country's political system is closely tied to its extant politico-economic system. The Putin years witnessed the emergence of a state-capitalist system in which political figures assumed leadership positions in the Russian corporate sector, especially in strategic sectors such as banking, mining, energy, and defense. This intra-elite cohesiveness, largely managed by Putin himself, was responsible for Russia's stable politico-economic order over the past decade or so.

However, the current global financial crisis has resulted in a split between the reform-minded Medvedev and the status quo–oriented Putin

[43] Nikolai Petrov, Masha Lipman, and Henry E. Hale, "Overmanaged Democracy in Russia: Governance Implications of Hybrid Regimes," Carnegie Papers, no. 106, February 2010. The discussion above draws from this paper.

[44] Richard Rose, William Mishler, and Neil Munro, *Russia Transformed: Developing Popular Support for a New Regime* (Cambridge: Cambridge University Press, 2006).

[45] Yu-Shan Wu, "Russia and the CIS in 2009: Pillar of the System Shaken," *Asian Survey* 50, no. 1 (2010): 76–88.

factions. Although Russia has begun slowly to emerge from the current financial crisis as a consequence of rising energy prices and massive spending of state reserves to bail out politically connected firms, the country's long-term growth prospects depend on both the implementation of major structural-economic reforms and the reduction of national dependence on energy exports. Yet, in order to succeed, Medvedev's reform plans must target the economic oligarchy of Russia and, as such, will challenge Putin's state-capitalist political system.[46] Given that economic and political reforms are thus interlinked in Russia, Medvedev's economic modernization strategy is unlikely to succeed, despite the rhetoric.[47] Instead, Russia's hybrid regime will likely maintain political and economic power, at least for the time being.

As a consequence of the political and economic trends underway in China and Russia, an authoritarian state-led developmental model that embraces a version of state capitalism has acquired widespread appeal across Asia. In particular, China's phenomenal economic growth under an authoritarian regime for more than three decades has led many analysts to argue that this combination is a viable alternative to liberal democratic capitalism in Asia.[48] But how sustainable is this model in China itself, and are other states in Asia and beyond willing and able to adopt it?

The CCP's ability to reinvent itself suggests that China's authoritarian system may be sustainable for at least the near-term.[49] The central tenet of modernization theory—that economic development and political liberalization are correlated—has been turned on its head by the success of China's model. Yasheng Huang, a professor and China economy specialist at the Massachusetts Institute of Technology, has argued that China was more liberal, politically as well as economically, in the decade before the 1989 Tiananmen Square massacre than in the two decades following it, even as the country's economy has clocked double-digit growth rates.[50] Yet Huang remains critical of this growth, which has generated large inequalities, and

---

[46] Jeffrey Mankoff, "Internal and External Impact of Russia's Economic Crisis," Russia/ NIS Center, Russie.Nei.Visions, no. 48, March 2010, 12, http://www.ifri.org/downloads/ ifriengeconomiccrisisinrussiamankofffevrier2010.pdf.

[47] Sinikukka Saari and Katri Pynnöniemi, "Medvedev's Take on Vertical Power," Briefing Paper, no. 51 (January 28, 2010): 1–8, http://www.upi-fiia.fi/assets/publications/UPI_Briefing_Paper_51_2010.pdf.

[48] For example, see Naazneen Barma and Ely Ratner, "China's Illiberal Challenge," *Democracy: A Journal of Ideas*, no. 2 (Fall 2006): 56–68; see also Naazneen Barma, Ely Ratner, and Steven Weber, "Letters to the Editor—Chinese Ways," *Foreign Affairs* 87, no. 3 (May/June 2008): 166.

[49] See Shambaugh, *China's Communist Party*; Nathan, "Authoritarian Resilience"; and Walder, "Unruly Stability."

[50] Yasheng Huang, *Capitalism with Chinese Characteristics: Entrepreneurship and the State* (New York: Cambridge University Press, 2008).

argues that the absence of political and economic liberties may impede China's further economic development.

That said, as has already been mentioned, several countries in Asia and beyond have shown an interest in China's model of development. Significantly, China has also begun to export its model through aid and developmental assistance, in sharp contrast to the two Asian democratic powers. Tsuneo Akaha, a specialist on Japan, argues that "a cultural bias against exporting political values" has prevented Japan from exporting democracy to other parts of Asia.[51] Japan's reluctance to interfere in the internal affairs of other states in Asia may also be a consequence of its history of brutal intervention and colonization in the first half of the twentieth century, a past that many states in Asia bitterly remember. Indian leaders have similarly argued that their country is "not inclined to export ideologies, even ideologies it believes in and follows," preferring instead to "promote democracy in the region by precept and example."[52] Guided by a national security calculus, India's promotion of democracy in Asia has been selective, with New Delhi supporting democracy in countries such as Afghanistan and Nepal but not in places such as Myanmar.

China has not only emerged as the largest lender to Africa, but its aid to a range of Southeast and Central Asian countries, such as Cambodia and Uzbekistan, outstrips that of democratic powers.[53] Beijing's policy of non-interference in the internal affairs of other states means that its developmental assistance comes without any strings attached. China's major interest in most of these countries is accessing their natural resources and expanding its own geopolitical influence. Importantly, China has organized large-scale programs to train police, judges, and other security officials in countries across Africa and Asia. Such programs promote the Chinese model of development among these countries' emerging elite. Furthermore, China is also training and sharing its censorship technology with media officials in these countries.[54]

Other countries are seriously studying the Chinese model for suitability to their political and economic environments. According to Halper, this model is believed to present a fast developmental path without regime

---

[51] Tsuneo Akaha, "Japan: A Passive Partner in the Promotion of Democracy," in *Exporting Democracy: Rhetoric vs. Reality*, ed. Peter J. Schraeder (Boulder: Lynne Rienner, 2002), 89–107.

[52] Pranab Mukherjee, "India's Strategic Perspectives" (speech at the Carnegie Endowment for International Peace, Washington, D.C., June 27, 2005), 5, http://www.carnegieendowment.org/files/Mukherjee_Speech_06-27-051.pdf.

[53] This section largely draws from Joshua Kurlantzick and Perry Link, "China: Resilient, Sophisticated Authoritarianism," in "Undermining Democracy: 21st Century Authoritarians," Freedom House, Radio Free Europe/Radio Liberty, and Radio Free Asia, June 2009, 25.

[54] Ibid., 15.

change or ideological compromise. At the same time, its authoritarian tenets ensure domestic political stability.[55] Consequently, China's dramatic economic development under an authoritarian regime poses a serious challenge for democratization in Asia and beyond.

The Appeal of Political Islam

Apart from the challenge of authoritarian development, democracy in Asia also confronts the challenge of political Islam. Though the more radical manifestations of political Islam have seized the popular imagination since the tragic events of September 11, in actuality the resurgence of Islam in politics took place in Asia as early as the late 1970s and early 1980s. In large part, the underlying causes of this phenomenon in recent times can be traced to a number of developments in the Middle East—specifically, the Iranian revolution, the war against the Soviet occupation of Afghanistan, and the growth of oil prices. The first two provided political inspiration for a host of regional and local political activists. The third development contributed financial support, especially from Saudi Arabia, for various Islamist political organizations. It is vital to bear in mind that the transnational character of political Islam as well as the institutional choices of the individual regimes, which range from Pakistan to Indonesia, mean that the impact and future of political Islam across the region will vary considerably.

Political Islam in South Asia, for example, has sprung from different origins and followed different trajectories. In Pakistan, where the state has long been complicit in utilizing Islamist forces to pursue strategic aims in Afghanistan and India, the dangers are considerable. Although the Pakistani state does not yet face an existential crisis from the very forces that it helped unleash, it cannot wholly control these forces either. Nevertheless, owing to the highly fragmented features of the country's political institutions and the dominance of the military and the intelligence apparatus, elements of the state continue their dalliance with groups that they deem to be furthering Pakistan's strategic interests. Hence, the state is not fully committed to bringing its coercive power to bear on the Taliban and allows groups such as the Jaish-e-Mohammed and, most importantly, the Lashkar-e-Taiba to wreak havoc in the disputed state of Kashmir and elsewhere in India. Before Pakistan can transition to democracy, the Pakistani military and intelligence agencies, both of which have a history of embracing Islamic radicalism, must be reformed and depoliticized.

---

[55] Halper, *The Beijing Consensus*, 128.

in the southern Philippines.[60] In recent years, following the assassination of ASG leader, Abubakar Janjalani, about a decade ago, the group lost much of its ideological momentum and turned to criminal activities in order to sustain its operations. The Moro rebellion will continue, however, as long as meaningful negotiations between the Philippine government and the disaffected groups fail to materialize.

Political Islam will doubtless remain a significant part of the landscape of Asia for the foreseeable future. Whether or not some of the extant local conflicts that have religious overtones will become enmeshed with transnational jihadi organizations such as al Qaeda remains an open question. If such links do develop, the possibilities of conflict resolution could become considerably more problematic, especially in southern Thailand, the Philippines, and Pakistan. Finally, a more general question persists in the region: namely, if Islamist parties were to rise to power through electoral means, would they be willing to relinquish their radical religious agenda once ensconced in office? This question, of course, has been raised elsewhere and, given the limited array of cases, is difficult to answer with any certainty.

Democratization has clearly stalled in Asia, as is evidenced by the region's preference for economic development under authoritarian regimes over political liberalization, on the one hand, and the growing appeal of political Islam, on the other. At the same time, the political and economic developments taking place in Asia's most important rising power, China, do not bode well for democratization either.

Conclusion

This chapter has analyzed the prospects for democracy and democratization in Asia. The analysis here shows that though democracy is not at risk in the region's established democracies, notably Japan and India, the global wave of democratization has seemingly stalled in most other states in Asia. To begin with, Asia's established democracies have followed multiple paths toward democratization that may not be easily replicable elsewhere in the region. Moreover, authoritarian development and political Islam are two important factors impeding the onward march of democratization. In addition, the phenomenal rise of China over the past three decades has made the authoritarian state-market economy model for development a viable competitor to liberal democratic capitalism in Asia.

---

[60] Angel Rabasa, *Political Islam in Southeast Asia: Moderates, Radicals and Terrorists*, Adelphi Paper 358 (London: International Institute of Strategic Studies, 2003).

Somewhat paradoxically, the stalling of democratization in Asia in and of itself does not threaten U.S. strategic interests in the region. For example, the Singaporean leader Lee Kwan Yew recently stated that it is important for the United States to retain a base in Okinawa to balance China's growing power: "If there is no base in Japan, then they [the United States] cannot deploy their weaponry and project their power sufficiently."[61] In fact, even authorities in China seem to believe that the United States "as an Asia-Pacific nation…contributes to peace, stability and prosperity in the region."[62] Guided by their national interests, the region's non-democracies are in large part comfortable with the U.S. presence and contribution to military stability and economic prosperity in the Asia-Pacific.

While this may seem somewhat counterintuitive, it should be noted that a state's policy toward another state is driven by the pursuit of national interests, not by the similarity or differences between the two states' domestic political orders. For example, throughout most of the Cold War, India and the United States—the world's largest and oldest democracies, respectively—remained estranged, believing that they had divergent national interests. Similarly, democratic Japan's phenomenal economic performance toward the end of the Cold War had led many Americans to view Japan's economic power as a greater threat to U.S. security than Soviet military power. In other words, U.S. interests in the region are threatened less by the stalling of democratization in Asia than by the changing power dynamics, notably the rise of China. For example, China has become more assertive in enforcing its claims to disputed island territories in East Asia as well as in the country's dealings with India. China has also put high-level military ties with the United States on hold—including a trip to China by Secretary of Defense Robert Gates—in response to Washington's arms pact with Taiwan that was announced in January 2010.[63]

Importantly, while the stalling of democratization in Asia may not in itself pose a serious strategic challenge to U.S. foreign policy, two important factors that are impeding democratization in the region—state capitalism and political Islam—have significant negative consequences for U.S. interests. As a result of state capitalism, some of the world's largest corporations in sectors as diverse as oil, mining, telecommunications, and power generation are state owned or operated.[64] Supported by their governments, state-backed

---

[61] Quoted in Kwan Weng Kin, "MM Lee: US Base in Japan Boosts Stability," *Straits Times*, May 21, 2010.

[62] "U.S.-China Joint Statement," Embassy of the United States, Beijing, Press Release, November 17, 2009, http://beijing.usembassy-china.org.cn/111709.html.

[63] Craig Whitlock, "Gates Criticizes Chinese Military for Blocking Talks in Beijing," *Washington Post*, June 3, 2010.

[64] Bremmer, "State Capitalism Comes of Age."

firms distort the normal functioning of the market in countries where they compete with U.S. corporations by paying higher rates, especially if their governments have a strategic interest in those countries. At the same time, backed by governments in their drive to access natural resources, state-backed firms from countries such as China are entering into long-term contracts with countries such as Iran, Myanmar, Sudan, and Zimbabwe.[65] China's foray into these countries is further reducing Washington's influence over states that are already unfavorably disposed toward the United States. Whether free-market capitalism bounces back as a serious alternative to state-capitalism depends in large measure on the actions of the United States. After all, as a consequence of the current global financial crisis, U.S. (and other Western) firms "went cap in hand to the state."[66]

The rise of political Islam threatens not only U.S. security interests in the region but also the security of the United States itself. Pakistan, a key ally of the United States in the war in Afghanistan, is perhaps the most glaring example. There were 2,586 terrorist-insurgent and sectarian attacks in Pakistan in 2009 alone that resulted in the deaths of approximately 3,000 people.[67] The emergence of the Pakistani Taliban not only threatens the stability of this key U.S. ally but also complicates the war in Afghanistan and Pakistan's frontier regions. More perniciously, the Pakistani Taliban is now threatening the United States itself and is believed to have directed the recently foiled Times Square bombing while actively recruiting more agents to carry out attacks in the United States.[68] According to one prominent analyst, there is "a very serious possibility that the next mass casualty terrorist attack on the United States will be postmarked Pakistan."[69] The struggle against political and radical Islam will be a long-term one in which the United States will need a global strategy that is sensitively adjusted to meet local conditions as well as the help of U.S. friends and allies around the world. At the same time, the United States cannot selectively target al Qaeda while ignoring other radical Islamist organizations such as the Pakistani Taliban, Lashkar-e-Taiba, and their affiliates in other parts of the world.

---

[65] Joshua E. Keating, "Beijing's Most Embarrassing Allies," *Foreign Policy*, May 24, 2010, http://www.foreignpolicy.com/articles/2010/05/24/beijing_s_most_embarrassing_allies?page=0,0.

[66] Halper, *The Beijing Consensus*, 35.

[67] Terrence Smith and Teresita Schaffer, "Pakistan: In the Cauldron," Center for Strategic and International Studies, South Asia Monitor, no. 139, March 3, 2010.

[68] Anne E. Kornblut and Karin Brulliard, "U.S. Blames Pakistani Taliban for Times Square Bomb Plot," *Washington Post*, May 10, 2010.

[69] Interview with Bruce O. Riedel, "U.S. Options Limited in Pakistan," Council on Foreign Relations, May 11, 2010, http://www.cfr.org/publication/22099/us_options_limited_in_pakistan.html?bread crumb=%2Fissue%2F135%2Fterrorism.

STRATEGIC ASIA 2010–11

INDICATORS

TABLE OF CONTENTS

Indicators

Strategic Asia
by the Numbers

The following twelve pages contain tables and figures drawn from NBR's Strategic Asia database and its sources. This appendix consists of fourteen tables covering politics, economies, trade and investment, energy and the environment, security challenges, and nuclear arms and nonproliferation. The data sets presented here summarize the critical trends in the region and changes underway in the balance of power in Asia.

The Strategic Asia database contains additional data for all 37 countries in "Strategic Asia." Hosted on the program's website (http://strategicasia.nbr.org), the database is a repository for authoritative data for every year since 1990. The 70 strategic indicators are arranged in ten broad thematic areas: economy, finance, trade and investment, government spending, population, energy and the environment, communications and transportation, armed forces, nuclear arms, and politics. The Strategic Asia database was developed with .NET, Microsoft's XML-based platform, which allows users to dynamically link to all or part of the Strategic Asia data set and facilitates easy data sharing. The database also includes additional links that allow users to seamlessly access related online resources.

The information for "Strategic Asia by the Numbers" was compiled by NBR Next Generation Research Fellow Ryan Zielonka.

Economies

Asia's rebound from the global financial crisis was a crucial factor in the decision of the International Monetary Fund (IMF) to revise its global forecasts for 2010 after markers of future economic growth in the region reached pre-crisis levels. Based on the region's strong performance in early 2010, the IMF predicted 9% growth across Asia's developing economies.

- In mid-2010, China's economy surpassed Japan's, becoming the second-largest economy in the world behind the United States.
- IMF models forecasted 10.5% GDP growth for China in 2010, 6.4% for the ASEAN-5 economies, and 9.2% for India.
- Japan's economic recovery from the global financial crisis showed signs of vulnerability. Japan suffered an 8.1% loss in current account surplus between 2009 and 2010 and a precipitous 9.1% drop in core machinery orders, a leading indicator of capital spending.
- In anticipation of the June 2010 G-20 Summit, China and India took modest steps toward economic reform, ranging from nominal currency valuation to strategic commodity price adjustments.

TABLE 3   Gross domestic product

	GDP ($b constant 2000)				Rank	
	1990	2000	2008	2008 growth (%)	1990	2008
United States	7,055.0	9,764.8	11,513.9	1.3	1	1
Japan	4,111.3	4,667.4	5,166.3	-0.4	2	2
China*	444.6	1,198.5	2,602.6	9.8	4	3
Canada	535.6	724.9	872.8	0.6	3	4
India	269.4	460.2	817.9	6.6	8	5
South Korea	283.6	511.7	750.8	2.5	6	6
Australia	280.5	399.6	521.5	2.2	7	7
Russia	385.9	259.7	430.1	6.0	5	8
Taiwan	–	303.2	383.3	0.1	–	9
Indonesia	109.2	165.0	247.2	6.1	9	10
Hong Kong	108.4	169.1	241.3	2.8	10	11
Thailand	79.4	122.7	177.9	3.6	11	12
Malaysia	45.5	90.3	139.2	1.2	13	13
Singapore	44.7	92.7	135.5	5.1	14	14
Philippines	55.8	75.9	110.7	4.6	12	15
World	23,996.7	31,876.3	40,231.9	3.1	N/A	N/A

SOURCE: World Bank, "World Development Indicators," 2010; and data for Taiwan is from CIA, *The World Factbook*, 2010.

NOTE: These values show GDP converted from domestic currencies using 2000 exchange rates. Figures for Taiwan are calculated using current exchange rates. Dash indicates no data available. Asterisk indicates that in 2010 China's economy surpassed Japan's to become the second-largest economy in the world.

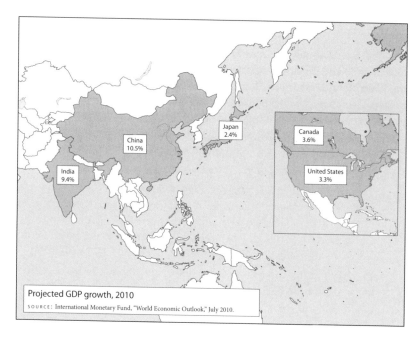

Projected GDP growth, 2010

SOURCE: International Monetary Fund, "World Economic Outlook," July 2010.

TABLE 4   GDP growth and inflation rates

	Average GDP growth (%)			Average inflation rate (%)		
	2000–04	2005–08	2009	2000–04	2005–08	2009
United States	3.0	2.3	-2.4	2.5	3.4	-0.3
Japan	1.3	1.7	-5.3	-0.5	0.5	-1.4
China	8.4	11.2	8.7	0.8	3.6	-0.7
Canada	3.0	2.3	-2.5	2.4	1.8	0.3
India	5.7	8.4	6.5	5.0	6.2	10.9
South Korea	5.7	4.2	0.2	3.0	3.1	2.8
Australia	3.9	3.0	1.0	2.1	3.3	1.8
Russia	5.7	7.1	-7.9	15.9	11.3	11.7
Taiwan	3.4	4.1	-2.5	0.6	2.1	-0.9
Indonesia	4.1	5.9	4.5	9.1	10.3	4.8
Hong Kong	4.6	5.9	-3	0.4	1.8	-0.5
Thailand	4.7	4.6	-2.8	1.8	4.2	-0.9
Malaysia	5.0	5.6	-2.2	1.5	3.6	0.6
Singapore	3.8	5.9	-2.1	1.0	2.0	0.2
Philippines	4.2	5.5	0.9	4.5	6.5	3.3

SOURCE: CIA, *The World Factbook*, 1990–2010.

Trade and Investment

China contributed to a renewed confidence in regional markets, buoyed by demand from European partners. The trade disparity between China and the United States continued to climb and contributed to an increase in the overall U.S. trade deficit. India made its own regional contribution as the country exported goods to the United States at record-setting rates.

- China's trade surplus grew due to a surprising rebound in exports, more than doubling to $20 billion. Overseas sales increased 43.9% mid-year and returned to a pre-crisis level of $137.4 billion.

- The share of foreign exchange reserves held by Asian economies grew, further enhancing central banks' control over currency exchange. As of June 2010, Asia held nearly half of the world's $10 trillion reserves. China held $2.4 trillion, Japan $990 billion, and Taiwan, India, South Korea, Hong Kong, and Singapore collectively held $1.3 trillion.

- In response to the global financial crisis, many Asian countries enacted stimulus packages to boost domestic economies and forestall potential contraction.

TABLE 5   Trade flow and trade partners

	Trade flow ($b constant 2000)			Trade partners	
	2000	2008	2007–08 growth (%)	Top export partner, 2008	Top import partner, 2008
United States	2,572.1	3,398.3	5.1	Canada (20%)	China (16%)
China	530.2	1,498.8	-24.0	U.S. (18%)	Japan (13%)
Japan	957.6	1,380.0	5.6	U.S. (18%)	China (19%)
Hong Kong	475.3	868.2	2.6	China (51%)	China (46%)
South Korea	401.6	792.9	0.5	China (20%)	China (18%)
Canada	617.4	714.5	2.5	U.S. (78%)	U.S. (52%)
Russia	176.8	461.1	8.8	Netherlands (12%)	China (13%)
India	130.5	409.4	16.1	UAE (12%)	China (11%)
Malaysia	206.7	305.6	0.0	Singapore (14%)	China (14%)
Australia	178.0	268.3	9.4	Japan (22%)	China (15%)
Thailand	153.3	253.2	8.5	U.S. (11%)	Japan (19%)
Indonesia	117.9	221.3	10.0	Japan (20%)	Singapore (17%)
Philippines	82.7	115.8	0.0	U.S. (18%)	Japan 13%
Vietnam	35.1	93.8	-25.1	U.S. (19%)	U.S. (22%)
New Zealand	36.6	49.8	6.6	Australia (23%)	Australia (18%)

SOURCE: World Bank, "World Development Indicators," 1990–2010; and CIA, *The World Factbook*, 2010.
NOTE: Data for the United States, Japan, Canada, Malaysia, and New Zealand is for 2007 rather than 2008. No comparable data from the "World Development Indicators" is available for Singapore or Taiwan.

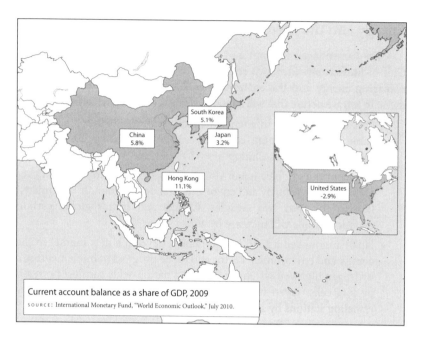

Current account balance as a share of GDP, 2009

SOURCE: International Monetary Fund, "World Economic Outlook," July 2010.

TABLE 6 Flow of foreign direct investment

	FDI inflows ($b)				FDI outflows ($b)	
	1990–2000 annual avg.	2008	2007–08 growth (%)	2008 rank	1990–2000 annual avg.	2008
United States	109.5	316.1	35.8	1	92.0	311.8
China	30.1	108.3	29.7	2	2.2	52.1
Russia	2.4	70.3	33.9	3	1.6	52.4
Hong Kong	13.8	63.0	5.2	4	20.4	59.9
Australia	7.0	46.7	109.8	5	3.2	35.9
Canada	15.7	44.7	-58.9	6	15.8	77.6
India	1.7	41.5	80.8	7	0.1	17.7
Singapore	9.2	22.7	-5.9	8	4.8	8.9
Kazakhstan	1.0	14.5	41.5	9	0.0	3.8
Thailand	3.2	10.1	5.5	10	0.4	2.8
Malaysia	4.7	8.1	-3.6	11	1.6	14.1
Indonesia	1.5	7.9	14.5	12	0.6	5.9
South Korea	3.1	7.6	190.1	13	3.1	12.7
Pakistan	0.5	5.4	1.3	14	0.0	0.0
New Zealand	2.3	2.0	-27.5	15	0.5	0.5
World	495.4	1,697.3	-7.4	N/A	492.6	1,996.5

SOURCE: UN Conference on Trade and Development, *World Investment Report*, 2009.

Security Challenges

The challenges of the post–September 11 world persisted as the United States and its partners made incremental progress in Iraq and Afghanistan, punctuated by isolated threats around the world.

- In March, the South Korean vessel *Cheonan* was sunk near a disputed sea border with North Korea, escalating tensions on the peninsula and fueling international debate on how to deal effectively with North Korea.
- In Afghanistan, key military developments included deployment of an additional 30,000 U.S. soldiers, the appointment of General David Petraeus as commander of U.S. Forces in Afghanistan, and an agreement by NATO countries to recall all troop deployments by 2014.
- Worldwide, high-profile cyberattacks and security intrusions have increased in frequency and complexity, giving rise to a number of new cyberdefense institutions, including U.S. Cyber Command.
- China retaliated against U.S. arms sales to Taiwan by suspending bilateral military exchanges and threatening sanctions on firms selling arms to Taiwan.

TABLE 9   Total defense expenditure

	Expenditure ($b)				Rank	
	1990	2000	2008	2007–08 growth (%)	1990	2008
United States	293.0	300.5	696.2	26.0	1	1
China	11.3	42.0	150.0	7.9	3	2
Russia	–	7.3	58.0	-28.8	–	3
Japan	28.7	45.6	46.0	12.2	2	4
India	10.1	14.7	31.5	18.9	6	5
South Korea	10.6	12.8	24.2	-8.7	4	6
Australia	7.3	7.1	22.1	9.4	8	7
Canada	10.3	11.5	19.8	7.6	5	8
Myanmar	0.9	2.1	11.2	60.0	13	9
Taiwan	8.7	8.9	10.5	9.6	7	10
Singapore	1.7	4.8	7.6	8.4	11	11
Indonesia	1.6	1.5	5.1	18.6	12	12
Pakistan	2.9	3.7	4.4	-2.9	9	13
Malaysia	1.7	2.8	4.4	9.5	10	14
Vietnam	–	1.0	2.9	-21.6	–	15
World	954.0	811.4	1,547.8	21.0	N/A	N/A

SOURCE: International Institute of Strategic Studies, *The Military Balance*, various editions; data for 1990 world total is from SASI Group and Mark Newman, "Military Spending 1990," 2007; and data for China is based on the average of various sources.

NOTE: Estimates for China vary widely. Dash indicates that no data is available.

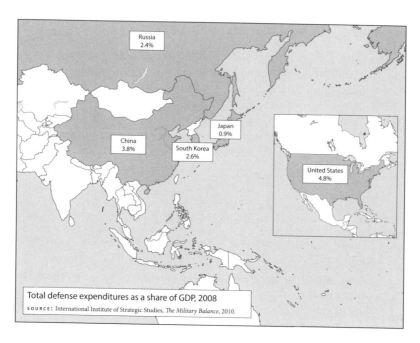

Total defense expenditures as a share of GDP, 2008

SOURCE: International Institute of Strategic Studies, *The Military Balance*, 2010.

TABLE 10 Manpower

	Armed forces (th)				Rank	
	1990	2000	2010	2009–10 change (th)	1990	2010
China	3,030	2,470	2,285	100	2	1
United States	2,118	1,366	1,580	40	3	2
India	1,262	1,303	1,325	44	4	3
North Korea	1,111	1,082	1,106	0	5	4
Russia	3,988	1,004	1,027	0	1	5
South Korea	750	683	687	0	7	6
Pakistan	550	612	617	0	8	7
Vietnam	1,052	484	455	0	6	8
Myanmar	230	344	406	0	13	9
Thailand	283	301	306	-1	10	10
Indonesia	283	297	302	0	10	11
Taiwan	370	370	290	0	9	12
Japan	249	237	230	0	12	13
Sri Lanka	65	–	161	10	14	14
Bangladesh	103	137	157	0	15	15
World	26,605	22,237	20,734	193	N/A	N/A

SOURCE: International Institute of Strategic Studies, *The Military Balance*, various editions.

NOTE: Active duty and military personnel only. Data value for Russia in 1990 includes all territories available for the Soviet Union. Dash indicates that no data is available.

Nuclear Arms and Nonproliferation

In 2010 the United States advanced the debate on nuclear arms, energy, and nonproliferation. The new Nuclear Posture Review aimed to refocus international efforts on arms control and nonproliferation, and in April the United States convened a summit on nuclear arms and nonproliferation that was the largest gathering of heads of state on U.S. soil since the end of World War II. The summit resulted in a series of pledges that range from the creating a new nuclear security institution to transferring highly enriched uranium.

- Barack Obama and Dmitry Medvedev signed the new Strategic Arms Reduction Treaty (START II) in April 2010. Pending ratification, the treaty limits the number of strategic nuclear warheads deployed by each side to 1,550, approximately one-third the number START I allowed.

- China and Russia backed a UN resolution in June 2010 sanctioning Iran for its pursuit of a uranium enrichment center.

- China agreed to sell two civilian reactors to Pakistan, which the United States claimed was in violation of China's participation in the Nuclear Suppliers Group. China claimed the sale adheres to its original accession conditions.

TABLE 11 Nuclear weapons

	Nuclear weapons possession				Total inventory
	1990	1995	2000	2010	2010
Russia	√	√	√	√	~12,000
United States	√	√	√	√	~9,400
China	√	√	√	√	~240
India	√	√	√	√	~60–80
Pakistan	–	–	√	√	~70–90
North Korea	?	?	?	√	<10

SOURCE: *Bulletin of the Atomic Scientists*, July/August 2010.
NOTE: Table shows confirmed (√) and unknown (?) possession of nuclear weapons. Dash indicates that no data is available. Total inventory includes both active and stockpiled arms.

TABLE 12 Intercontinental ballistic missiles

	Number of ICBMs			
	1990	1995	2000	2010
United States	1,000	580	550	450
Russia	1,398	930	776	430
China	8	≥ 17	≥ 20	50
India	–	–	–	In development
Pakistan	–	–	–	–
North Korea	–	–	–	?

SOURCE: International Institute of Strategic Studies, *The Military Balance*, various editions.
NOTE: Dash indicates that no data is available. Question mark indicates unconfirmed possession.

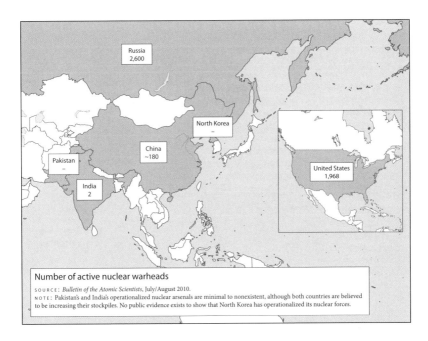

Number of active nuclear warheads

SOURCE: *Bulletin of the Atomic Scientists*, July/August 2010.
NOTE: Pakistan's and India's operationalized nuclear arsenals are minimal to nonexistent, although both countries are believed to be increasing their stockpiles. No public evidence exists to show that North Korea has operationalized its nuclear forces.

TABLE 13 Nonproliferation treaties

	NPT	Additional Protocol	CTBT	CWC	BTWC
Russia	Ratified	Signatory	Ratified	Ratified	Ratified
United States	Ratified	Signatory	Signatory	Ratified	Ratified
China	Ratified	Ratified	Signatory	Ratified	Ratified
India	–	–	–	Ratified	Ratified
Pakistan	–	–	–	Ratified	Ratified
North Korea	Withdrew	–	–	–	Acceded

SOURCE: Nuclear Threat Initiative; and Monterey Institute for International Studies.
NOTE: NPT = Nonproliferation Treaty. Additional Protocol = IAEA Additional Protocol. CTBT = Comprehensive Test Ban Treaty. CWC = Chemical Weapons Convention. BTWC = Biological and Toxic Weapons Convention. Dash indicates nonparticipation.

TABLE 14 WMD-export control regimes

	Nuclear Suppliers Group	Australia Group	Wassenaar Arrangement	Zangger Committee	MTCR
United States	Member	Member	Member	Member	Member
Russia	Member	–	Member	Member	Member
China	Member	–	–	Member	–
India	–	–	–	–	–
Pakistan	–	–	–	–	–
North Korea	–	–	–	–	–

SOURCE: Nuclear Threat Initiative; and Monterey Institute for International Studies.
NOTE: Dash indicates nonparticipation.

About the Contributors

Richard A. Bitzinger is a Senior Fellow with the S. Rajaratnam School of International Studies (RSIS) at Nanyang Technological University in Singapore, where his work focuses on military and defense issues relating to the Asia-Pacific region, including defense transformation and military modernization, regional armaments production, and weapons proliferation. Mr. Bitzinger was previously an Associate Professor with the Asia-Pacific Center for Security Studies (APCSS), Honolulu, and has also worked for the RAND Corporation, the Center for Strategic and Budgetary Affairs, and the U.S. government. In 1999–2000, he was a Senior Fellow with the Atlantic Council of the United States. He has written several articles, monographs, and book chapters, and has been published in *International Security*, *Survival*, and *Orbis*. He is the editor of *The Modern Arms Industry: Political, Economic, and Technological Issues* (2009) and author of *Towards a Brave New Arms Industry?* (2003).

Abraham M. Denmark is a Fellow with the Center for a New American Security (CNAS), where he directs the Asia-Pacific Security Program and the Contested Commons Project. Prior to joining CNAS, Mr. Denmark was Country Director for China Affairs in the Office of the Secretary of Defense, where he was responsible for developing and implementing strategies and plans vis-à-vis China and the Asia-Pacific region. He is the recipient of numerous government recognitions, most recently an Award for Excellence from the Office of the Secretary of Defense in January 2009. He has authored and edited several CNAS reports, including "Crafting a New Vision: A New Era of U.S.-Indonesia Relations" (2010), "The Contested Commons: The Future of American Power in a Multipolar World" (2010), and "China's Arrival: A Strategic Framework for a Global Relationship" (2009). He is also the American editor and lead author of *The U.S.-ROK Alliance in the 21st Century* (2009). Mr. Denmark has testified before the U.S.-China Economic and Security Review Commission and has been featured in major media publications in the United States and Asia.

Nicholas Eberstadt (PhD, Harvard University) holds the Henry Wendt Chair in Political Economy at the American Enterprise Institute. Dr. Eberstadt is also a Senior Advisor to The National Bureau of Asian Research, a member of the visiting committee at the Harvard School of Public Health, and a member of the Global Agenda Council at the World Economic Forum. He researches and writes extensively on issues in demographics, development, and international security. Dr. Eberstadt authored chapters on the Koreas and demography in the first four volumes of the *Strategic Asia* series. His many books and monographs include *Poverty in China* (1979), *Foreign Aid and American Purpose* (1988), *The End of North Korea* (1999), and *Russia's Peacetime Demographic Crisis: Dimensions, Causes, Implications* (2010).

Richard J. Ellings (PhD, University of Washington) is President and Co-founder of The National Bureau of Asian Research (NBR). Prior to serving with NBR, from 1986–89, he was Assistant Director and on the faculty of the Jackson School of International Studies of the University of Washington, where he received the Distinguished Teaching Award. He served as Legislative Assistant in the United States Senate, office of Senator Slade Gorton, in 1984 and 1985. Dr. Ellings is the author of *Embargoes and World Power: Lessons from American Foreign Policy* (1985); co-author of *Private Property and National Security* (1991); co-editor (with Aaron Friedberg) of *Strategic Asia 2003–04: Fragility and Crisis* (2003), *Strategic Asia 2002–03: Asian Aftershocks* (2002), and *Strategic Asia 2001–02: Power and Purpose* (2001); co-editor of *Korea's Future and the Great Powers* (with Nicholas Eberstadt, 2001) and *Southeast Asian Security in the New Millennium* (with Sheldon Simon, 1996); founding editor of the *NBR Analysis* publication series; and co-chairman of the *Asia Policy* editorial board. He established the Strategic Asia Program and AccessAsia, the national clearinghouse that tracks specialists and their research on Asia.

Charles D. Ferguson (PhD, Boston University) is President of the Federation of American Scientists. He also holds an adjunct teaching position in the Security Studies Program at Georgetown University. Prior to joining the Federation of American Scientists, he served as the Philip D. Reed Senior Fellow for Science and Technology at the Council on Foreign Relations. From 2002–04, he was the scientist-in-residence at the Monterey Institute's Center for Nonproliferation Studies, where he co-directed a project on how to prevent and respond to nuclear and radiological terrorism. Dr. Ferguson has been a Foreign Affairs Officer in the Bureau of Nonproliferation at the Department of State and has consulted for the U.S.

Department of Energy. While in the navy, he served as an officer on a fleet ballistic missile submarine and studied nuclear engineering. Dr. Ferguson is co-author of *The Four Faces of Nuclear Terrorism* (2004) and has written numerous articles on energy policy, missile defense, nuclear arms control, nuclear energy, nuclear proliferation, and nuclear terrorism.

Aaron L. Friedberg (PhD, Harvard University) is a Professor of Politics and International Affairs at Princeton University, where he also is Co-director of the Center for International Security Studies in the Woodrow Wilson School of Public and International Affairs. He joined Princeton in 1987, and from 1992–2003 served as Director of the Research Program in International Security. From June 2003 to June 2005, Dr. Friedberg was a Deputy Assistant for National Security Affairs in the Office of the Vice President. He has since served as a member of the Department of Defense Policy Board, the Secretary of State's Advisory Committee on Democracy Promotion, and the National Intelligence Council Associates Group. In 2001–02, Dr. Friedberg was the first Kissinger Scholar at the Library of Congress. He is a former fellow at the Woodrow Wilson International Center for Scholars, the Norwegian Nobel Institute, the Australian Strategic Policy Institute, and Harvard University's Center of International Affairs. Dr. Friedberg is the author of *The Weary Titan, 1895–1905: Britain and the Experience of Relative Decline* (1988) and *In the Shadow of the Garrison State: America's Anti-Statism and Its Cold War Grand Strategy* (2000), and he is co-editor (with Richard Ellings) of the first three volumes in the *Strategic Asia* series. His latest book, on the emerging U.S.-China rivalry, will be published in 2011 by W.W. Norton.

Sumit Ganguly (PhD, University of Illinois–Champaign) is a Professor of Political Science and holds the Rabindranath Tagore Chair in Indian Cultures and Civilizations at Indiana University, Bloomington. He has previously served on the faculty of James Madison College of Michigan State University, Hunter College and the Graduate Center of the City University of New York, and the University of Texas–Austin. He has also taught at the School of International and Public Affairs at Columbia University and held fellowships at the Woodrow Wilson International Center for Scholars, the Center for International Security and Cooperation, and the Center on Democracy, Development, and the Rule of Law at Stanford University. In the spring of 2010 he was the Ngee Ann Professor of International Relations at the Rajaratnam School of International Studies (RSIS) at Nanyang Technological University in Singapore. In the fall term of 2010 he will be a Senior Visiting Fellow at the Institute of Defense Studies and Analysis in New Delhi. Dr. Ganguly is a member of the Council on Foreign

Relations and the International Institute of Strategic Studies. He serves on the editorial boards of *Asian Affairs, Asian Security, Asian Survey, Current History, India Review, Journal of Democracy, and Security Studies,* and he is the founding editor of *India Review* and *Asian Security.* He is the author, editor, or co-editor of twenty books on South Asia, including *The State of India's Democracy* (co-edited with Larry Diamond and Marc Plattner, 2007) and *Fearful Symmetry: India and Pakistan Under the Shadow of Nuclear Weapons* (co-authored with Devin Hagerty, 2005). He is nearing completion of a new book (with Rahul Mukherji) entitled *India Since 1980* and is at work on a single-authored work, *Deadly Impasse: India-Pakistan Relations at the Dawn of a New Century.*

Mikkal Herberg is a Senior Lecturer on international and Asian energy in the Graduate School of International Relations and Pacific Studies at the University of California–San Diego. He is also Research Director on Asian energy security at The National Bureau of Asian Research and the BP Foundation Senior Research Fellow for International Energy at the Pacific Council on International Policy. Previously, Mr. Herberg spent twenty years in the oil industry in senior planning roles for ARCO, where from 1997–2000 he was Director for Global Energy and Economics and responsible for worldwide energy, economic, and political analysis. He also headed country risk management and held positions that include Director of Portfolio Risk Management and Director for Emerging Markets. Mr. Herberg writes, speaks, and testifies extensively on Asian and global energy issues to the energy industry, governments, research institutions, and the media in the United States, Asia, and Europe. His recent publications include "China's 'Energy Rise' and the New Geopolitics of Global Energy" (2010), "Energy Security in the Asia-Pacific Region and Policy of the New U.S. Administration" (2008), "The Rise of Asia's National Oil Companies" (2007), and "China's Search for Energy Security: Implications for U.S. Policy" (co-authored with Kenneth Lieberthal, 2006).

Andrew Marble (PhD, Brown University) serves as Editor at The National Bureau of Asian Research (NBR), where he is responsible for all editorial and managerial aspects of publications. He helped launch NBR's peer-reviewed academic journal, *Asia Policy,* which promotes bridging the gap between academic research and policymaking. He is also co-editor of *Strategic Asia 2009–10: Economic Meltdown and Geopolitical Stability* (with Ashley J. Tellis and Travis Tanner, 2009) and *Strategic Asia 2008–09: Challenges and Choices* (with Ashley J. Tellis and Mercy Kuo, 2008). Before joining NBR in January 2005, Dr. Marble was the Editor of *Issues & Studies: A Social Science*

Quarterly on China, Taiwan, and East Asian Affairs. Special issues of *Issues & Studies* that he edited include "Studies of Taiwan Politics" (September/December 2004), "The State of the China Studies Field" (December 2002/March 2003), "The Taiwan Threat?" (March 2002), "The 'China Threat' Debate" (March 2000), and "The Clash of Civilizations" (October 1998). Dr. Marble spent eight years in Asia, having studied, worked, researched, and traveled in Taiwan, China, Hong Kong, Singapore, Malaysia, and Thailand.

Richard A. Matthew (PhD, Princeton University) is Founding Director of the Center for Unconventional Security Affairs and an Associate Professor of International and Environmental Politics in the Schools of Social Ecology and Social Science at the University of California–Irvine (UCI). He studies the climate, environmental, and natural resource dimensions of conflict and peace-building, and has done extensive fieldwork in conflict and post-conflict zones in South Asia and East and West Africa. Dr. Matthew has consulted for numerous United Nations and government agencies. In addition to his positions at UCI, he is also a Senior Fellow at the International Institute for Sustainable Development in Geneva; a member of the UN Expert Advisory Group on Environment, Conflict and Peacebuilding; and a member of the World Conservation Union's Commission on Environmental, Economic and Social Policy. He has over 130 publications including six books, the most recent of which is *Global Environmental Change and Human Security* (co-edited with Jon Barnett, Bryan McDonald, and Karen O'Brien, 2009).

Manjeet S. Pardesi is a PhD student in the Department of Political Science at Indiana University, Bloomington. His dissertation work focuses on the origins and escalation of strategic rivalries, and his research interests include great-power politics in Asia and Indian foreign and security policy. He obtained his MS in Strategic Studies in 2002 from the Institute of Defence and Strategic Studies (IDSS), now the S. Rajaratnam School of International Studies (RSIS), Singapore. After completing his MS, Mr. Pardesi worked as an Associate Research Fellow at IDSS, where he focused on the institute's projects on the revolution in military affairs (RMA) and India. He has lectured, conducted tutorials, and led discussion groups at the Singapore Armed Forces Training Institute (SAFTI) Military Institute, Singapore. His articles have appeared in the *Air & Space Power Journal* (USAF), *The Fletcher Forum of World Affairs*, *World Policy Journal*, *India Review*, *Asian Security*, *Defense and Security Analysis*, and in several edited book volumes. He has also written commentaries on the RMA and India's foreign and security policy, which have appeared in the *Straits Times* (Singapore), *Korea Herald* (South Korea), *Indian Express*, *Daily News & Analysis* (India), *Times of India*, and *Asia Times Online*.

Peter A. Petri (PhD, Harvard University) is the Carl J. Shapiro Professor of International Finance at the International Business School (IBS) at Brandeis University and a Senior Fellow at the East-West Center. He served as Dean of IBS from its founding in 1994 until 2006. Dr. Petri has held appointments as a Fulbright Research Scholar and Visiting Scholar at the Organisation for Economic Co-operation and Development (OECD), Brookings Institution, Keio University, and Fudan University. He has consulted for the World Bank, the OECD, the Asian Development Bank, APEC, and agencies of the United Nations, the United States, and other countries. He serves on the editorial boards of several journals dedicated to Asia-Pacific research and is Convener of the East-West Center's East-West Dialogue. He is a member of the board of the U.S. Asia Pacific Council and the Pacific Trade and Development Forum (PAFTAD) International Steering Committee, and is a former chair of the U.S. APEC Study Center Consortium. Dr. Petri's research focuses on international trade, finance, and investment, with primary applications to the Pacific Rim, and has been supported by the U.S. Departments of State, Education, and Health and Human Services; the World Bank; the United Nations; and several major foundations. He is the author of approximately one hundred research contributions in these fields.

Travis Tanner is Senior Project Director at The National Bureau of Asian Research (NBR) and Director of NBR's Kenneth B. and Anne H.H. Pyle Center for Northeast Asian Studies. In these roles, Mr. Tanner creates and pursues business opportunities for NBR, determines significant and emerging issues in the field, manages project teams, and is responsible for the success of research projects. Prior to joining NBR, he was Deputy Director and Assistant Director of the Chinese Studies Program at the Nixon Center in Washington, D.C. He also worked as a research assistant at the Peterson Institute for International Economics. Mr. Tanner's interests and expertise include Northeast Asian regional security, China's economy and foreign affairs, and Taiwanese politics. His publications include *Strategic Asia 2009–10: Economic Meltdown and Geopolitical Stability* (co-edited with Ashley J. Tellis and Andrew Marble, 2009), *The People in the PLA: Recruitment, Training, and Education in China's Military* (co-edited with Roy D. Kamphausen and Andrew Scobell, 2008), and *Taiwan's Elections, Direct Flights, and China's Line in the Sand* (co-authored with David M. Lampton, 2005). Mr. Tanner holds an MA in International Relations from the Paul H. Nitze School of Advanced International Studies (SAIS) at the Johns Hopkins University.

Ashley J. Tellis (PhD, University of Chicago) is Senior Associate at the Carnegie Endowment for International Peace, specializing in international security, defense, and Asian strategic issues. He is also Research Director of the Strategic Asia Program at NBR and is co-editor of the six most recent annual volumes in the series, including *Strategic Asia 2009–10: Economic Meltdown and Geopolitical Stability* (with Andrew Marble and Travis Tanner, 2009). While on assignment to the U.S. Department of State as Senior Adviser to the Undersecretary of State for Political Affairs (2005–08), Dr. Tellis was intimately involved in negotiating the civil nuclear agreement with India. Previously he was commissioned into the Foreign Service and served as Senior Advisor to the Ambassador at the U.S. embassy in New Delhi. He also served on the National Security Council staff as Special Assistant to the President and Senior Director for Strategic Planning and Southwest Asia. Prior to his government service, Dr. Tellis was Senior Policy Analyst at the RAND Corporation and Professor of Policy Analysis at the RAND Graduate School. He is the author of *India's Emerging Nuclear Posture* (2001) and co-author of *Interpreting China's Grand Strategy: Past, Present, and Future* (with Michael D. Swaine, 2000). His academic publications have also appeared in many edited volumes and journals.

About Strategic Asia

The **Strategic Asia Program** at The National Bureau of Asian Research (NBR) is a major ongoing research initiative that draws together top Asia studies specialists and international relations experts to assess the changing strategic environment in the Asia-Pacific. The Strategic Asia Program transcends traditional estimates of military balance by incorporating economic, political, and demographic data and by focusing on the strategies and perceptions that drive policy in the region. The program's integrated set of products and activities includes:

- an annual edited volume written by leading specialists

- an Executive Brief that is tailored for public- and private-sector decisionmakers and strategic planners

- an online database that tracks key strategic indicators

- briefings and presentations for government, business, and academe that are designed to foster in-depth discussions revolving around major, relevant public-policy issues

Special briefings are held for key committees of Congress and the executive branch, other government agencies, and the intelligence community. The principal audiences for the program's research findings are the U.S. policymaking and research communities, the media, the business community, and academe.

The Strategic Asia Program's online database contains strategic indicators—economic, financial, military, technological, energy, political, and demographic—for all the countries in the Asia-Pacific region.

To order a book or access the database, please visit the Strategic Asia website at http://www.nbr.org/strategicasia.

Previous Strategic Asia Volumes

Over the past ten years this series has addressed how Asia is increasingly functioning as a zone of strategic interaction and contending with an uncertain balance of power. *Strategic Asia 2001–02: Power and Purpose* established a baseline assessment for understanding the strategies and interactions of the major states within the region—notably China, India, Japan, Russia, and South Korea. *Strategic Asia 2002–03: Asian Aftershocks* drew upon this baseline to analyze the changes in these states' grand strategies and relationships in the aftermath of the September 11 terrorist attacks. *Strategic Asia 2003–04: Fragility and Crisis* examined the fragile balance of power in Asia, drawing out the key domestic political and economic trends in Asian states supporting or undermining this tenuous equilibrium. Building on established themes, *Strategic Asia 2004–05: Confronting Terrorism in the Pursuit of Power* explored the effect of the U.S.-led war on terrorism on the political, economic, social, and strategic transformations underway in Asia. *Strategic Asia 2005–06: Military Modernization in an Era of Uncertainty* appraised the progress of Asian military modernization programs and developed a touchstone to evaluate future military changes to the balance of power. *Strategic Asia 2006–07: Trade, Interdependence, and Security* addressed how increasing levels of trade and changing trade relationships are affecting the balance of power and security in the region. Turning to focus on the factors that motivate states' choices, *Strategic Asia 2007–08: Domestic Political Change and Grand Strategy* examined internal and external drivers of grand strategy and evaluated their impact on Asian foreign policymaking. Returning to the themes found in the first volume, *Strategic Asia 2008–09: Challenges and Choices* examined the impact of geopolitical developments on Asia's transformation over the previous eight years and then assessed the major strategic choices on Asia facing the new U.S. president. *Strategic Asia 2009–10: Economic Meltdown and Geopolitical Stability* analyzed the impact of the global economic crisis on key Asian states and explored the strategic implications for the United States.

Research and Management Team

The Strategic Asia research team consists of leading international relations and security specialists from universities and research institutions across the United States. A new research team is selected each year. The research team for 2010 is led by Ashley J. Tellis (Carnegie Endowment for International Peace). General John Shalikashvili (former Chairman of the Joint Chiefs of Staff), Aaron Friedberg (Princeton University, and Strategic Asia's founding research director), and Richard Ellings (The National Bureau of Asian Research, and Strategic Asia's founding program director) serve as senior advisors.

The Strategic Asia Program depends on a diverse base of funding from foundations, government, and corporations, supplemented by income from publication sales. Major support for the program in 2010 comes from the

Lynde and Harry Bradley Foundation and the National Nuclear Security Administration at the U.S. Department of Energy.

Attribution

Readers of *Strategic Asia* and visitors to the Strategic Asia website may use data, charts, graphs, and quotes from these sources without requesting permission from NBR on the condition that they cite NBR and the appropriate primary source in any published work. No report, chapter, separate study, extensive text, or any other substantial part of the Strategic Asia Program's products may be reproduced without the written permission of NBR. To request permission, please write to:

NBR Editor
The National Bureau of Asian Research
1414 NE 42nd Street, Suite 300
Seattle, Washington 98105
publications@nbr.org

The National Bureau of Asian Research

The National Bureau of Asian Research is a nonprofit, nonpartisan research institution dedicated to informing and strengthening policy. NBR conducts advanced independent research on strategic, political, economic, globalization, health, and energy issues affecting U.S. relations with Asia. Drawing upon an extensive network of the world's leading specialists and leveraging the latest technology, NBR bridges the academic, business, and policy arenas. The institution disseminates its research through briefings, publications, conferences, congressional testimony, and email forums, and by collaborating with leading institutions worldwide. NBR also provides exceptional fellowship and internship opportunities to graduate and undergraduate students for the purpose of attracting and training the next generation of Asia specialists. NBR was started in 1989 with a major grant from the Henry M. Jackson Foundation.

Index